The Social Causes of Husband-Wife Violence

The John K. Fesler Memorial Fund provided assistance in the publication of this volume, for which the University of Minnesota Press is grateful.

The
Social Causes
of
Husband-Wife
Violence

Murray A. Straus
and Gerald T. Hotaling
Editors

UNIVERSITY OF MINNESOTA PRESS □ MINNEAPOLIS

Copyright © 1980 by the University of Minnesota.
All rights reserved.
Published by the University of Minnesota Press,
2037 University Avenue Southeast,
Minneapolis, Minnesota 55414

Library of Congress Cataloging in Publication Data
Straus, Murray Arnold, 1926-
    The social causes of husband-wife violence.

    Bibliography: p.
    Includes indexes.
    1. Conjugal violence — Social aspects — United States —
Addresses, essays, lectures. I. Hotaling, Gerald T.,
joint author. II. Title.
HQ809.3.U5S88   306.8'7   79-27071
ISBN 0-8166-0886-5
ISBN 0-8166-0955-1 pbk.

The University of Minnesota
is an equal-opportunity
educator and employer.

Foreword

Despite the lip service ritualistically paid to the need to integrate sociological theory and empirical research, too often research on the causes and consequences of social problems lacks theoretical guidance. Much theorizing in such areas, on the other hand, proceeds in blissful ignorance of scientific data. The virtue of this book is that it avoids these pitfalls. It presents research findings within a firmly held theoretical framework, at the same time that some of the empirical findings refine existing theories. These findings, to borrow Robert K. Merton's formulation, help to initiate, reformulate, deflect, and clarify theories, rather than simply testing them; and thus contribute not only to empirical knowledge but also to the consolidation of the theoretical propositions in the area of family relationships and in the general field of social conflict and violence.

What I like particularly in the approach of Murray Straus and his associates is their commitment to an ironic perspective. They have a fine sense of the incongruities between the public image of an institution, in this case the family, and the underlying reality. Just as medical research has shown that hospitals, which are supposed to make people well, may make them sick and produce iatrogenic diseases, so the authors show that family living, supposedly predicated on consensus, integration, and harmony, may lead to forms of conflict and violence rarely found outside the family context. The very features of family life that contribute to intimacy, it turns out, also facilitate high degrees of violence between spouses.

Murray Straus and his associates are finely attuned to the need to attend to the unanticipated as well as the anticipated consequences of social actions. They are aware that although evil intents may lead to desirable consequences, good intentions may lead to undesirable ones.

v

We learn here, for example, that more egalitarian relations between husbands and wives may have the ironic consequence of increasing rather than decreasing conflict between them, at least in the short run. The authors' orientation to the ironic perspective on human affairs yields significant insights that could probably could not have been reached without this stance.

Throughout this book, the authors eschew what Georg Simmel once called the "fallacy of separateness." That is, they never succumb to the temptation to regard family conflicts in terms of the personalities of husbands and wives. They are successful at conveying the idea that family conflicts, as all types of interactions within the family, cannot be understood without the realization that they tend to derive from social structures and cultural norms. The high incidence of conflict and violence in contemporary families, they argue persuasively, must be understood in terms of fundamental contradictions built into the foundations of family life. They argue, for example, that when the resources of a spouse are low--when that spouse has, for example, a low status position in the occupational world--the chances are higher that he or she will resort to violence in marital quarrels. They draw attention to the interfamilial consequences of the deprivation of valued status position with attendant losses of ego identity and symbolic reinforcement of self-worth. Hence, the ironic finding that working-class husbands, who tend to cling to an ideology of male dominance more determinedly than middle class husbands, in fact possess fewer resources for exercising power in the family and thus resort to violence more frequently to compensate.

An ironic perspective, alert to the ambivalence of human relationships, especially in intimate settings, has borne considerable fruit in this work. Aware that (to borrow from Bronislaw Malinowski) aggression like charity begins at home, they have documented with instructive thoroughness that, contrary to the prevailing image, family relations are the breeding ground of both love and hostility, of selfless devotion and of destructive violence. What is more, they have shown that to decrease the level of violence in family settings involves more than counseling and therapy. It involves no less than a restructuring of relations between men and women, which, in its turn, is largely dependent on a fundamental restructuring of the allocation of power and status in the society at large. I hope that their seminal contribution will find an echo among scholarly investigators and social practitioners alike.

Stony Brook, N.Y.   Lewis A. Coser

Acknowledgments

This book is a product of the Family Violence Research Program at the University of New Hampshire. The program began as a result of the stimulus provided by the 1970 annual meeting of the National Council on Family Relations. The theme of that conference was "Violence And The Family." Preparing a paper for the conference (Straus, 1971) and the discussion that followed, made us see both the theoretical and the practical importance of research on physical violence in families. We are now even more convinced that such research will increase our general understanding of the human family and will provide knowledge that will reduce a source of vast human misery.

The Family Violence Research Program also illustrates what can be accomplished when a group of graduate students and faculty focus on a single topic over even a relatively short period of time. We hope it confirms the faith in our work shown in the financial support provided by the University of New Hampshire and by the National Institute of Mental Health (grants number MH27557, MH13050, and MH15161). A list of publications from the Family Violence Research is available on request.

We also want to express our appreciation to the anonymous referees who reviewed the book, and to many colleagues, both at the University of New Hampshire and elsewhere, whose comments, criticisms, and suggestions have been important to the development of the Family Violence Research Program in general and/or the specific chapters in this book. A special thanks to Sieglinde Fizz for her conscientious typing of this manuscript and for her patience and good nature throughout this project.

Durham, New Hampshire   Murray A. Straus
                                               Gerald T. Hotaling

Contents

Part I Overview

Chapter 1

Culture, Social Organization, and Irony in the Study of Family Violence

Gerald T. Hotaling and Murray A. Straus

That acts of physical violence are common--even typical--of American marriages has been well established (see Chapter 2 and Straus, Gelles, and Steinmetz, 1979). What is not known is why violence occurs, or what to do about it. The perspective of this book is simple: that physical violence between husbands and wives is socially patterned.*1

The chapters are deliberately diverse, but all share the perspective that violence grows out of the nature of social arrangements. In part, the diversity is inevitable because the authors are different. The major differences, however, are built into the plan of the book--to present major differences in viewpoint. Most of the chapters present theories to explain the prevalence of violence in the family. Since the social causes of husband-wife violence are diverse and complex, the different chapters seek to show how different sets of these factors might operate to produce violence.

The chapters also differ because, no matter how cogent the theory, it must be supported by empirical evidence. Consequently, five of the chapters report such data. Here also deliberate diversity exists, illustrating such different methods as case studies, content analysis of popular literature, brief questionnaire studies, and a survey of a nationally representative sample of couples. Each of these theories, and each of these methods, has limitations and advantages. Together, they help unravel the paradox of marital violence.

MARITAL VIOLENCE AND THE SOCIAL STRUCTURE

Any attempt to understand why physical violence occurs so often in American marriages must take into account the way society structures the interaction of husbands and wives. Of course, a proposition that simple is necessarily deceptive. Our intention is not to convince the reader that the aspects of social patterning to which this book gives attention are the only causes of marital violence. We acknowledge the complexity of married life, but temporarily narrow our focus so that we can gain a clearer understanding of that part of the complex whole of husband/wife conflict that is created by the very nature of our society.

Physical violence among family members usually is considered an infrequent occurrence; when violence does erupt, the husband or wife who resorts to it is thought to be defective or abnormal. Neither view seems to be correct. Wars and riots aside, physical aggression occurs more often among family members than among any others. Moreover, the family is the predominant setting for every form of physical violence from slaps to torture and murder. In fact, some form of physical violence in the life cycle of family members is so likely that it can be said to be almost universal (see the section on "Family Socialization in Violence" in Chapter 2). If this is indeed the case, then violence is as typical of family relationships as is love.

The available evidence suggests that, with rare exceptions, family members using violence are not mentally ill. Instead, violent acts by one family member against another are the result of socially learned and socially patterned behavior.

The aspects of causation this book describes are what sociologists refer to as "social structure." The concept of social structure is almost as elusive as it is important for understanding how society works and how social life affects our relationships. A recent volume (Blau, 1975) gives ample testimony to the wide variety of ways in which the concept is used. But amidst this diversity of definition, a general interpretation exists, as stated in the program of the 1974 meeting of the American Sociological Association:

> Whatever the specific orientation, the structural approach is designed to explain, not the behavior of individuals, but the structure of relations among groups and individuals that finds expression in this behavior. (Blau, 1975:2)

Our specific approach to social structure contains two main elements. First, we use the term to mean those aspects of society that are relatively enduring and that transcend

the individual and the particular moment. Not that social
structure is fixed; indeed, it constantly changes. But
compared with other factors being examined, it is relatively
stable. Second, we identify two different but interrelated
processes of social patterning: culture and social
organization. In reality, culture and social organization
cannot be separated, but for analytical purposes it is an
important distinction.

The following two sections summarize the concepts of
culture and of social organization. These will be familiar
to many readers of this book, especially sociologists, and
can be skipped over. However, we want to address those in
other professions concerned with family violence, such as
psychologists, social workers, psychiatrists, police
officers, and lawyers. These sections will help alert them
to these crucial aspects of the sociological perspective.
This is particularly important because it contrasts sharply
with the more usual psychological explanations for violence.

The Concept of Culture

When we describe "cultural influence" we are really
talking about causes. The question addressed in Part II of
this book is the extent to which culture causes violence
between family members. Before that question can be
answered, one must first be clear about what culture is.

The term culture means something roughly similar to
social heredity, that is, the total legacy of past human
behavior effective in the present or what is available to be
learned from others (Williams, 1970). That concept covers a
vast domain, ranging from how to hold a spoon or say the
word father to the complexities of matrix algebra. Thus a
great deal of the culture of a society is not of direct
interest to those concerned with understanding the family.

The aspect of culture of direct interest is what are
called social norms. A social norm prescribes the correct
thing to do when interacting with another person. To be
cultural norms, these norms must be prescriptions shared by
the society or sector of a society in which the behavior
takes place. They also must be rules of behavior that are
learned from others.

Cultural norms in large part account for differences
between the family patterns of people in different societies
and in different subgroups within one society (for example,
differences between social classes or between groups such as
French-speaking and English-speaking Canadians).

Cultural norms regulate almost all aspects of family
life. They provide a blueprint of the behavior appropriate
for husbands, wives, children, grandfathers; in fact, for

each of the relationships within a family. Thus, the culture contains norms specifying how marriages are to be arranged (and, if necessary, dissolved), who is to be regarded as a member of the family, what activities a husband should carry out in relation to the wife and vice versa, how children should be brought up, and so on.

If the idea of cultural norms as causes of family behavior were taken literally, all families within a given society would be expected to act in the same way. Obviously, that is not the case: every family is in some ways unique. Therefore, even though culture does, on the average, define what family life is like, it cannot tell the whole story. We must round out the story somewhat by considering what sociologists call social organization.

Social Organizational Influences

Social organization refers to the pattern of relationships among individuals and among groups--how the parts are related to each other and to the whole. Some aspects of social organization are dictated by the culture, many are not. Whether or not it is prescribed by culture, each aspect of social organization has consequences that are distinct from the cultural influences. For example, a family might contain one, two, three, four, or eight children. Cultural "rules" specify how many children one should have; the middle-class rules of the recent past tended to specify two or three children. Anyone who had no children was under considerable cultural pressure. The pressure is often subtle, but may be expressed openly: "Why don't you have any children?" or "How come you have six children?" But subtle or not, social pressures to conform do exist and most of us follow the rules of the culture.

Now the number of children in a family is an important aspect of its social organization and makes a difference to what goes on in that family, no matter whether the parents had that number of children because of cultural rules, biological limits on fertility, or contraceptive failure. To take a simple example, if the family eats the evening meal together, the number of children present will influence how long any one child can, on the average, talk at the dinner table. Assume that each child gets an equal chance and that the meal lasts 30 minutes. If there are two children, each child can talk for ten minutes (allowing ten minutes for the parents to say something). But if there are four children, each child's limit is cut to five minutes.

THE SOCIAL STRUCTURAL CAUSES OF HUSBAND-WIFE VIOLENCE

The preceding two sections preface the shared ideas of the authors of this volume. This is not to say that they are in complete agreement as to the social structural causes of husband-wife violence, but all focus on the cultural and organizational features of American marriages and their relation to conflict and violence.

Each chapter in this book, whether it is a deduction from an existing theory, a case study, or a statistical analysis, attempts to clarify some aspect of the social causes of husband-wife violence. The chapters are deliberately diverse in approach because we believe that case studies, statistical analyses, and theoretical deduction all are necessary in the search for an explanation of marital violence.

One of the difficulties in research on family violence has been too heavy an emphasis on fact-gathering relative to testing causal theories. Since this is partly because promising theories have not been formulated, half of the chapters attempt to fill that void. But in no case is the purpose of any chapter to set forth an integrated or complete explanation of husband-wife violence. That task is at the present stage of our knowledge clearly beyond what can be accomplished, even though preliminary steps have been taken (Gelles and Straus, 1979).

With this general understanding, the authors of the various chapters spare the reader a repetitious disclaimer about the partial nature of the theory examined and, in the case of the strictly theoretical chapters, do not repeat that the conclusions are intended to stimulate empirical research, not to substitute for such data. Thus, for example, in the first two chapters we try to show that some factor in the family system not only produces a high level of aggression, but also makes wives the most frequent victims of that aggression. The third chapter, although admitting the organizational features of family life that contribute to this high level of aggression, examines through popular culture and other materials the prevailing sexist attitudes about the role of violence in the family system. The result is to make explicit the implicit set of cultural norms and values that legitimate, and at times encourage, violence between husbands and wives.

Conversely, Farrington (Chapter 7) and Hotaling (Chapter 9) both recognize the existence of cultural norms, but focus on the organizational features of married life that contribute to violence. Farrington presents a theory of intrafamily violence based on the notion of optimum stress level. He defines stress as an imbalance between the demands with which an individual or family is faced and the

capability of responding appropriately to them. He argues
that all individuals and families develop personal and
unique optimum stress levels at which they function most
comfortably. Similarly, Hotaling specifies the particular
combinations of family rules and family structural
characteristics which produce a high probability that a
family member will attribute malevolent intent to the rule
violations of other family members.

The History of the Study of Family Violence

        Describing a "history" of the sociological study of
intrafamily violence may be premaure; it has been a very
short time since sociologists first turned a critical eye on
the phenomenon.   But the period has been long enough to
point out some differences between "earlier" work and the
present volume. Previous efforts were aimed at establishing
the prevalence, the correlates, and, most important, the
socially patterned nature of family violence (Steinmetz and
Straus, 1974;   Gelles, 1974).   Intrafamily violence was
established as a widespread phenomenon, appearing in many
forms besides the more spectacular crimes of murder and
child abuse.   Studies of husbands and wives revealed
varying, but substantial, amounts of spousal violence.

        The most accurate measure, to date, of the extent of
husband-wife violence comes from the analysis of data from
the representative sample of American families presented in
Chapter 2.   Straus finds that, during the survey year, one
of every six couples (16 percent) reported violence between
spouses.   If the reference period is the duration of the
marriage, the figure is between one of four and one of three
couples (27.8 percent). Straus warns, however, that these
figures are probably affected by substantial underreporting.
It is almost certain that not everyone "told all." Pilot
studies and informal evidence (where some of the factors
leading to underreporting were less) indicate that these
figures could easily be twice as large.

        Previous work on intrafamily violence also has negated
the comfortable notion that family violence can be explained
solely by psychopathology. The sheer amount, as well as the
patterned variation in rates of intrafamily violence among
various social groups, belies an explanation anchored in the
abnormalities of individual members.

        Besides establishing the prevalence of violence in the
home and the extent of sociological causes, earlier
investigators also have paid attention to the particular
social factors related to family violence. For example,
some of the factors found to be associated with different
rates of family violence were subcultural norms (Coser,
1967;   Wolfgang and Ferracuti,   1971), social class
(Levinger, 1966;   Kohn, 1969), and a husband's lack of the

"resources" necessary to legitimate his position as family head (Goode, 1971; O'Brien, 1971).

These writers point to factors that may make certain couples more or less likely to engage in physical aggression; the present volume focuses attention on the nature of married life itself. The orienting question becomes: what cultural and social organizational processes make the marital dyad a potentially violent social relationship?

A good way to begin the search for an answer is to examine the "social construction of marriage" (Berger and Kellner, 1964). The marital relationship has always been viewed with ambivalence. Arlene Skolnick (1973) points out that, in the social sciences, prevailing models of marriage highlight this ambivalence. There is a tendency, on the one hand, to see marriage as a one-way ticket to paradise; a minority sees marriage as a battleground, stressing conflict and competition. Either view, of itself, is narrow, at best a poor reflection of the everyday realities of married life. Novelists and playwrights over the years have avoided this false dichotomy by depicting marriages not so much as happy or unhappy, loving or uncaring, but as relationships in which seemingly contradictory feelings and processes coexist.

A few sociological investigators as well have recognized certain incongruities in marriage. For example, Cuber and Haroff's study (1965) of middle-class marriages reveals a type characterized by arguments and fights. The "conflict-habituated" marriage basically relies on hostility to bind the couple together and to lend stability to the marriage.

Hicks and Platt (1970), in a review of studies of marital happiness, find that low happiness often may be associated with marital stability. Similar findings that appear contrary to common sense are those of Blood and Wolfe (1960) and Pineo (1961), who stated that marriages over time experience a decline in companionship, affection, and common values and beliefs; as couples become more familiar with each other, they become more estranged. Lastly, Simmel's (1950) classic analysis of the marital dyad sees the two-person bond as the most intimate and, at the same time, the most unstable social relationship.

Herein lies the important contribution of logically organized, probing theoretical and empirical analyses: they are typically counterintuitive, that is, they reveal the existence of phenomena and relationships contrary to common sense.

The chapters contained in this volume emphasize in
large part the ironic nature of married life and violence.
The intriguing question, which all these chapters address,
is why the social group that society most often looks to for
warmth, intimacy, help, and love, is also characterized by
cruelty and violence. It is to an examination of this and
other ironies about husband-wife violence that we now turn.

IRONY AND FAMILY VIOLENCE

The recognition and study of family violence has
blurred apparently simple ideas about the relationship
between the family and deviance. Once we recognize that
families are not easily classified as either normal or
abnormal, healthy or sick, the picture becomes complicated.
These complications, though, lead to a fuller appreciation
of the complexity of family life. As David Matza has argued
in his interpretation of theories of deviance and their
handling of the distinction between conventional and deviant
phenomena:

> Once the distinction between good and evil is
> made problematic, once their interpenetration is
> stressed, a similar insight may develop with
> respect to the relations between phenomena and
> their purported causes. (1969:69)

If we accept the notion that the family is a social
group capable of generating conflict and violence just as
easily as intimacy and love, we can accept the idea of irony
in the relation of family life to violence.

What do we mean by irony? Most simply, irony refers to
a point of view, the ability to see phenomena related to one
another in curious ways. As Matza notes:

> ...irony refers to the complicated--and
> suprising--relations between good and evil
> phenomena in sequence. Irony is a state of
> affairs or a result opposite to, and as if in
> mockery of, the appropriate result. (1969:69)

In a sociological sense, irony is a point of view that
recognizes the coexistence of incongruities in the culture
and organization of social life. Thus, the marital
relationship is organized according to certain cultural
values that are intended to maximize love, support, and
happiness. However, because of this very same mode of
organization and because of the influence of these same
cultural values, conflict and violence coexist with these
more benign aspects of married life. Again, as Matza tells
us, "a key element of irony is latency" (p. 70). Qualities
inherent in social norms and social organization, despite

their hidden nature, lead to unexpected results in the family setting.*2

Irony also points to the existence of patterning in relationships where no patterning is obvious. For example, Reinhold Niebuhr has defined irony as "apparently fortuitous incongruities in life which are discovered, upon closer examination, to be not merely fortuitous" (1952:viii). The incongruities surrounding husband-wife violence are ironic in Niebuhr's sense of the word, for the existing evidence supports the claim that husband-wife violence is not the result of random events, but is patterned into the very structure of marital and family relations.

Before we specify the ironies apparent in husband-wife violence, it would be useful to point out why there is such a resistance to viewing husband-wife violence as a patterned aspect of married life.

The Myth of Family Nonviolence

The family is usually thought to be a group committed to nonviolence between its members. Family members are supposed to maintain benevolent and loving relationships. From what is known about the prevalence of family violence in American society, there seems to be a discrepancy between the idealized picture of the family and what actually goes on (Steinmetz and Straus, 1974: Chapter 1; Straus, 1974b). This idealization is a useful, perhaps necessary social myth. Its usefulness derives from the family's position as a tremendously important social institution. Elaborate precautions are taken to strengthen and support it. In Western countries, one of these supportive devices is the myth of familial love and gentleness. The ideal encourages people to marry and stay married despite the stresses and strains of family life (Ferreira, 1963). Thus from the standpoint of preserving the integrity of a crucial institution, such a mythology is highly useful.

This myth is transmitted through cultural norms and values as reflected in literature, motion pictures, and television. For example, Huggins and Straus (Chapter 4) find the myth of family nonviolence a pervasive theme of children's literature between 1850 and 1970. While the authors find that the typical children's classic book is marked by a number of violent acts, including killings, almost no intrafamily family violence is depicted. This seems remarkable in light of the fact that in society generally, physical violence between family members is more common than between any other aggressor-victim relationship.

As the myth of family nonviolence makes clear, a set of cultural norms promulgates an image of the family as a place of love and gentleness. At the same time, as already

mentioned, a set of norms exists that legitimates, and at
times encourages, the use of violence on family members.
This is an excellent example of a cultural contradiction.
Cultural contradictions are found in most, perhaps all
societies. They are by no means entirely undesirable. In
fact, cultural contradictions help prevent societies from
stagnating, open possibilities for social change, and allow
for a measure of individual autonomy. Without them, we
might be slaves to the dictates of culture. Each individual
and each family must manipulate many, often conflicting,
norms and values to work out a strategy appropriate to their
own circumstances and aspirations. The process of selecting
from and reconciling the different aspects of a culture is
one of the reasons why, despite cultural norms, families
differ.

The choice of norms for guiding one's life leads to
diversity, but there is no guarantee that one will recognize
all of the implications of that choice. Certain unexpected
results, or latent features of these choices, make
individual and family life a complicated matter.

This complexity is especially true for violence in the
family. Knowing that our family system is a violent system,
rational people certainly would not choose this situation.
Yet over 90 per cent of Americans marry, and many marriages
are marked by conflict and violence. Perhaps what is
important for understanding the relationship between
violence and the family is not individual choice but the
ironies that seem to underlie the norms and organization of
family life.

> Irony 1. Cultural norms that legitimate and, at
> times, encourage violence between family
> members are instrumental in maintaining the
> family system; but these same norms
> perpetuate violence as an integral part of
> family life.

A set of norms exists that legitimize the striking of
family members, at least under certain conditions. These
norms sometimes are used to justify the use of violence to
maintain the family system. In no way should this statement
be interpreted to mean that we favor any type of family
system over another. Whether our present family structure
should be maintained or changed is not at issue here. In
most forms of social organization, whether it is a whole
society, a bureaucracy, or the family system, there is an
emphasis on maintaining the status quo. Even though social
organization constantly changes, group well-being is
adversely affected if no provision is made for a relatively
stable framework for action.

Our interest here is understanding the relationship
between the norms that legitimize violence and the role
these norms play in family life. Goode (1971) argues that
those who desire to maintain the present family system may
use force or its threat as a form of social control. In
other words, norms legitimizing violence maintain order in
the family group by imposing strong sanctions when an
individual tries to play by other "rules." For many in
American society, force or the threat of force in the family
is seen as a permitted technique for preventing or
controlling certain behaviors of family members. As Goode
notes:

> ...the mother who abandons her children, the father
> who runs off with the children, the wife or husband
> who takes a second spouse, the child who beats up
> his mother, the adolescent girl who wishes to spend
> a weekend with her boyfriend against the will of her
> parents, the wife who wishes to change the family
> domicile without the consent of her husband, all can
> be and sometimes are restrained by either force or
> its threat, if not from family members then at their
> request by the community through its command over
> force (1971:626).

Most Americans see a moral obligation for parents to
use physical punishment as a means for controlling children
if other means fail (Stark and McEvoy, 1970), and a good
proportion see it as the most desirable means for
controlling children. Although the legal right of a husband
to physically punish a wife no longer exists (Calvert,
1974), the informal norms of certain social groups (and
specific families in all segments of society) still
legitimize the use of physical force to control an errant
spouse.

Of the modalities that ensure that the family functions
as an efficient social group, violence is seen to have high
instrumental value. It works--at least in the short run.

This kind of violence is what Gelles and Straus (1978)
call "legitimate-instrumental" violence, violence that is
permitted or required by the norms of society. Physical
force is used to induce some desired act or to prevent some
undesired behavior. Legitimate-instrumental violence occurs
in all role-relationships of the nuclear family with greater
or lesser frequency. The greatest frequency is in the
parent-child relationship in the form of physical
punishment, but as Straus shows in Chapter 3, the marriage
license also tends to be a hitting license.

Violence can also take a "legitimate-expressive" form.
By expressive violence we mean the use of physical force to
cause pain or injury as an end in itself. Examples of this
type of violence in the family include the widespread

beliefs that it is better to spank a child than to "hold in" one's anger and better to let siblings "fight it out" than to interfere.

At times violence in the family setting goes beyond sanctioning by cultural norms; it is illegitimate. This most widely recognized type of violence in the family includes the most spectacular and extreme forms: child abuse and murder.

Whenever physical force is used within the family, for whatever reason, there are certain unexpected outcomes. Chapter 2 points to three such unexpected outcomes. The first is the association of love with violence. The child learns that those who love him/her most are also those who hit and have the right to hit. The second unintended consequence is the lesson that when something is really important, it justifies the use of physical force. Finally, and most important, these indirect lessons become so fundamental to the individual's personality and world view that they are generalized to social relationships, and especially to the relationship closest to that of parent and child-- that of husband and wife.

This last point is examined in detail in Joseph Carroll's chapter on the differential role of violence in Mexican-American and Jewish subcultures. He attempts to show how general family norms and values operating within these two divergent ethnic groups act to influence the actual use of violence as well as its perpetuation in future generations.

The irony here is that these norms, seen to be necessary in maintaining the family group, also guarantee that violence will become a regular feature of family life in the future. This guarantee is ensured by simple membership in the family group. As Gelles (1974) notes:

> "...the family serves as basic training for violence by exposing children to violence, by making them victims of violence, and by providing them with learning contexts for the commission of violent acts" (p. 170).

Indeed, the evidence is clear that early experiences with physical punishment lay the groundwork for the normative legitimacy and actual use of intrafamily violence. Owens and Straus (1975), in a study of exposure to violence and violence approval, show that the more violence experienced by a child, the greater the tendency to favor the use of violence as an adult. Gutmacher (1960) states that a common experience among a group of murderers he studied was the high level of violence their parents inflicted on them when they were growing up. Tanay's (1969) study of homicidal offenders finds that 67 percent had histories of violent

child-rearing. Gelles (1974) finds that respondents who had
seen their parents engaging in physical violence were much
more likely to physically fight with their own spouses than
were people who never saw their parents physically fight
(p. 173).

Welsh (1976) explored the relationship between severe
parental punishment and juvenile delinquency. He defines
severe parental punishment as any type of physical
discipline using an object capable of inflicting physical
injury. Welsh's analysis of three samples of delinquent
children led him to conclude that the recidivist male
delinquent who had never been exposed to a belt, board,
extension cord or fist was nonexistent. In addition, Welsh
finds among male delinquents a strong relationship between
severe parental punishment and aggression.

Increasing evidence indicates that a high price is paid
for maintaining order in the family through violence. The
norms that legitimate violence assure a family institution
and a society characterized by violence for years to come.

> Irony 2. The social organizational features of
> family life that contribute to intimacy also
> facilitate the occurrence of a high rate of
> intraspousal violence.

Though the family shares certain characteristics with
other social groups, as a social group and as an institution
the family has distinctive characteristics. Gelles and
Straus (1978) have catalogued certain of these features of
the family to point out that a special theory of violence is
necessary for the family group. Some of these
characteristics, and others mentioned by authors in this
volume, serve a dual role in the family. On the one hand,
they contribute toward making the family a warm, supportive,
and intimate environment; on the other hand, they suggest
reasons why this social group may be especially prone to
violence. We list eleven such factors:

1. _Time at Risk_. An elementary characteristic
accounting for the high incidence of violence is that so
many hours of the day are spent interacting with other
family members. However, although this factor is important,
the ratio of intrafamily violence to violence experienced
outside the family far exceeds the ratio of time spent in
the family to time spent outside. Comparing the family with
another group in which large amounts of time are spent, such
as a work group, provides a concrete example that far more
is involved than "time at risk."

2. _Range of Activities and Interests_. Most nonfamily
social interactions are focused on a specific purpose or
issue; family interactions cover a vast range of
activities. In practical terms, this means more "events"

take place over which a dispute or a failure to meet
expectations can occur.

3. Intensity of Involvement. Not only is there a wider
range of possibilities for disputes or dissatisfactions,
but, in addition, the degree of injury felt in such
instances is likely to be much greater than if the same
issue were to arise in relation to someone outside the
family. Foss (Chapter 7) considers this factor especially
important in generating hostility among family members as
well as in creating the strategies for dealing with
conflicts of interest among family members.

4. Infringing Activities. Many family activities have
a "zero sum" aspect. Conflict arises from such decisions as
whether to play Bach or Mendelssohn on the family stereo,
whether to go to a movie or bowling, or how to line up for
the bathroom. Less obvious, but equally important, is the
infringing of one's personal space or self-image by the life
style and habits of others in the family, such as those who
leave things around versus those who put everything away, or
those who eat quickly and those who like leisurely meals.

5. Right to Influence. Membership in a family carries
with it an implicit right to influence the behavior of
others. Consequently, the dissatisfaction over undesirable
or impinging activities of others is further exacerbated by
attempts to change the behavior of the other.

6. Age and Sex Discrepancies. The differences in age
and sex of family members (especially during the
child-rearing years), coupled with the existence of
generational and sex differences in culture and outlook,
make the family an arena of culture conflict. This conflict
is expressed in such phrases as "the battle of the sexes"
and "the generation gap."

7. Ascribed Roles. Compounding the problem of age and
sex differences, family statuses and roles are assigned, to
a considerable extent, on the basis of biological
characteristics rather than on the basis of competence and
interest. One aspect of this structuring has traditionally
been a focus of contention -- socially structured sexual
inequality or, in contemporary language, the sexist
organization of the family. Straus (Chapter 6) argues that
a male-dominated family has especially high conflict
potential when it exists in a society with an egalitarian
ideology. But, as Allen and Straus point out (in Chapter
12), even without such an ideologic inconsistency, the
conflict potential is high, because inevitably not all
husbands can fulfill the culturally prescribed leadership
roles.

8. **Family Privacy**. In many societies the normative kinship and household structure insulates the family from social controls and social assistance in coping with intrafamily conflict. This characteristic is most typical of the conjugal family system of urban-industrial societies (Laslett,1973). Both Foss (Chapter 8) and Hotaling (Chapter 9) mention that the nuclear structure of American family life makes less likely the dampening effects of the presence of third parties in husband-wife arguments and disputes.

9. **Involuntary Membership**. Birth relationships are obviously involuntary, and under-age children cannot themselves terminate such relationships. In addition, Sprey (1969) shows that the conjugal relationship also has nonvoluntary aspects. First, the social expectation is that marriage is a long-term commitment, as expressed in the phrase "until death do us part." In addition, emotional, material, and legal rewards and constraints often make membership in the family group inescapable, socially, physically, or legally. So, when conflicts and dissatisfactions arise, the alternative of resolving them by leaving often does not exist--at least in the perception of what is practical or possible.

10. **High Level of Stress**. Paradoxically, in light of the previous paragraph, nuclear family relationships are unstable. A number of circumstances bring about this instability, beginning with the general tendency for all diadic relationships to be unstable (Simmel,1950:118-144). In addition, the nuclear family continually undergoes major changes in structure because of processes inherent in the family life cycle--the birth of children, maturation of children, aging, and retirement. The crisis-like nature of these changes has long been recognized (LeMasters,1957). All of this, combined with the huge emotional investment typical of family relationships, means that the family is likely to be the locus of more, and more serious, stresses than other groups. A reading of Chapter 7 emphasizes the important role of internal and external stresses on family life in the explanation of intrafamily violence.

11. **Extensive Knowledge of Social Biographies**. Because of the intimacy of the marital relationship, spouses usually have an in-depth kowledge of each other's social histories--their abilities and shortcomings, their strengths and vulnerabilities, their likes and dislikes (Hepburn 1973). In effect, the members of marital relationships have at their disposal information that can be used to support and enhance each other's identities because each knows about the things that matter to the other. At the same time, this information can be used to damage the identity of either spouse. Goode (1971) suggests that intimates are able to launch verbal assaults on the partner's vulnerable points because the nature of marriage exposes each other's weaknesses. Hotaling (Chapter 9) specifically refers to the

extensive knowledge of partners as predisposing them to mistakenly attribute malevolent intent to the actions of spouses.

These eleven factors, and no doubt there are others, have been posited by authors of this volume and others as important characteristics of the family group that contribute to its high rate of conflict and violence. The irony here is that many of these same features encourage warmth, intimacy, and support; for example, large amounts of time spent together, deep emotional involvement, privacy, and in-depth knowledge of one another.

The relationship of these unique characteristics of the family to violence as well as to intimacy has not been verified empirically. But the theoretical work on this issue suggests many intriguing questions for research. The most important is whether changes in these unique characteristics can make the family a less violent group without sacrificing the benefits of an intimate environment. For example, if we compare nuclear family structures with various combinations of extended family structures, will there be a higher level of support between members in the latter form, as well as a lower level of stress? Straus' comparison of supportiveness between spouses in nuclear and in joint households (1975) suggests that lack of stress may be gained at the expense of support. And what role do grandparents play in terms of the occurrence of intrafamily violence when they live in the same households as their sons and daughters and grandchildren?

Investigations also could be focused on specific characteristics. For example, the effect of involuntary family membership on violence could be studied by comparing nonmarried couples who live together with married couples, controlling for relevant factors. Also, does intense involvement among family members facilitate or dampen the occurrence of violence? Do families with extensive community interests or involvements with nonfamily members experience less violent interaction at home? These examples suggest only a few of many such questions that could be brought to bear on the special social organizational features and their influence on husband-wife violence.

> Irony 3. The change to an egalitarian structure
> of marriage leads to the destruction of the
> sexist organization of the family but also
> seems to lead to higher rates of violence.

The two previous ironies could be called macro ironies. They were concerned with the family as an institution and social group as compared with other institutions and social groups in terms of its proclivity to high rates of violence. The last two ironies presented here are concerned with micro level processes, that is, with characteristics that differentiate families from each other.

The first of these ironies concerns the sexist organization of the family (Straus, Chapter 6). This chapter cites nine specific ways in which the male-dominated structure of society and family creates and maintains a high level of marital violence. One of the many ways in which male domination can lead to family violence occurs when the male is threatened. In our society, where male-superiority norms are in the process of transition, and in which the presumption of superiority must be validated by "resources" such as valued personal traits and material goods and services, ascribing superior authority to men is a potent force in producing physical attacks on wives. A husband who wants to be the dominant person in his family, but who has little education, a job that is low in prestige and income, and a lack of interpersonal skills, may resort to physical violence to maintain his position.

Empirical evidence supports these notions. For example, in families where the husband's achieved status is lower than his wife's, O'Brien (1971) found a greater tendency to use force and violence on family members than when the husband had the "resource" of a higher prestige occupation. Also, Allen and Straus (Chapter 12) found that among working class husbands who were high in economic or personal resources, there was no correlation between power in the family and violence. However, among those working class husbands who were low in resources, the correlation between male power and violence was 0.49.

The expectation of male dominance is graphically illustrated in the case history of Joe and Jennifer reported by La Rossa (in Chapter 10). This couple depicts the conflict between men and women in the transition from male superiority to egalitarian family norms, most clear in the dialogue between Joe and Jennifer about Jennifer's employment outside of the home, which Joe perceives as a threat to his right to be the dominant member of the relationship.

The issue of wife employment, perhaps the most direct threat to male domination in the society as well as in the family, is investigated by Brown (Chapter 11) to determine its potential impact on husband-wife violence. In a more general vein, Brown probes the conflict between emerging sexual equality and existing norms that promote male domination.

Logically, we would assume that the increasing breakdown of the sexist organization of the family would also lead to a decrease in husband-wife violence. But this decrease may not be the case, at least in the short run. During this transition period, as the family restructures its power distribution, conflict and violence may actually

be increased as men feel threatened by their loss of power.
Ironically, attempts by women to increase their power in
society and the family may serve to victimize women further,
at least temporarily.

In the long run, the egalitarian ethos should lead to a
decrease in husband-wife violence, but it will not decrease
until men begin to accept egalitarian norms as legitimate.

> Irony 4. The suppression of conflict, widely
> felt to decrease violence, may actually
> increase it.

Most people fear conflict and try to avoid it.
Sociologists and psychologists do research to find out why
conflict occurs, ostensibly to be able to provide
information that will enable people to avoid conflict.
Marriage counselors and other professionals concerned with
the family, with a few exceptions such as Bach and Wyden
(1968) and Shostrom and Kavanaugh (1971), focus much of
their efforts on helping families to avoid conflict. The
implicit assumption here is that the suppression of conflict
will lead to the avoidance of hostility and violence.

However, conflict theorists have presented a convincing
case for exactly the opposite assumption; they argue that
conflict is an inevitable part of all human associations
(Coser, 1956; Dahrendorf, 1959; Sprey, 1969).
Furthermore, they hold that any social unit that attempts to
suppress conflict runs a high risk of collapsing, either
because it fails to adapt to changing circumstances or
because hostility accumulates, eroding group solidarity.

The application of conflict theory to family violence
has assumed that conflict is central to, or even a
prerequisite for, violence. However, a delineation of how
conflict processes and violence are related has not received
adequate attention. Foss takes on this issue in Chapter 8.

Foss contends that certain unique features of the
husband-wife relationship, that is, the high frequency of
interaction between spouses, total personality involvement,
and the difficulty in simply leaving the family setting,
will produce hostility and generate attempts to suppress or
ignore hostility. Foss proposes that the avoidance of
conflict situations ironically tends to increase hostility
as well as the probability of violence.

If suppressing conflict leads to violence does this
imply the more conflict the better for marital
relationships? The question of how much conflict is
desirable in the family setting is an uninvestigated and
important empirical challenge. Straus (1978) has suggested
that there is a curvilinear relation between the amount of
conflict and group well-being. That is, the absence of

conflict in the sense of conflicts of interest is
theoretically impossible; even if it could be brought
about, suppression of conflict would be fatal for group
well-being. At the same time, very high levels of conflict
can create such a high level of stress and/or such rapid
change that group welfare is adversely affected.

If Straus' hypothesis is correct, that a certain level
of conflict is indeed healthy for the marital relationship,
how could the appropriate level be determined? Certain
theoretical deductions made by authors in this volume and
others suggest that the level of intimacy in marital
relationships may be a key factor in the amount of conflict
experienced. Several writers have suggested that the more
intimate the relationship, the more likely the occurrence of
conflict (Simmel,1950; Sprey,1969; Foss, Chapter 8;
Hotaling, Chapter 9; Brown, Chapter 11). Perhaps, then,
the lessening of those factors that contribute to intimacy
also would reduce the amount of conflict in the family.

Foss' chapter points out that in some patterns of
family life a less intimate or intensive involvement is
characteristic. An excellent case in point is described by
Cuber and Haroff (1965) as the "passive-congenial" marriage,
a life-style in which all emotional and instrumental
satisfaction does not derive from the marriage. In
marriages in which creative energies and the satisfaction of
interests and emotional needs are not exclusively directed
to the marital relationship, less intensive patterns of
involvement will occur. Whether this type of marriage also
has less conflict and violence is a crucial question for the
study of family violence.

                THE IRONIC NATURE OF INTRAFAMILY VIOLENCE

When this book was planned, the key ideas to be
presented were those of culture and social organization. As
the book began to come together, what might be called the
"ironic nature of intrafamily violence" kept cropping up.
This in no way undercuts the importance of culture and
social organization as interpretive tools. The dual
influence of culture and social organization is described
throughout this volume as revealing the socially patterned
nature of marital violence. The individual personalities of
married couples, without considering the socially
constructed nature of marriage itself, cannot explain why
marriage as a social institution is characterized by a high
incidence of strife and violence.

But culture and social organization are somewhat static
notions and do not force one to face up to the dynamic and
emergent nature of family interaction. In the context of
this book, it is largely the notion of irony that provides
the needed dynamic. We have pointed to four such ironies.

At first glance, these ironies may seem to be only amusing oddities. They are more than this. Recognizing the existence of these counterintuitive processes sensitizes us to the complexity of family life. Ironies highlight the fundamental contradictions that reside in the cultural norms and social organization of family life. They force us to be wary of accepting the common-sense dichotomy between vice and virtue, good and evil, love and conflict.

Lastly, the exploration of ironic relationships naturally leads to the opening up of new and interesting research questions on family violence. Rather than viewing irony as residing in nature or in the universe, a sociological perspective on irony leads us to focus on the complex relationship between culture and social organization and its role in generating the contradictions of family life.

NOTES

*Part of the first section of this chapter is a revised version of part of "Cultural and Social Organizational Influences on Violence Between Family Members" (Straus 1974b).

1. For the purposes of this chapter, violence is defined, following Gelles and Straus (1978), as "an act carried out with the intention of, or perceived as having the intention of, physically hurting another person." The "physical hurt" can range from slight pain, as in a slap, to murder. Although this is the basic definition of violence used in our research, it is usually also necessary to take into account a number of other characteristics of the violent act, such as whether it is "instrumental" to some other purpose or "expressive," that is, an end in itself; and whether it is a culturally permitted or required act versus one that runs counter to cultural norms (legitimate versus illegitimate violence). Thus, the basis for the "intent to hurt" may range from a concern for a child's safety (as when a child is spanked for going into the street) to hostility so intense that the death of the other is desired. The former would be an example of "legitimate instrumental violence" and the latter of "illegitimate expressive violence."

2. Certain authors in this volume, e.g., Foss (Chapter 7), use the term paradox rather than irony. As Matza (1969) notes: there are two meanings of paradox--the general and the technical. In the general meaning of paradox, something can be both paradox (a tenet contrary to common sense) and irony (an outcome of events that mocks the fitness of things). Foss uses the term paradox in the general and not the technical sense of an apparent internal contradiction.

Chapter 2

Wife-Beating: How Common and Why?

Murray A. Straus

* *

Chapter 1 made frequent references to the high rates of physical violence that characterize American marriages. Until recently, such assertions had to be based on impressionistic evidence, or on studies of small or perhaps unrepresentative samples, for example, couples seeking divorce or couples involved in "domestic disturbance" police calls. This chapter, however, reports the results of a study of a large and nationally representative sample of couples. The rates of violence found in this study were somewhat lower than expected for "ordinary" pushing, slapping, and shoving, but astoundingly high for "wife-beating." In addition to documenting the high incidence of wife-beating, data on "husband-beating" is also presented and used to illustrate a recurring theme of this volume: that marital violence cannot be understood in terms of a single factor such as sexism, aggressiveness, lack of self-control, or mental illness of husbands who beat their wives. Each of these factors is important but does not account for the rate of assault by wives on husbands.

* *

The first objective of this chapter is to present some of the findings on violence between spouses from a recently completed study of American couples. These findings are unique, being the first such data on a nationally representative sample. Although the findings have limitations, they give at least some indication of the extent to which wife-beating is part of the way of life of American families.*1

The second objective is to explain further the irony that the group to which most people look for love and gentleness is also the most violent civilian group in our society.

The first of these objectives poses tremendous technical problems. The second objective, in addition to the technical problems, poses theoretical problems fundamental to our understanding of human society. Therefore, what follows should be taken as highly tentative, beginning answers to these questions.

Data will be presented on a sample of 2,143 couples. This sample was chosen in a way that makes it extremely likely that they are representative of all American couples. The age, race, and socioeconomic status of the couples in the sample correspond quite closely with census data for the nation as a whole. So far so good. But what about the data on wife-beating?

WHAT IS WIFE-BEATING?

To do research on the incidence of wife-beating, one must be able to define it in a way that can be measured objectively. One soon realizes that "wife-beating" is a political rather than a scientific term. For most people, wife-beating refers only to those instances in which severe damage is inflicted. Other violence is treated as normal or laughed off with remarks such as "Women should be struck regularly, like gongs." Or take the following:

> Concord, N.H. (AP) The New Hampshire Commission on the Status of Women has rejected a plan to help battered wives, saying that wife-beating is caused by the rise of feminism.
>
> "Those women libbers irritate the hell out of their husbands," said Commissioner Gloria Belzil of Nashua.
>
> At a meeting Monday, commission members, appointed by Gov. Meldrim Thomson, said any program to help battered wives would be "an invasion of privacy." (Portsmouth Herald, Sept. 13, 1977)

This statement suggests that a certain amount of violence in the family is "normal violence" in the sense that it is deserved (for example by "irritating the hell" out of one's spouse) and that, contrary to its position on violence outside the family, the state should not interfere.

A recent conversation with a student who had decided to do a term paper on violence in the family suggests the same conclusion. She came to see me for help on how to narrow the topic to something manageable. I suggested that she could choose to concentrate on husband-wife violence, parent-child violence, or violence between the children in a family. She was astounded at the last possibility and said "Well, I never thought of my brother hitting me as violence." There seems to be an implicit, taken-for-granted cultural norm that makes it legitimate for family members to hit each other.

At what point does one exceed the bounds of "ordinary" marital violence? When does it become "wife-beating?" To solve this problem that Richard Gelles and I took for our research, we gathered data on a continuum of violent acts, ranging from a push to using a knife or gun. This allows readers to draw the line at whatever place seems most appropriate for their purpose.

MEASURING WIFE-BEATING

But this "solution" can also be a means of avoiding the issue. So besides data on each violent act, we combined the most severe acts into what can be called a "severe violence index" or, for purposes of this chapter, a "Wife-Beating Index."

The Conflict Tactics Scales (CTS) were used to gather these data (Straus, 1979). These scales provide data on how family members attempt to deal with conflicts between themselves. The Physical Violence Index of the CTS contains the following eight items:

K. Throwing things at the spouse
L. Pushing, shoving, or grabbing
M. Slapping
N. Kicking, biting, or hitting with the fist
O. Hit or tried to hit with something
P. Beat up
Q. Threatened with a knife or gun
R. Used a knife or gun

The overall Violence Index consists of the extent to which any of these acts were carried out during the previous 12 months. The Wife-Beating Index consists of the extent to which acts N through R occurred.

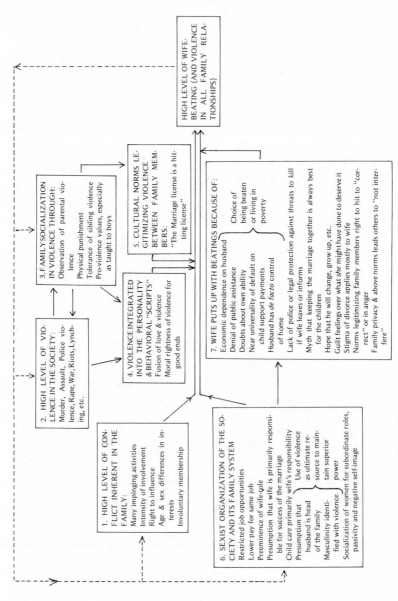

Figure 1. Flow chart illustrating some of the factors accounting for high incidence of wife beating (solid lines) and positive feedback loops maintaining the system (dashed lines)

The choice of acts N through R as the Wife-Beating Index does not reflect our conception of what is permissible violence. I find none of these to be acceptable for relationships between any human beings, including parent and child, brother and sister, husband and wife, student and teacher, minister and parishioner, or colleagues in a department. In short, I follow the maxim coined by John Valusek: "People are not for hitting."

What, then, is the basis for selecting items N through R to make up the Wife-Beating Index? It is simply that these are all acts that carry with them a high risk of serious physical injury to the victim. With these considerations in mind, we can turn to the question of trying to estimate the extent of wife-beating in the United States.

THE EXTENT OF WIFE-BEATING

The procedures for measuring violence just described were used in a study of a nationally representative sample of American families, made possible by a grant from NIMH. A probability sample of 2,143 families was studied. In approximately half the cases the person providing the information was a woman and in half a man. To be eligible for inclusion in the study, the respondent had to be one member of a male-female couple, aged 18 to 70. The couple did not have to have children, nor did they have to be legally married. Our sample contains couples with and without children, and married and unmarried couples in about the same proportion as are found in the population.

Yearly Incidence. The most direct, but in some ways also a misleading, statistic emerging from the data on the 2,143 couples in our sample is that, for the 12-month period preceding the interview, 3.8 percent of the respondents reported one or more physical attacks that fall under our operational definition of wife-beating. Applying this incidence rate to the approximately 47 million couples in the United States means that, in any one year, approximately 1.8 million wives are beaten by their husbands.

I mentioned that this can be a misleading figure; two other facts must be considered: how often these beatings occur, and how they fit in with the overall pattern of violence in the family.

Table 1. Violence Rates per Hundred Marriages, 1975

CRT Violence Item	Incidence Rate for Violence by		Frequency*			
			Mean		Median	
	H	W	H	W	H	W
Wife-Beating and Husband-Beating (N to R)	3.8	4.6	8.0	8.9	2.4	3.0
Overall Violence Index (K to R)	12.1	11.6	8.8	10.1	2.5	3.0
K. Threw something at spouse	2.8	5.2	5.5	4.5	2.2	2.0
L. Pushed, grabbed, shoved spouse	10.7	8.3	4.2	4.6	2.0	2.1
M. Slapped spouse	5.1	4.6	4.2	3.5	1.6	1.9
N. Kicked, bit, or hit with fist	2.4	3.1	4.8	4.6	1.9	2.3
O. Hit or tried to hit with something	2.2	3.0	4.5	7.4	2.0	3.8
P. Beat up spouse	1.1	0.6	5.5	3.9	1.7	1.4
Q. Threatened with a knife or gun	0.4	0.6	4.6	3.1	1.8	2.0
R. Used a knife or gun	0.3	0.2	5.3	1.8	1.5	1.5

*For those who engaged in each act, i.e., omits those with scores of zero.

Frequency During the Year. Among those couples in which a beating occurred, it was typically not an isolated instance, as can be seen from the "Frequency" columns of Table 1. However, the mean frequency of occurrence overstates the case; in a few cases violence was almost a daily or weekly event. For this reason, the median gives a more realistic picture of the typical frequency of violence in the violent families. This is 2.4, that is, the typical pattern is over two serious assaults per year. But of course there is great variation. For about a third of the couples who reported an act that falls in our category of wife-beating, beating occurred only once during the year. At the other extreme were cases in which it occurred once a week or more often. About 19 percent reported two beatings during the year, 16 percent reported three or four, and 32 percent reported five or more.

A more literal interpretation of the data can be obtained from looking at the figures in Table 1 for each type of violent act. When the category of "wife-beating" is restricted to those who used the term "beat up" to describe what happened (item P), the figure is 1.1 percent, with a median of 1.7 beatings per year. While this is much lower than the 3.8 percent figure that takes into account all the severe violent acts, it still represents over half a million families.

Duration of Marriage Rates. Another aspect of wife-beating that must be considered is the proportion of families in which a beating ever occurred. Unfortunately, our data for events before the year of the survey do not identify the assailant and the victim. All that can be reported is that 28 percent of the couples in the study experienced at least one violent incident and 5.3 percent experienced violence that we consider a beating.

In some of these cases, it was a single slap or a single beating. However, there are several reasons why even a single beating is important. First, in my values, even one such event is intrinsically a debasement of human life. Second, physical danger is involved. Third, many, if not most, such beatings are part of a family power struggle. Often only one or two slaps fix the balance of power in a family for many years--or perhaps for a lifetime.

Physical force is the ultimate resource that most of us learn as children to rely on if all else fails and the issue is crucial. As the husband in the family described in Chapter 10 said when asked why he hit his wife during an argument:

> ...She more or less tried to run me and I said no, and she got hysterical and said, "I could kill you!" And I got rather angry and slapped her in the face three or four times and I said

"Don't you ever say that to me again!" And we
haven't had any problem since.

Later in the interview, the husband evaluated his use
of physical force as follows:

You don't use it until you are forced to it. At
that point I felt I had to do something physical
to stop the bad progression of events. I took
my chances with that and it worked. In those
circumstances my judgment was correct and it
worked.

Since superior strength and size gives the advantage to men
in such situations, the single beating may be an extremely
important factor in maintaining male dominance in the family
system.

Accuracy of Estimates. How much confidence can be
placed in these figures? I am reasonably confident that the
sample is representative of American couples generally. But
that is only one aspect of the accuracy question. The other
main aspect is whether our respondents "told all." Here I
have doubts for the following reasons:

1. Underreporting of domestic violence is likely to
occur among two groups of people, for opposite reasons. For
a large group, violence is so much a normal part of the
family system that a slap, push, or shove (and sometimes
even more severe acts) is simply not noteworthy or dramatic
enough to be remembered. Such omissions are especially
likely when we ask about events over the entire length of a
marriage.

2. Paradoxically, there is also underreporting at the
other end of the violence continuum--those who experienced
such severe violent acts as being bitten, hit with objects,
beaten up, or attacked with a knife or gun. These acts go
beyond the "normal violence" of family life. Such acts are
admitted reluctantly, because of the shame involved if one
is the victim, or the guilt if one is the attacker.

3. A final reason for regarding these figures as
drastic underestimates lies in the nature of our sample.
Since a major purpose of the study was to investigate the
extent to which violence is related to other aspects of
husband-wife interaction, we sampled only couples living
together. Divorced persons were asked only about the
current marriage (again because of interview time limits and
recall accuracy problems). Since "excessive" violence is a
major cause of divorce, and since our sample is limited to
couples living together, these data probably omit many of
the high violence cases.

These considerations, plus the higher rates in our pilot studies and informal evidence (where some of the factors leading to underreporting were less) suggest that the true incidence for violence in a marriage is probably closer to 50 or 60 percent of all couples than it is to the 28 percent who were willing to describe violent acts in a mass interview survey.

WIFE-BEATING IS NOT RESTRICTED TO WIVES

Although this chapter is concerned primarily with wife-beating, an adequate understanding of the phenomenon requires that we consider it in a wider context. We must recognize that one does not have to be married to be the victim of physical violence by a partner. Our national survey (Yllo and Straus, 1980) a study by Hennon (1976) of students living together, and much informal evidence suggest that couples who are not married have rates of violence that are as high or higher than those married. In fact, couples do not have to live together. Once a step is taken toward a marriage-like arrangement, as in a boyfriend-girlfriend relationship, and especially if regular sex is involved, the violence rate jumps dramatically. Violence can no longer be figured in the rates per 100,000 characteristic of assaults in general. Instead, simple percentages, that is, rates per hundred, are more logical. Why this happens is important in itself and also because it throws a great deal of light on the situation of wives.

HUSBAND BEATING

Now we come to findings that may be surprising to some readers. The national sample data confirm what all of our pilot studies have shown (Gelles, 1974; Steinmetz, 1977; Straus, 1974): that violence between husband and wife is not a one-way street. The old cartoons of the wife chasing a husband with a rolling pin or throwing pots and pans are closer to reality than most of us (especially those of us with feminist sympathies) realize. This can be seen from an inspection of the wife columns in Table 1.

Violence Rates. The overall figures in the second row of Table 1 show that, for all violent acts during the survey year, the incidence is only slightly higher for husbands than for wives (12.1 percent versus 11.6 percent). In addition, those wives who were violent tended to engage in such acts somewhat more often than did the husbands in this sample median (3.0 times in the year compared with 2.5 times for the husbands). Moreover, the first row of Table 1, which gives the data on severe violence, suggests that the wives were more violent even in this traditional sense of the word violence.

Specific Violent Acts. If we look at the specific
types of violent acts sampled by the CRT, there is evidence
for the pot and pan throwing stereotype, since the number of
wives who threw things at their husbands is almost twice as
large as the number of husbands who threw things at their
wives. For half of the violent acts, however, the rate is
higher for the husband; the frequency is higher for the
husbands in all but two of the items. The biggest
discrepancy in favor of wives occurs in kicking and hitting
with objects. Such acts are less dependent on superior
physical strength. This seems to support the view that an
important difference between male and female domestic
violence stems from the smaller size, weight, and muscle
development of most women, rather than from any greater
rejection of physical force on moral or normative grounds.

Policy Implications. Although these findings show high
rates of violence by wives, this fact should not divert
attention from the need to give primary attention to wives
as victims as the immediate focus of social policy. There
are a number of reasons for this:

(1) A validity study carried out in preparation for
this research (Bulcroft and Straus, 1975) shows that
underreporting of violence is greater for violence by
husbands than it is for violence by wives. This is probably
because the use of physical force is so much a part of the
male way of life that it is typically not the dramatic and
often traumatic event that the same act of violence is for a
woman. To be violent is not unmasculine. But to be
physically violent is unfeminine according to contemporary
American standards. Consequently, if it were possible to
allow for this difference in reporting rates, even in simple
numerical terms, wife-beating probably would be the more
severe problem.

(2) Even if one does not take into account this
difference in underreporting, the data in Table 1 show that
husbands have higher rates of the most dangerous and
injurious forms of violence (beating-up and using a knife or
gun).

(3) Table 1 also shows that when violent acts are
committed by a husband, they are repeated more often than is
the case for wives.

(4) These data do not tell us what proportion of the
violent acts by wives were in response to blows initiated by
husbands. Wolfgang's data on husband-wife homicides (1957)
suggest that this is an important factor.

(5) The greater physical strength of men makes it more likely that a woman will be seriously injured when beaten up by her husband than the reverse.

(6) A disproportionately large number of attacks by husbands seem to occur when the wife is pregnant (Gelles, 1976), thus posing a danger to the as yet unborn child.

(7) Women are locked into marriage to a much greater extent than men. Because of a variety of economic and social constraints, they often have no alternative to putting up with beatings by their husbands (Gelles, 1976; Martin, 1976; Straus, 1976a, 1977b).

In short, wives are victimized by violence in the family to a much greater extent than are husbands and should therefore be the focus of the most immediate remedial steps. However, these data also indicate that a fundamental solution to wife-beating cannot be restricted to the immediate problem of the assaulting husbands. Rather, violence is embedded in the structure of the society and the family system itself (Straus, 1976a). The particularly brutal form of violence known as wife-beating is likely to end only with a change in the cultural and social organizational factors underlying parent-to-child, child-to-child, and wife-to-husband violence as well. Some of the specific steps to accomplish this change are outlined in Chapter 13.

THE CAUSES OF WIFE-BEATING

Now I turn to the proposition that the causes of wife-beating are to be found in the structure of American society and its family system. Demonstrating this, even in principle, is a vast undertaking. Indeed, that is what this book is about. In this chapter, I will simply identify seven of the main factors and the general tenor of the argument. Figure 1 gives an overview of these factors and some of their interrelationships.

A combination of these factors (plus others not diagrammed for lack of space) makes the family the most violent of all civilian institutions and accounts for that aspect of family violence which we call wife-beating. Let us look briefly at each of these factors.

1. High Level of Family Conflict. An essential starting point for any understanding of family violence is the high level of conflict characteristic of families. In Chapter 1, eleven reasons for the typical high level of conflict within the family were identified and briefly explained. These reasons included the broad range of activities shared by family members, with consequent greater

opportunity for conflicts of interest than in more narrowly focused groups; the age and sex differences built into the structure of the family; and the assignment of family roles on the basis of age and sex rather than interest and competence. All four chapters in Part III consider various aspects of intrafamily conflict. Chapter 8 considers these conflicts in the light of conflict theory and the paradox of the love-hate relationship so often found in families.

2. High Level of Violence in the Society. The high level of conflict inherent in the family, combined with the huge emotional investment typical of family relationships, means that the family is likely to be the locus of more, and more serious, conflicts than other groups. But conflict and violence are not the same. Violence is only one means of dealing with conflict. What accounts for the use of violence to deal with conflicts within the family? A fundamental starting place is that we are part of a violent society. There is a carry-over from one sphere of life to another, as I have tried to show in a paper comparing levels of family violence in different societies (Straus, 1977a). However, granting the carry-over principle, this explanation is by no means sufficient. Conflict is also high, for example, in academic departments. But there has never been an incident of physical violence in any of the six departments in which I have taught during the past 25 years. In fact, I have only heard of one such incident occurring anywhere. Clearly, other factors must be present.

3. and 4. Family Socialization in Violence. One of the most significant of these other factors is that the family is the setting in which most people first experience physical violence, and the setting that establishes the emotional context and meaning of violence.

Learning about violence starts with physical punishment, which is nearly universal (Steinmetz and Straus, 1974). When physical punishment is used, several consequences can be expected. First, most obviously, is learning to do or not do whatever the punishment is intended to teach. Less obvious, but equally or more important, are three other lessons that are so deeply learned that they become an integral part of one's personality and world view.

The first of these unintended consequences is the association of love with violence. Physical punishment typically begins in infancy with slaps to correct and teach. Mommy and Daddy are the first and usually the only ones to hit an infant, and for most children this continues throughout childhood. The child therefore learns that those who love him or her the most are also those who hit.

Second, since physical punishment is used to train the child or to teach about dangerous things to be avoided, it establishes the moral rightness of hitting other family members.

The third unintended consequence is the lesson that
when something is really important, it justifies the use of
physical force.

These indirect lessons are not confined to providing a
model for later treatment of one's own children. Rather,
they become such a fundamental part of the individual's
personality and outlook that they are generalized to other
social relationships, especially to the relationship closest
to that of parent and child--that of husband and wife.

Thus, early experiences with physical punishment lay
the groundwork for the normative legitimacy of all types of
violence but especially intrafamily violence. As suggested
by box 4, it provides a role model--indeed, a specific
"script" (see Chapter 4 and Gagnon and Simon, 1973)--for
such actions. Many children do not even need to generalize
this socially scripted pattern of behavior from the
parent-child nexus in which it was learned to other family
relationships: if our estimates are correct, millions of
children can directly observe physical violence between
husbands and wives (see also Owens and Straus, 1975).

5. Cultural Norms. The preceding discussion has
focused on the way in which violence becomes built into the
behavioral repertory of husbands and wives. Though
important, early experience could not account for the high
level of family violence, were it not also supported by
cultural norms legitimizing such violent predispositions.
Since most of us tend to think of norms that call for love
and gentleness within the family, it is difficult to
perceive that there are both de jure and de facto cultural
norms legitimizing the use of violence between family
members. Chapter 3 documents the evidence for the existence
of such norms and Chapter 5 illustrates the indirect effect
of cultural norms.

6. and 7. Sexual Inequality and Coping Resources of
Women. The last two causal factors, boxes 6 and 7 of Figure
1, can be considered together and summarized in the
proposition that the sexist organization of the society and
its family system is one of the most fundamental factors in
the high level of wife-beating. Chapter 6 and Part IV
demonstrate this proposition. Policy recommendations aimed
at preventing wife-beating are examined in Chapter 13. Some
aspects also have been presented earlier in this chapter.
Since these issues are discussed in depth in other chapters,
I will note only that boxes 6 and 7 of Figure 1 summarize
the main elements of sexism that lead to wife-beating.

Perhaps devoting an inappropriately small part of the
text of this chapter to sexual inequality--one of the most
important causal factors in wife-beating,--will dramatize

that sexism is only one part of the complex causal matrix of family violence (outlined in Figure 1). That male dominance does not protect men from violence by other men also illustrates this complexity.

If true equality between the sexes were somehow to be achieved tomorrow, all forms of family violence (including wife-beating) would continue to exist--though probably at a somewhat lower incidence--unless steps also are taken to alter the factors identified in boxes 2, 3, 4, and 5 of Figure 1. The level of non-family violence also must be lowered to end the training in violence that is part of growing up in a typical American family. Violence is truly woven into the fabric of American society, and into the personality, beliefs, values, and behavioral scripts of most of our population. Elimination of wife-beating depends not only on eliminating sexual inequality, but also on altering the system of violence on which so much of American society depends.

NOTE

1. This chapter, originally presented at the conference on "Battered Wives: Defining the Issues," Center for Research on Women, Stanford University, May 20, 1977; and at the Second World Congress, International Society on Family Law, Montreal, June 14, 1977, is a shortened and revised version of "Wife-Beating: How Common and Why," reprinted with permission from Victimology Vol. 2, Number 3, 1977, (c) 1977 Visage Press, Inc. The materials in this chapter will be presented more fully in a forthcoming book, Behind Closed Doors: Violence in the American Family (Straus, Gelles, and Steinmetz, 1980).

Part II Cultural Norms and Family Violence

The cultural norms and values permitting husband-wife violence resemble what Bem and Bem (1970) call "nonconscious ideology." This idea points out that on some issues (the Bems examined the role of women in American society) our perspective is so deeply held and so subtle that we cannot even imagine alternative beliefs and attitudes. Only when "nonconscious ideologies" are challenged are people apt to display the depth of such a belief system. Only under challenge is the rationale of the ideology likely to surface.

As the chapters in the following section make clear, our society fails to recognize the massive cultural "scripting" (Gagnon and Simon, 1973) that makes it more permissible to strike a family member than to hit a friend, co-worker, or stranger. One of the reasons these cultural norms or scripts are ignored is a deeply held belief that violence is an integral part of human nature. This belief blinds people to seeing that cultural norms specify who may be hit and who may not, and how hard, and under what circumstances.

Another factor blinds people to the culturally patterned nature of family violence (see Chapter 1): the irony that the manifest ideology (as contrasted with the "nonconscious ideology") emphasizes peace, harmony, and gentleness among family members. The reality to which the chapters in Part II testify is that norms legitimizing intrafamily violence are present and powerful. They may not be easily recognized, but "nonconscious ideologies" seldom are. Recognizing these taken-for-granted cultural norms is critical to understanding the social causes of family violence; family violence must be seen as a mode of behavior _acquired_ through years of cultural and family socialization.

Chapter 3

The Marriage License as a Hitting License: Evidence from Popular Culture, Law, and Social Science

Murray A. Straus

* *

This chapter emphasizes a theme that
underlies many of the other chapters. It is the
ability to see through or probe behind the
official version of reality. Official norms may
exalt the family as a group devoted to
gentleness and love, but this chapter provides
evidence that these norms coexist with a more
subtle set of norms that legitimate the use of
force and violence in the family setting.

The chapter also raises a number of
critically important questions for understanding
violence in the family system. Although it
demonstrates the existence of pro-violence
norms, the question of how such norms come into
existence in the first place is not answered.
Why are they being maintained, sometimes with
great fervor, by men and women alike?
Throughout this volume there are hints to
answers to these questions. For example, the
chapter on violence in children's books (Chapter
4) illustrates one of the ways that cultural
norms are transmitted from generation to
generation. The chapters in Part III show some
of the ways that the nature of families creates
a high level of conflict, and the conditions
under which conflict turns into violence.
Finally, Part IV helps us avoid the trap of
fixing on any one factor as the cause, or even
the main cause, of husband-wife violence. Each
of those chapters shows that neither cultural
norms nor family structure alone can account for
the high rate of husband-wife violence. But
together they form an explosive combination.

* *

In Chapters 1 and 2, and in a series of other papers and books (Gelles, 1974, 1977; Steinmetz and Straus, 1974; Straus, 1973), evidence was presented that the family is preeminent in all types of physical violence, from slaps to torture and murder. These studies suggest that the first priority for those concerned with the level of violence in American society should not be violence in the streets, but violence in the home, and the factors that lead to it.

The most appropriate place to begin is with a discussion of the physical punishment of children. We believe that physical punishment serves as the primary mechanism by which members of our society learn to use both verbal and physical aggression. Parental use of physical punishment is remarkably similar to many experiments on aggression using electric shocks. Even more important, physical punishment provides a powerful role model through which the child learns that if one truly wishes to influence another, physical force is effective and socially acceptable; that it is legitimate, often morally necessary to use physical violence on those one presumably loves; and that one should respond to aggression with aggression.

Since studies in the United States and Great Britain show that at least 93 percent of all parents use physical punishment (Steinmetz and Straus, 1974), and that at least half continue to use it through the senior year in high school (Straus, 1971; Steinmetz, 1974), it is an almost universal social learning experience. Moreover, this role modeling is supplemented for an amazingly large number of children by explicit instigation to aggression. Exhortation to violence is not restricted to slum families. Parents typically permit or urge a child to fight back if a sibling is aggressive. Moreover, 70 percent of the respondents in one national sample survey felt that "When a boy is growing up, it is very important for him to have a few fist fights" (Stark and McEvoy, 1970).

As for husband-wife aggression, this chapter will attempt to show that a marriage license is an implicit hitting license. The available evidence shows that the typical adult is more likely to be attacked--verbally, physically, or even morally--by his or her own spouse than by any other person. Data on homicides in at least a dozen different countries (Curtis, 1974; Wolfgang, 1956; Bohannan, 1960) show that murderers and their victims were more often members of the same family than of any other murder-victim relationship. In fact, when women are murdered, it is overwhelmingly by their husbands. And, to complete the picture, when husbands murder wives they tend to do so with great brutality, as indicated by such things as multiple stab wounds or multiple gun shots, as compared with the single stab or single shot typical when wives murder husbands (Wolfgang, 1956).

Therefore, something in the family system not only produces a high level of physical aggression, but also makes wives the victim of that aggression. Chapter 6 examines this high rate of aggression against women in terms of the sexist organization of society and the family, and identifies nine of the processes that link sexual inequality to physical aggression against women, starting with the most obvious linkage: the use or implicit threat of physical intimidation to keep women subordinate.

This chapter focuses on some of the ways that these patterns are reflected in the norms and values of the society. Specifically, I will present evidence that covert, largely unrecognized, but nonetheless powerful cultural norms permit and, in some cases, encourage physical aggression between spouses. Such norms are powerful instigators to husband-wife aggression because, in the absence of third parties, they provide the social expectations for behavior in situations of marital conflict.

THE PARADOX OF FAMILY VIOLENCE NORMS

As noted in Chapters 1 and 2, the norms and values relating to intrafamily violence pose a paradox. On the one hand, there is the "myth of family nonviolence" (Steinmetz and Straus, 1974; Straus, 1974b) that reflects cultural norms and aspirations for the family to be characterized by love, gentleness, and harmony. On the other hand, social norms exist that imply the right of family members to strike each other, therefore legitimizing intrafamily assaults, at least under certain conditions.

As noted in our discussion of The Myth of Family Nonviolence in Chapter 1, cultural contradictions and discontinuities of this type are present in every society to a greater or lesser extent (Benedict, 1938; Embree, 1950; Ryan and Straus, 1954). Physical aggression is a prime example of this in American society. Although there are clear norms and values restricting violence and emphasizing the value of peace and harmony, especially between family members, simultaneously a high level of actual violence exists, along with norms glorifying aggression and violence. In respect to the family, the legitimation of violence is sometimes explicit or even mandatory--as in the case of the right and obligation of parents to use an appropriate level of physical force to train and control a child. In fact, parents are permitted to use a level of physical force that is denied prison authorities in controlling inmates. In the case of husband-wife relations, similar norms are present and powerful, but largely implicit, unrecognized, or covert. What is the evidence that such norms exist?

INFORMAL MANIFESTATIONS OF CULTURAL NORMS
PERMITTING OR APPROVING MARITAL VIOLENCE

Ingeborg Dedichen, who lived with Aristotle Onassis for 12 years, describes an incident in which Onassis beat her severely until he quit from exhaustion:

> The following day instead of apologizing, Onassis explained, "All Greek husbands, I tell you, all Greek men without exception, beat their wives. It's good for them." And then he laughed (Shearer, 1975:4).

Most of the American or English public reading this might dismiss it as a Greek peculiarity. But, just as Onassis' statement is an exaggeration for Greek men, our denial of this norm exaggerates in the other direction. Once one is aware that there are norms legitimizing marital (and especially husband-to-wife) violence, instances such as the above pop up constantly. One amazing example is the ancient (and flagrantly sexist) joke told on the BBC women's program "Pettycoat Lane" in the spring of 1974. One woman asked another why she felt her husband didn't love her anymore. Her answer: "He hasn't bashed me in a fortnight."

At a higher literary level, plays provide many examples of the marriage license as a hitting license, including several by George Bernard Shaw, and the recent play about a Lesbian couple, "The Killing of Sister George," in which June makes threatening motions toward Alice:

> Alice: Don't touch me. You've got no right.
>
> June: I've got every right.
>
> Alice: I'm not married to you, you know.

The above are, of course, only literary reflections of the cultural norms that can be observed in everyday life. These examples range from casual remarks such as that of the railway conductor who, when asked by a woman for help with a stubborn seat, did so and remarked, "Some of these seats are just like women: you have to kick them to make them work" (protest letter to The New York Times, July 14, 1974:5). Other examples appear in the media with at least tacit approval of their contents, as in the following section of the widely read column by Ann Landers (October 29, 1973):

> Dear Ann Landers: Come out of the clouds, for Lord's sake, and get down here with us humans. I am sick to death of your holier-than-thou attitude toward women whose husbands give them a well-deserved belt in the mouth.

Don't you know that a man can be pushed to the
brink and something's got to give? A crack in
the teeth can be a wonderful tension-breaker.
It's also a lot healthier than keeping all that
anger bottled up.

My husband hauls off and slugs me every few
months and I don't mind. He feels better and so
do I because he never hits me unless I deserve
it. So why don't you come off it?-Feal Happy

Dear R.H.: If you don't mind a crack in the
teeth every few months, it's all right with me.
I hope you have a good dentist.

A number of husbands and wives interviewed by Gelles
expressed similar attitudes, so that Gelles developed a
classification of types of "normal violence" that includes
such categories as "I asked for it," "I deserved it," "She
needed to be brought to her senses," etc.   (Gelles,
1974:58). Other examples occur in connection with family
disturbance police calls, with wives as well as husbands
often asserting their right to hit each other because they
are married (Parnas, 1967; Yorkshire Post, May 23, 1974:9).
These same attitudes are widely shared by officials of the
criminal justice system. Sometimes this presumed right to
hit is linked to the race or social class of the couple, as
shown in many of Parnas' examples and in an English judge's
remark, "if he had been a miner in South Wales I might have
overlooked it" (London Daily Mirror, January 29, 1974:1).
This remark made headlines, but only because Welsh miners
protested.

A final example is provided by a marriage counseling
case (Straus, 1973:120) in which the husband hit his wife on
numerous occasions. He and his wife felt that he could not
help himself because, in the heat of the tremendous
arguments, he "lost control." The counselor, however, tried
to persuade the couple that the husband's behavior was not
simply a reversion to "primitive" levels, but in fact was
under normative control.   He did so by asking the husband
"Why didn't you stab her?" This conversation brought out the
implicit, unrecognized, but nonetheless operating norm that
permitted the husband to hit his wife but not to stab her.
This unrecognized norm legitimizing intrafamily violence,
unless it produces severe injury, parallels the California
"wife-beating" statute cited below.

Legitimation of Husband-Wife Violence
by the Courts and Police

There is considerable evidence that even though laws
giving husbands the right to "chastise" an erring wife are
no longer with us, the underlying spirit of such laws
lingers. That spirit is now primarily extralegal, but in
important ways it is still embodied in the legal system.

Immunity from Suit. One of the most important of these
legitimizations of husband-wife violence is to be found in
the doctrine of "spousal immunity" that, to this day, in
many jurisdictions prevents a wife from suing her husband
for assault and battery. In other jurisdictions, the law
has been changed only recently. Truninger (1971:269) cites
the following example:

> In Self vs. Self (1962) the wife alleged that
> the defendant husband..."unlawfully assaulted
> plaintiff and beat upon, scratched and abused
> the person of plaintiff," and that as a result
> plaintiff "sustained physical injury to her
> person and emotional distress, and among other
> injuries did receive a broken arm." The
> husband's motion for a summary judgment was
> granted by the trial court.
>
> On appeal, the California Supreme Court reversed
> the trial court's judgment, thus overruling
> several older California cases supporting
> interspousal immunity. The rationale of courts
> retaining the common law spousal immunity
> doctrine fear was that allowing the tort action
> "would destroy the peace and harmony of the
> home, and thus would be contrary to the policy
> of the law."

Failure of the Police to Act. As Truninger also points
out, it is doubtful whether a wife gains much, other than
the principle, from ability to sue her husband for assault
and battery; the actual operation of both the civil and
criminal justice systems puts up enormous obstacles and, in
any case, it typically does nothing to prevent immediate
repetition of the offense while the case is being
adjudicated. Usually the only way in which a violent spouse
can be removed from the home is by arrest, but the police
make such arrests rarely. In fact, until the 1976 revision,
the International Association of Police Chiefs' training
manual recommends that arrests not be made in such cases.

The no-arrest guideline probably is more closely
followed than any other in the training manual because it so
clearly fits the experience and values of the police. In
general, the police seem to share the belief in the
legitimacy of spousal violence, provided the resulting

injuries or destruction are within limits. Some police
departments have informal "stitch rules" whereby the wound
requires a certain (high) number of stitches before an
officer makes an arrest (Field and Field, 1973:229). Parnas
(1967) cites case after case of the police avoiding arrests
in situations mandating one were the parties not husband and
wife. Almost any policeman can cite numerous examples of
husbands' claiming the right to strike their wives, and many
police themselves believe this to be the law (Truninger,
2972:272; Coote, 2974).*1

     Obtaining even basic physical protection is often
difficult as is graphically shown in the following instance
(New York Times, June 14, 1976):

          It was about 4 o'clock in the afternoon when a
          call came into the 103rd Precinct station house
          in Jamaica, Queens, from a woman who said her
          husband had beaten her, that her face was
          bleeding and bruised. She thought some of her
          ribs had been broken.

          "Can you help me?" she pleaded to the police
          officer who answered the phone. "My husband's
          gone now, but he said he would come back and
          kill me." She was also frightened, she said,
          that he would start beating the children when he
          returned.

          "It's not a Police Department thing," the
          officer told her. "It's really a family thing.
          You'll have to go to Family Court tomorrow.
          There's nothing that I can do."

     Failure of Prosecutors to Act. Despite the repeated
nature and frequent severity of marital violence, it is
endured for long periods--often many years--by large numbers
of women. Some of the reasons that so many wives tolerate
this situation follow from the variables analyzed in this
paper. Other factors have been identified in Gelles' paper
"Abused Wives: Why Do They Stay?" (1976). Sooner or later,
however, the situation brings large numbers of women to the
point of desperation. Some respond to this by leaving, or
even by killing the husband; others attempt to secure a
warrant for the arrest of their husbands. For obviously
different reasons, each of these alternatives is typically
unsatisfactory. If the wife attempts to bring charges, she
faces being "cooled out" at every step by officials of the
criminal justice system. This process is illustrated by
Field and Field's tabulation of the approximately 7,500 such
attempts in Washington, D.C. in 1966:

          Invariably, the police had told them that, in
          order to protect themselves, they had to "get a
          warrant from the district attorney." They

announced typically, "I have come to get one."
To them this implied an automatic process, like
dropping nickels into a vending machine, and
they expected a routine procedure culminating in
the issuance of a warrant for their husband's
arrest. Their heightened feeling of precipitate
danger reinforced this expectation, and their
sense of grievance and desperation was further
solidified by the long wait they endured before
talking with the initial screening policeman or
the district attorney. Of these 7,500 women,
fewer than 200 left having secured their
objective (1973:232).

Finally, even when the circumstances are such that the
police and district attorney cannot avoid bringing charges,
few such cases get to trial.

A survey of the assault cases in the District of
Columbia showed that over three-fourths of the
cases not involving husbands and wives went to a
disposition of the merits of guilt or innocence.
The enforcement pattern was reversed in
husband-wife cases. Only about one-sixth of all
arrests involving marital violence ultimately
ended at trial or with a guilty plea, and the
crime charged by that time was invariably a
misdemeanor rather than a felony (Field and
Field, 1973:224).

Victim Compensation. Another way in which the law
continues, in effect, to legitimize husband-wife assault
crops up in connection with the workings of boards and
commissions that have been set up in England and a few
American states to compensate victims of crimes. The
English board explicitly ruled against compensation when the
victim is a spouse (Williams, 1974) and this also seems to
be the case with the California law (Edelhertz and Geis,
1974:278; Truninger, 1971:270).

The Legal System and Cultural Approval of Intrafamily
Violence. The situation described in this section is well
summarized by the phrase used as the subtitle of Field and
Field's article (1973) on the criminal process in cases of
marital violence: "Neither Justice Nor Peace." A situation
so pervasive is not likely to be a result of historical
accident. Nor is it likely to be a consequence of the many
difficulties in dealing legally with marital violence and
the low rate of success achieved by invoking criminal law.
These difficulties and uncertainties, after all, do not
deter the police and courts from invoking criminal
adjudication processes for many crimes--such as
prostitution--with an even lower rate of success in control.
Rather, the failure to invoke criminal penalties reflects
historical continuities in the cultural norms that make the

marriage license a hitting license. This is almost clear in
the California Penal Code section on wife-beating, which
prohibits an assault only if it results in severe physical
injury. But the most clear contemporary legal expression of
the right of husbands to use physical force is found in the
immunity of husbands from prosecution for rape of their
wives.

Experimental and Survey Evidence on
Approval of Marital Violence

There is a slowly growing body of empirical research on
intrafamily aggression and violence, some of which provides
evidence on the cultural norms we are considering. The
survey conducted for the United States National Commission
of the Causes and Prevention of Violence found that about
one quarter of the persons interviewed said they could
approve a husband or wife hitting each other under certain
circumstances (Stark and McEvoy, 1970). That figure is
probably a considerable underestimate because of the
existence of opposite norms--the more socially acceptable
anti-violence norms and the implicit or covert pro-violence
norms.

The contradictory and covert nature of the norms
approving marital violence makes experimental and
observational studies particularly appropriate, because
these studies do not depend on the willingness or ability to
verbalize norms and values. Unfortunately, for practical
reasons, all the observational studies have been of
parent-child violence (Bellak and Antell, 1974). But there
have been experimental studies of marital aggression or
studies that bear on marital aggression.

The first of these studies also reflects the more
general phenomenon of male hostility to women:

> One of the least recognized indices of male
> hostility to females is the reaction of men who
> watch a violent act against women, rather than
> committing or initiating it themselves. Three
> psychologists from Michigan State University
> staged a series of fights that were to be
> witnessed by unsuspecting passersby. The
> researchers found, to their amazement, that male
> witnesses rushed to the aid of men being
> assaulted by either women or men, and that men
> helped women being hit by other women. But not
> one male bystander interfered when a male actor
> apparently beat up a woman (Pogrebin, 1974:49-55
> and 80).

In addition to the interpretation of these findings as reflecting male hostility to women, it also seems likely that they reflect the norm permitting assaults between spouses. That is, the male bystanders did not come to the aid of a female victim of a male assailant because they inferred that he was the woman's husband. This, in fact, is the reason a number of bystanders gave for not intervening as Kitty Genovese was murdered (Rosenthal, 1964). This conclusion is further given credence because it agrees with experimental studies of "bystander intervention," such as the experiments reported and summarized by Bickman (1975). Bickman concludes that the social definition of what actions are right for the bystander is a more powerful determinant of intervention than the severity of the crime or concern for the welfare of the victim.

Closely related to these findings is an unpublished experiment by Churchill and Straus in which the subjects were given a description of an assault and asked to indicate what punishment they felt was appropriate. In the course of the assault, the victim was knocked unconscious. In half the descriptions the assailant was described as the woman's husband. In the other half, the description was identical except that the couple was described as "going together" for a year. The mean punishment score when the victim was not married to the assailant was 4.15, compared with 2.65 when the victim was the wife. Moreover, this experiment probably understates the difference, in that it specified that the unmarried couple had been going together for a year. The difference probably would have been much greater if the unmarried couple had not been described as having a quasimarital relationship.

In a final set of experiments bearing on this issue, couples interacted in a standardized laboratory task involving conflict. The data for married couples was compared with the data for unmarried couples in the same task situation. A study by Ryder (1968) found that strangers were treated more gently than were spouses. Similarly, using an experimental task that required the couple to reach a decision, Winter, Ferreira, and Bowers (1973) found the unrelated couples listened respectfully to one another whereas married couples were often rude to one another. Although there is a long distance between rudeness and violence, it seems likely that what is manifested in these two experiments is the beginning of the journey that for many couples ultimately ends in violence (Straus, 1974a).

THE CYCLE OF INTRAFAMILY VIOLENCE

In Chapter 2 the role-modeling function of physical punishment was described, and especially the implicit lesson that it is permissible, even mandatory, to use physical violence on those one loves most. But the learning of social scripts for aggression between family members takes place in many other ways, and I will conclude by briefly mentioning just one of these: observation by children of aggressive behavior between the parents themselves, and physical violence in particular.

When the Family Violence Research Program began, we were under the impression that violence between spouses is rare, and that middle class parents take pains to avoid physical fights in the presence of their children. The idea that physical violence between spouses is rare was the first of the myths about intrafamily violence that the data from the program forced us to abandon. Subsequently, a study by Bulcroft and Straus (1975) suggested that the idea of parents' being able to hide physical fights may also be incorrect.

In this study, 121 university students and their parents each separately completed parallel questionnaires, including one section that dealt with conflicts between the parents. There was a series of items concerning modes of coping with these conflicts (the Conflict Tactics Scales described in Straus, 1979 and used in Chapters 2 and 12). These items were arranged in order of coerciveness, starting with discussing things calmly, and ending with hitting the other with a hard object. A violence index was computed from the latter questions.

We found a surprisingly high correlation between the scores computed on the basis of data obtained from the student and the scores obtained on the basis of the questionnaire completed by each parent: the correlation between the parent-report data and the child-report data for husband's violence was .64, and for the wife's violence index the correlation was .32. The significance of this finding in the present context is that it indicates the degree to which children do know about acts of physical aggression between their parents, at least during the year the child is a senior in high school. Consequently, parents seem again to be serving as role models for intrafamily physical aggression and for learning the social norms which--to repeat the opening statement of this chapter--make the family the most frequent setting for aggression of all types, ranging from insults, to slaps, to beating, torture, and murder.

NOTES

Part of this chapter is reprinted with permission from
Murray A.   Straus, "Sexual Inequality, Cultural Norms, and
Wife-Beating," originally published in Victimology, 1976;   1
(Spring):54-76,   (c) 1976 Visage Press, Inc.; and in Emilio
C. Viano, editor, Victims and Society, Washington, D.C.,
Visage Press, 1976.

1. Programs to inform and train police to deal more
effectively with family disturbances have been initiated in
several cities. See Bard, 1969, 1971, and Chapter 13.

Chapter 4

Violence and the Social Structure as Reflected in Children's Books from 1850 to 1970

Martha D. Huggins and Murray A. Straus

* *

The previous chapter showed that cultural norms make the marriage license a hitting license. The research reported in the present chapter was designed to see if this approval of violence between family members is a theme in books written for children. The results show that children's books do depict a great deal of violence, including killings. In addition, they reinforce the lesson of physical punishment by depicting violence as an effective means of securing justice or of achieving some valued end.

However, although this chapter shows that children's books describe and justify violence, for __family__ violence the findings are not what we expected. Given the high rates of family violence pointed out in Chapters 1 and 2, it is ironic that in these stories little of the violence takes place between members of the same family. There is a wide discrepancy between the reality of family life and the idealized picture implied by the lack of family violence in children's books. As in television, physical aggression is largely depicted as something that occurs between strangers. The chapter concludes with a discussion of the discrepancy between the violent reality of family life and the media's avoidance of showing violence between family members.

* *

Of the highly industrialized nations of the world, the
United States is clearly one of the most violent (Palmer,
1972:15). Many explanations have been offered for this
phenomenon (Graham and Gurr, 1969), and undoubtedly a number
of factors operate to maintain physical violence as a
continuing aspect of American social structure. One factor
that has been a subject of considerable controversy is the
mass media.

Some investigators argue that violence in the media
reflects the violence of the society (discussed in Lynn,
1969). Others maintain that violence in the mass media and
in sports serves as a safety valve, permitting aggressive
drives to be drained off--the "drive discharge" and
"catharsis" models (Bettelheim, 1967; Freud, 1959;
Feshbach and Singer, 1971; Lorenz, 1966). Both the
"reflection" and the "catharsis" theories see violence in
the media and in sports as having either a neutral or a
neutralizing role. They therefore contrast sharply with
theories that hold that violence in the media is part of the
process of transmitting and encouraging violence. Among the
latter are the "cultural pattern" theory of Sipes (1973),
"social learning" theory (Bandura, 1973), and "general
systems theory" (Straus, 1973).

The theoretical and methodological issues underlying
this controversy are so complex that an eventual resolution
will require, at the minimum, an accumulation and
"triangulation" of evidence from a variety of
investigations. Historical studies of a variety of cultural
forms are particularly needed. A study of children's books
therefore seemed desirable because (1) Most of the available
research on the mass media and violence focuses on
television. Children's books, however, may be just as
important or more important. Our informal observation is
that the impact of a book read by a child (or to a young
child by a significant person such as a parent) is extremely
powerful. (2) The availability of children's books for over
one hundred years enables a degree of historical depth not
possible for any of the other mass media.

Theoretical Perspective. We believe that the relation
between literature and society is "dialectic": literary and
other artistic productions reflect the culture and social
organization of the society, especially its dominant strata.
However, once it is in existence, literature serves to
control and mold that culture and social structure. If the
artist's work is to be accepted, he or she must draw on the
cultural heritage of society and appeal to important
elements in the lives of members of society. At the same
time, the work of an artist--once accepted--becomes a part
of that cultural heritage and is one of many elements
influencing and controlling what goes on in the society.

Previous content analysis studies have given some indication of the relationship between changes in society and changes in literary contents. Straus and Houghton (1960), for example, found that, in issues of a youth magazine from 1925 to 1956, appeals to the value of individual achievement declined slowly but steadily. Their study helped verify what many observers had noted, but for which no firm evidence existed, namely, that American society has been placing less emphasis on the value of individual achievement. Content analysis may also invalidate or question a widely held belief, as in Furstenberg's study (1966) of the presumed greater power attached to the husband-father role in nineteenth-century America. But we should note that neither the studies cited nor the present study provide proof (or even a modestly rigorous test) of our assumptions about the dialectical interplay of literature and society. This would require time series data on both societal events and literary content and the use of techniques such as lagged and cross-lagged correlation. Since we will not be presenting such data, the present chapter is not offered as a test of these assumptions. Our aim is more modest; simply to present the results of our historical analysis, together with our interpretation of the trends.

Specific Objectives. One of the purposes of the study is to determine if the level of interpersonal physical violence depicted in children's books has been increasing or decreasing during the 120-year span from 1850 to 1970. We pose no hypothesis about the direction of change, because the available evidence does not suggest any overall increase or decrease in the level of violence in the United States during this period (Graham and Gurr, 1969).

The second objective is to gain information on the way society defines and labels physical violence for its next generation. The study examines the extent to which violence in literature is depicted as an "expressive" act (carried out to cause pain or injury as an end in itself) or an "instrumental" act (carried out to achieve some extrinsic purpose). Similarly, the proportion of violent acts presented by the authors as "legitimate" and "illegitimate" suggests how society evaluates and labels physical violence.

Finally, the content analysis was designed to obtain information on the statuses, roles, motives, and emotions of the characters involved in violence, and the precipitating conditions, outcomes, and consequences of violence. To the extent that violence in literature mirrors violence in the society, such information provides insight into this important aspect of social structure. To the extent that literature influences society, such information gives important clues to the "script" (Gagnon and Simon, 1973) for violent behavior presented to children.*1

SAMPLE AND METHOD

Sample. A three-step sampling process was used. The first step was the identification of what, for want of a better term, can be called "children's classics," books recognized by a literary elite of the society. We focused on this type of literature because, as Marx suggested (1964), the ideas of the elite strata tend to be the dominant and influential ideas in the society. From this perspective, it is not the moral evaluations of the population at large that give rise to a group's definitions of reality, but mainly the evaluations of the dominant class (Parkin, 1971:42). On the basis of these assumptions, we sought out lists of recommended and esteemed children's books, for example, the "Notable Children's Books: 1965-1972" prepared by the Book Evaluation Committee of the American Library Association.*2 The body of work compiled by this method is a chronologically ordered list of all books published between 1850 and 1970 that were included in any of the lists of recommended books.

The second step of the sampling process was designed to yield five books published in 1850, and five published every fifth year thereafter, in 1855, 1860, and so on, up to and including 1970, for a total of 125 books. For those years in which many books appeared, the sample of five was drawn by random numbers. If there were fewer than five books in the sample year (as sometimes happened in the early years), books from the closest adjacent year were included, for example, a book published in 1856 is included in the sample for 1855. Since these are all "classic" or "recommended" books we were able to find 115 of the originally selected 125 books in nearby libraries. The missing ten books were replaced by a random selection from among the other books published during the appropriate years.

The third step in the sampling process consisted of using a table of random numbers to select fifteen different pages from each book. We followed this procedure to prevent longer books from disproportionately influencing the results. Our data then describe any act of interpersonal physical violence that occurred on one of the sample pages in 125 "recommended" children's books published from 1850 through 1970.*3

Coding Methods. The basic unit of analysis consists of an act of interpersonal violence, which we define as the use, or threat to use, physical force for purposes of causing pain or injury to another person. Each time such an act occurred on a sample page, a coding form was completed identifying the book in which it occurred and providing space to code the type of information identified a few paragraphs back. More specific information on each of these variables will be given when the relevant data are presented.*4

FREQUENCY AND TRENDS IN VIOLENCE

Many observers of the American scene have suggested that America is a violent society. Palmer (1972:15), for example, contends that:

> "Since its inception, the United States has been in the front ranks of violent societies. Born in revolution, wracked by civil war, involved in numerous wars, it has also the tradition of bloody rioting, homicide and arrest."

According to the statistics cited by Palmer, each year there are 15,000 criminal homicides, 35,000 suicides, 300,000 serious assaults, and 50,000 forcible rapes, and these are minimum estimates. These more extreme forms of physical force only partially illustrate a more widespread pattern of violence in the United States. For example, physical fights between husband and wife may occur in half to three-quarters of all marriages (see Chapter 2), and physical fights between siblings are so common as to be almost universal (Straus, Gelles, and Steinmetz, 1979). Is the violence that is so much a part of American life found in the literature for children?

The answer to this rhetorical question is a clear "yes." More than three-quarters of the 15-page "book-segments" had one or more violent episodes, with a total of 264 such episodes. The largest number of violent episodes in a single book was 10 (in The Boys' King Arthur). The mean number of violent acts per book-segment was 2.1. The figure of 2.1 violent episodes per book-segment means that a 50-page book is likely to include about seven violent acts and a 150-page book, about 21 violent acts.

Modalities of Violence. The variety of methods used in these books to cause physical pain or injury to another covers most of those known to the human race. These ranged from merely shaking someone (two such incidents), to hitting and kicking (39 incidents), torture (6 incidents), burning (11 incidents), stabbing (43 incidents), and shooting (40 incidents). The most frequent type of violence involved pouncing on someone, grabbing them forcefully or causing them to fall (66 incidents or 25 percent of the total). However, such relatively mild forms were outnumbered by about two to one by more severe forms such as stabbing, shooting, torture, and burning.

This fact is also reflected in the classification of acts on the basis of the resulting physical injury; 22 percent of the 264 cases described a physical injury, and an

additional 33 percent described a violent death. Clearly,
we are not dealing with "kid stuff." The essentially adult
nature of the violence portrayed in these books will be
shown at greater length later.

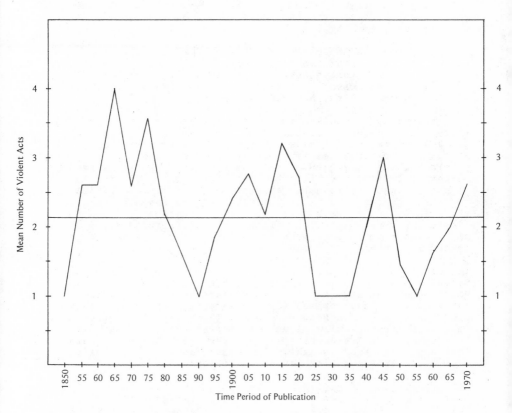

Figure 1. Mean number of violent acts per 15 pages by year published

Historical Trends. Figure 1 gives the mean number of
violent acts per book-segment for each five-year time
period. This chart reveals no long-term "secular" trend.
This finding is consistent with the conclusions of Graham
and Gurr (1969:628) concerning studies of actual rather than
fictional violence. At the same time, there is a pattern to
the highs and lows in fictional violence. The highs tend to
occur when the society is engaged in war. Thus, the highest
points in Figure 1 occurred during the American Civil War
(1865), World War I (1915), World War II (1945), and during
the peak of the Viet Nam demonstrations in the United States
(1970).*5

These data, showing that violence in children's fiction
is associated with the collective violence of the society,
are remarkably close to the findings of studies that show an
increase in actual violence within a society during periods
of war (Archer and Gartner, 1976; Henry and Short,
1954:102). The Archer and Gartner findings are particularly
impressive because they are based on data for 110 different
nations. The correspondence between the findings of our
content analysis with analyses based on actual levels of
violence is also of methodological interest in that it
provides additional support for using content analysis to
understand the operation of a society.

FICTIONAL VIOLENCE AND SOCIAL CONTROL OF DEVIANCE

The data just presented suggest that violence is an
integral part of "recommended" children's books. However,
since our interest is not in children's literature per se,
but in using children's books to gain a greater
understanding of the role of violence in American society,
our focus will be on the nature of violence and its
correlates. We have already presented one such
correlate--the association of fictional violence with
periods of national collective violence. This can be
interpreted as manifesting the principle that artistic
productions reflect the sociocultural matrix of the artist.

We suggested that fiction may serve to mold and control
society, and it is to this issue that we now turn. Durkheim
(1950) and Erikson (1966) hold that moral violations are
singled out for punishment and public disapproval as a means
of strengthening the commitment of the society to its moral
norms. Theoretically, the high incidence of violence in
these books could be a vehicle to expose and punish those
who use violence. Several of our findings, however, suggest
that this is not the case. In fact, the implicit message is
that violence is effective in resolving seemingly insoluble
problems.

The first evidence for this interpretation is the large proportion of the violent incidents classified as "instrumental violence" (defined as the use of violence to force another to carry out, or to hinder another from carrying out, some act). Some 72 percent of acts were classified as instrumental violence, compared with 28 percent classified as "expressive violence" (acts carried out to cause pain or injury as an end in itself).*6 Violence in these books is portrayed overwhelmingly as useful.

A second type of evidence against the theory that the violence is a vehicle for conveying moral disapproval of violence is shown in the outcomes. Of the 171 instrumental violent acts that could be coded for outcome, 60 percent were depicted as achieving the desired outcome.

Third, we classified each act according to whether the book's author portrayed it as legitimate or illegitimate. Of the 261 acts that could be coded on this dimension, 48 percent were presented as socially legitimate acts.

Finally, additional insight is gained when the instrumentality and the legitimacy dimensions are cross-classified, revealing that most of the acts of instrumental violence (55 percent) were depicted as socially legitimate whereas "only" 28 percent of the expressive acts of violence were depicted as legitimate. Thus, when violence is portrayed as a means of achievement, it tends to be given the stamp of social approval by the authors of these books. But when it is portrayed as an expression of emotion, it is depicted as illegitimate. We suggest that this relationship represents the combination of the historically important emphasis on achievement in American society coming together with the national heritage of violence.

Overall, the evidence suggests that the high frequency of violence in children's books is not part of a social control process restricting violence. The violence in these stories is typically carried out to achieve some end or solve some problem; it is usually successful; and, when used for such instrumental purposes, it is most often depicted as socially legitimate. Thus, to the extent that children's books are a means of social control and socialization, they contribute to the institutionalization of violence in American society.

A Vocabulary of Motives. Even if these books are not part of a process by which the society exposes and labels violence as a deviant act, other social control and socialization functions in relation to violence are not ruled out. We have suggested just the opposite--that these books play an important role in labeling violence as legitimate and in teaching the socially appropriate occasions for its use.

As Bandura (1973) shows, aggression and violence are, for the most part, socially scripted behavior. Among the most important elements of the script for violence taught in these children's books are "motives" or reasons that communicate to the child society's definition of the occasions on which violence may be used. Our initial analysis made use of 34 categories, some of which were predetermined and the remainder added as we came across reasons that did not fit the categories. These 34 categories then were grouped under six major headings.

In designing the study, we felt that violence in children's books often would be presented as a means of punishing or preventing socially disapproved behavior, especially on the part of children. To allow this hunch a fair opportunity to be proved or disproved, we combined all coding categories that could be considered violence used to enforce social norms or values. We included any indication that the purpose of violence was to enforce a legitimate authority; to punish violations of aesthetic norms (table manners, etc.), lack of thrift, lying, stupidity, wickedness, or greed; or to promote the general triumph of good over evil. The "Social Control" category in the accompanying tabulation shows that all these instances came to only 18 percent of the total number of violent acts.

TABLE 1.   MOST COMMON REASONS FOR INITIATING VIOLENCE

Reason	% (N=264)
Goal Blockage or Frustration	22
Emotional States	22
Social Control	18
Self-Defense	18
War	10
No Apparent	7
Other	3

The low percentage of violence for social control does not come about because any other rationale dominates the portrayal of violence in these books. In fact, the two categories that share top place, "Goal Blockage or Frustration" and "Emotional States," include only about 22 percent each of the total cases. The Goal Blockage category includes using violence to remove an obstacle; for example, to remove a barrier to the satisfaction of hunger, to attack a person blocking attainment of a goal, to assert one's

power in general. The other top category, "Emotional
States," includes violence motivated by some strong emotion
such as shame or humiliation, revenge, or rage over having
been insulted.

The Social Control, Self-Defense, and War categories
combined come to 46 percent of the motives or reasons for
violence. Thus, the types of violence for which a moral
case can be argued are slightly less frequent than the
combined frequency of violence to attain some other end,
gratuitous violence, or violence as a result of an emotional
state. Clearly, if these are morality tales, an important
part of the moral code being communicated is the "eye for an
eye, tooth for a tooth" aspect of the Old Testament. By and
large, these conclusions apply over the entire period from
1850 to 1970. However, the Social Control category tended
to be more common prior to 1930. In addition, one of the
subcategories occurred only in the period 1955 to
1970--violence used to punish the "stupidity" of others.
Perhaps the increasing bureaucratization of modern society
and the attendant demands for rationality, so well described
by Weber (1964), leads to depicting "sheer stupidity"
(irrationality) as one of the more serious moral
transgressions of our time.

     Capital Punishment. Another aspect of the vocabulary
of motives contained in these books concerns violent death.
The fact that someone was killed in 33 percent of the
book-segments provides an opportunity to gain insight into
the social definition of killing and death that is presented
to children. An important aspect of this depiction comes to
light because the death often occurs because the victim has
committed some moral wrong or crime. That is, although the
terms "capital punishment" and "death penalty" are not used,
these books graphically describe use of the death penalty.
And, as Bruno Bettelheim (1973) says about "...those great
American folk heroes, The Three Little Pigs" (in which the
big bad wolf is boiled alive for blowing the house down):
"Children love the story... But the important lesson
underlying the enjoyment and drama of the story equally
captures their attention."*7

     We felt that the books sampled contained many such
examples of the implicit use of the death penalty. To check
this, we cross-tabulated the variable indicating death or
other injury with the act that precipitated the violence.
The results show that capital punishment (the killing of a
character who committed a moral transgression or crime)
occurred in 22 percent of the instances in which a character
died. Since these are happenings of great dramatic
intensity, what Bettelheim calls "the important lesson
underlying the enjoyment and drama of the story" is likely
to make a strong impression on the child's mind. It is not
at all far-fetched to suggest that this literary background
is part of the basis for the widespread, seemingly

irrational commitment to the death penalty by so many
Americans (see Gelles and Straus, 1975).

RACE, SEX, AND FAMILY

Race. The racial identification of violent characters
in these books and their victims does not show any striking
deviation from the composition of the United States
population. Of the initiators of aggressive acts, 80
percent were white, 4 percent black, 1 percent Oriental, 7
percent Indian, and 8 percent "other." The distribution for
victims of these aggressive acts is approximately the same
(79, 7, 2, 5, and 6 percent).

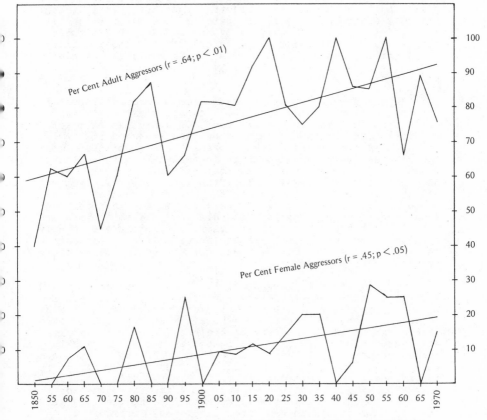

Figure 2. Regression of per cent adult aggressors and per cent female aggressors on year of publication

Sex. Most of the violence in this sample of books took place between men. Ninety-one percent of the aggressors were male, as were 86 percent of the victims. Thus, violence in these books is overwhelmingly depicted as a male activity. If the period covered by this study is one showing a gradual movement toward sexual equality, this trend should be reflected in a gradual increase in the proportion of female characters who engage in "masculine" acts of all types, including aggression. The lower line of Figure 2 does indicate just such a trend.

Although the proportion of women aggressors is growing, there are many ups and downs in Figure 2. Gecas (1972) did not find any such trend over time in a study of adult magazine fiction, and it may be that the "trend" we observed reflects a coincidence of random fluctuations. Arguing against this possibility is the fact that the correlation of 0.45 has a probability of chance occurrence of less than 0.05 when measured over 25 time periods. In addition, Figure 2 suggests a cyclical pattern within the general trend. A spectral analysis (Dixon, 1965) was therefore carried out to determine if a dependable cyclical pattern could be seen in the time series; this analysis revealed a cycle of four time periods (20 years), accounting for 38 percent of the variance.

In the absence of other information, it is difficult to interpret this 20-year cycle. One possibility is that a child reading these books at age 10 would have reached maturity and perhaps would be writing books of his or her own in 20 years. That generation's authors might then tend to produce works of fiction influenced by the depiction of female characters in the books they had read as a child. But whatever the explanation, the fact that this cyclical pattern, in combination with the upward secular trend, accounts for 58 percent of the variance in the proportion of female aggressors suggests that more than chance factors are shown in Figure 2. In addition, the increase in female aggressors is consistent with an increase in the proportion of women arrested for various crimes, especially violent crimes (Roberts, 1971).*8

Adults Versus Children. On the basis of actual and potential injuriousness, and in terms of the purposes depicted, we suggested that the violent incidents in these books are not "kid stuff." The most direct evidence is that 80 percent of the initiators of violent acts were adults. Nor was this figure often mitigated by use of an animal or other nonhuman characters: 80 percent of the aggressors were human characters. The image presented to children in these books is of adults being physically violent. Moreover, the percentage of acts in which the aggressor is an adult has gradually been increasing over the 120-year span of this study, as the upper line shows in Figure 2.

The preponderance of adult figures as physical aggressors is an instance of fiction that does not mirror reality, not because adults in our society are not violent, but because children are. Pushing, shoving, hitting, and physical fighting are more common among children than among adults, rather than the reverse.*9 This reversal may represent one of the myths concerning violence in American middle-class society, namely, that violence is approved only when its end is seen as socially worthy or valued, as punishment of wrongdoers or "preventative" air raids.*10

Family Violence. Another myth that these books transmit is the notion that physical violence between family members is rare. There is a wide discrepancy between the idealized picture of the family as a group committed to nonviolence between its members and what actually goes on. The available evidence suggests that violence is typical of family relations (Steinmetz and Straus, 1973; Straus, 1974b; Straus, Gelles, and Steinmetz, 1979). In childhood, the persons most likely to strike a child are siblings and parents. In adulthood, the victim of assault or murder is most likely a family member. As shown in Chapter 3, informal norms, largely unverbalized, make a marriage license a hitting license (see Gelles, 1974; Schulz, 1969).

Nevertheless, in these children's books, 91 percent of the violent incidents take place between persons who are not related. Two percent of the violence was by fathers and two percent by mothers. In only a single incident did a husband hit a wife and in none was the aggressor a wife or grandparent. These findings are parallel to those revealed in an informal search for instances of husband-wife violence in 20 novels for adults (Steinmetz and Straus, 1974).

The absence of husband-wife violence in adult fiction and the virtual absence of any intrafamily violence in children's fiction calls for an explanation, especially since so much contemporary fiction attempts to show reality in grim detail. Although these data do not permit a definitive answer, we suggest that the following processes may be at work.

First is a process of social control. The society does have a commitment to familial nonviolence, even though it exists side by side with more covert norms permitting and encouraging intrafamily violence (Chapter 3). Thus, the cultural representations of society tend to portray families in a way that will not encourage people to violate this norm.

Second is a process of social construction of reality. The society must have its members define the family as a place of love and gentleness rather than a place of violence because of the tremendous importance of securing commitment to the family as a social group. The myth of family nonviolence is one of the many ways that the institution of the family is strengthened and supported. It helps encourage people to marry and to stay married despite the actual stresses of family interaction.

Third, most speculatively, the _myth_ _of_ _family_ _nonviolence_ discourages members of the intellectual elite, whether novelists or sociologists, from probing into this aspect of the family. We have all been brought up on this literature and even read it as adults. Apparently, having accepted the literature's basic premises, novelists avoid writing about physical violence between family members, and sociologists have practiced "selective inattention" to research on this aspect of the family (Steinmetz and Straus, 1974).

SUMMARY AND CONCLUSIONS

Our study of 125 "classic" or "recommended" children's books published from 1850 to 1970 revealed an extremely high incidence of physical violence. Almost all the books described one or more acts of actual or threatened violence. The typical children's book can be expected to have one violent incident, a third of which is lethal, for every seven pages of text. There was no general increase or decrease over the 120 years studied. However, the portrayal of violence tended to be high during periods in which the society was engaged in war, and to be low during periods of economic difficulty.

If the depiction of violence were construed as a vehicle to express societal disapproval of violence, it would be presented as evil, and the perpetuators of violence would be punished. The opposite seems to be the case. For example, "instrumental" violence was frequent, and typically resulted in the attainment of the aggressor's purpose.

Nevertheless, the evidence suggests that these books do have important functions of socialization and social control. They provide scripts and role models through which generations of young Americans have learned how to behave violently. Among the elements of these complex scripts that must be learned are the motives that one can legitimately invoke to justify violence, the kinds of persons who can be violent and against whom violence is permissible, the level of socially acceptable injury, and the emotions that are appropriate or required on the part of the aggressor (for example, joy or remorse) and the victim (for example, rage, tears, or humiliation). All of these elements and their complex interrelations are depicted for the child in this sample of books.

Violence between family members is a major exception to the conclusion that children's books provide a script for violence. Violence within the family was rarely portrayed, reflecting the social mythology of familial nonviolence. The myth of family nonviolence may in turn reflect the high stake that society has in securing and maintaining commitment to the family as a social group.

NOTES

*Paper presented at the 1975 annual meeting of the Eastern Sociological Society. This research was partly supported by National Institute of Mental Health grant number MH-15521 and by a summer fellowship awarded to the senior author by the University of New Hampshire Graduate School. We would like to express our appreciation to Paul Kaplan for his work on coding the 125 books, to Loren Cobb for assistance with the spectral analysis, and to Paul Drew, Arnold Linsky, Stuart Palmer, and Donna Peltz for valuable comments and criticisms on an earlier draft.

1. Assuming that literature does influence society, a content analysis by itself can only indicate the nature of the message. It does not provide data on the intensity of the influence or on the specific sectors of the population that are most, least, or not at all influenced. In a complex modern society, both the intensity and the extent of influence are highly problematic, for the same reasons that "functional integration" in general is problematic in such societies (Cohen, 1969:151-156).

2. The following supplementary material is available on request: (1) List of books analyzed. (2) List of book lists used to locate books for each of the five year periods. (3) Code and code sheet used in the content analysis.

3. For 193 of the books, we were able to obtain information on the approximate age-of-child range for which the book was considered suitable. We coded the midpoint of the age range for each book. These median ages ranged from five books with a recommended age of six years to one book for 16 year olds. The mean of the median ages was 10.8 years and the mode was 10 years (26 percent of the cases).

4. Although we coded only acts of interpersonal violence that occurred on the pages drawn in the sample, we read as much of the rest of the book as necessary to determine such things as the social characteristics of the actors and their motives. A copy of the detailed content analysis code may be obtained from the National Auxiliary Publications Service. See footnote 1.

Two different coders made the content analysis. A test of the reliability of the content analysis procedure was carried out three days after the actual coding had begun. All books coded that day were done by both coders. For the 360 codings compared (10 books, 36 variables per book), there was an 87 percent agreement.

To prevent differences between coders from influencing the trend analysis, each coder analyzed only two or three of the books for a given year. Therefore, possible "drift" or changes in coding standards that might have occurred as the coding proceeded would not bias the time series analysis.

5. None of the books published during the peak years were "war stories." In addition, little of the violence portrayed in any of these books is the killing or wounding of an enemy soldier.

6. Our coding categories were primarily expressive, versus primarily instrumental, since both components may be present. See Straus, Gelles, and Steinmetz (1973) for a discussion of this and related issues in identifying types of violence. The coding of each act as either primarily instrumental or expressive was carried out separately from the coding of such variables as the specific reasons for initiating violence (see Table 1) and there is therefore a small discrepancy between the two variables. If the two noninstrumental categories are subtracted from Table 1, this produces 71 rather than 72 percent instrumental acts.

7. Bettelheim was referring to teaching the work-ethic in this quotation, but we feel it is equally applicable to the violence-ethic that is also presented.

8. Of course, as those familiar with crime statistics realize, this does not necessarily mean that women have engaged in more violent acts. Changes in the social definition of women similar to those occurring in these children's books may also characterize the perception of women by the police and public prosecutors, leading to an increase in arrest rate rather than an increase in incidence of violence.

9. However, if the unit of violence is homicide or those assaults that enter the official statistics, then the peak age is the middle to late twenties.

10. Asserting that this is one way in which children's literature reflects ideal rather than actual social patterns points up the weakness of the "dialectical interplay" theory, namely, that it is untestable: nothing can refute it. Correspondence can be claimed as an instance of support of the "reflection" process and a discrepancy can be claimed as part of the "influence" process. Nevertheless, as Cohen (1969:6) notes, untestable theories can have heuristic

value. In the present case it sensitizes us to finding instances that, in our judgment, reflect one or the other of these two processes and to speculate about the underlying reasons. If these speculations point to important social processes, it can be said that the theory has heuristic value, especially so if it leads to subsequent research to test these speculations.

Chapter 5

A Cultural-Consistency Theory of Family Violence in Mexican-American and Jewish-Ethnic Groups

Joseph C. Carroll

* *

Up to this point we have been considering cultural norms that deal directly with violence. However, this chapter suggests that even cultural norms that do not have a manifest reference to violence also affect the level of violence. For example, norms may structure family roles in a way that increases tension and hostility in the family, even though that is not what is intended. Carroll argues that the elements of a culture tend to be interdependent. He applies this "cultural consistency" theory to Mexican-American and Jewish-American families. For example, Carroll concludes that in Mexican-American families, norms call for male dominance in husband-wife relationships and father dominance in parent-child relationships, whereby it is not legitimate for a wife or child to contest the husband or father, are systematically linked to a high level of violence. In Jewish families, it is not illegitimate to argue with one's husband, wife, or father. Conflicts are not settled on the basis of ascribed power, but on the basis of discussion and knowledge (either scriptural or scientific). To the extent that this ideal is followed, conflicts can be settled without resorting to violence.

While this chapter examines only two ethnic subcultures, it is a promising beginning to the development of a typology of family subcultural norms and their role in permitting or discouraging the use of violence as a means of conflict resolution.

* *

The concept of the subculture of violence refers to norms that deal directly with the extent to which violence may be used and the conditions under which violence is permissible. However, this conceptualization does not deal with the question of how such norms and values come into being and why they persist as cultural patterns. One explanation of the development of these cultural patterns asserts that specific cultural elements reflect the operation of the culture as a system. White suggests that culture may have systemic properties, in that the structure of culture consists of integrated components related by cause and effect (1975:36). Thus, norms concerning violence tend to reflect and be consistent with the values characteristic of a group.

The purpose of this chapter is to develop such a cultural-consistency theory of violence and to apply this theory to Mexican-American and Jewish ethnic groups. These groups were selected because they seemed to have markedly different values and norms, allowing for examination of the theory from two different standpoints. The two groups may be seen as extremes on a cultural value continuum on which other ethnic groups may be placed and compared. Other theories besides cultural consistency assert that a culture reflects the typical personality of a society's members or that a culture reflects the pressures and limitations inherent in the organization of a society. These explanations are also important for a full understanding of a culture, but they are omitted from the present chapter to allow room to adequately develop a cultural-consistency theory.

A CULTURAL-CONSISTENCY THEORY OF VIOLENCE

Since the goal of this chapter is to explain the cause of family violence in certain ethnic groups in terms of cultural consistency, we must first define what we mean by a subculture. According to Wolfgang, subcultures arise when not all of the values, beliefs, or norms in a society are given equal status by all groups. Subcultural groups may partially accept or deny elements of the central or dominant values, yet remain within the cultural system (1967:99). Thus a group of people, for example, an ethnic group, may share values and norms regarding family life that are not identical to those generally accepted by the wider society. In our definition, values for family life refer to basic values of the ethnic group rather than to those that deal explicitly with violence. Examples of more basic values are those of power relations assigned by age and sex, or the practice of religion.

Although they are not concerned with specific ethnic
groups, Parsons and Shils' discussion of the consistency of
cultural patterns is relevant. They state:

> Cultural patterns tend to become organized into
> systems. The peculiar feature of this
> systematization is a type of integration which
> we may call consistency of pattern (1953:21).

> The consistency of pattern of such a system will
> exist to the extent to which the same
> combination of value judgments...runs
> consistently throughout the actors' responses to
> different situations; that is, to a different
> class of objects, different objects in the same
> class, and the same objects on different
> occasions (1953:172).

In a cultural system, as the term is used above,
orientations toward a particular nonsocial or social object
are interdependent. Social objects may be individuals or
collectivities (1953:5). Cultural patterns refer to the
extent to which systems of ideas or beliefs, and systems of
value orientations are shared by members of a culture.

According to Parsons and Shils, the problem for the
student of culture is to determine the value judgments that
lead to consistency of patterns.

> In order therefore to determine the existence of
> systematic coherence where there has not been
> explicit systematization, it is necessary for
> the student of culture to uncover the explicit
> culture and to detect whatever common premises
> may underlie apparently diverse and unconnected
> items of orientation (1953:22).

The position taken in this chapter is that each ethnic
group shares a set of "common premises" that constitute the
source of members' actions in all areas of life. These are
the basic values of the group. Thus, to arrive at the
actual level of family violence, we must examine the basic
family values of the ethnic group.

There is little doubt that norms for family violence do
exist in some ethnic groups. Lewis (1960) found that severe
punishment was traditional in Tepoztlan. Parents believed
in early punishment that began about the time a child
learned to walk, although the most severe punishment of
children occurred between the ages of five and twelve.
Lewis reported that although punishment in this village had
become less severe, it was not uncommon for fathers to beat
their children with a stick or rope.

In years past family violence was even within the bounds of the law.

> Canon Law in years past accepted wife-beating as a fair means of keeping a spouse in order. A hundred years ago it was an unquestioned pattern in many families, due in part to the lack of status of a woman, and in part to their chattel value in a marriage (Fennell, 1974:15).

The final question to be discussed in the development of a theory of ethnic family violence is how the norms of a group remain strong from generation to generation. Wolfgang believes that learning processes perpetuate the subcultural norms for violence.

> The development of favorable attitudes toward, and the use of, violence in a subculture usually involve learned behavior and a process of differential learning, association, or identification (1967:160).

Since imitation is a powerful learning process (Bandura, 1973), one could say that the greater the amount of violence in parents' behavior toward a child and toward each other, the greater the chance that the child will act violently later in life (see Chapter 12, section D).

At this point it may be appropriate to assess the idea that one's culture has a great deal to do with the development of personality. Perhaps in viewing culture as a cause of personality, we see only half of the picture. Personality may have a lot to do with the development of culture. Yinger (1965) has stressed this point in an examination of whether the sociocultural system affects individual action or whether individual action affects the sociocultural system, or both. He calls for a more careful specification of causal relationships in studies of culture and states that the relationship between cultural norms and personality is reciprocal. In other words, "individual responses to and interpretations of culture lead to normative variation" (1965:82). Also, Kardiner (1963) has reported that although culture and personality change each other in a cyclic process, institutional change tends to be followed by personality change. The following diagram illustrates the reciprocal nature of the relationship between cultural values, norms, and personality.

Values   Norms   Personality ────────▶ Action

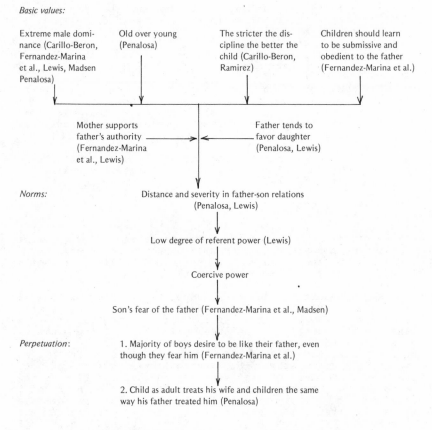

Basic values:

Extreme male domi-   Old over young   The stricter the dis-   Children should learn
nance (Carillo-Beron,   (Penalosa)   cipline the better the   to be submissive and
Fernandez-Marina   child (Carillo-Beron,   obedient to the father
et al., Lewis, Madsen   Ramirez)   (Fernandez-Marina et al.)
Penalosa)

Mother supports   Father tends to
father's authority ─────────►◄───────── favor daughter
(Fernandez-Marina   (Penalosa, Lewis)
et al., Lewis)

Norms: Distance and severity in father-son relations
                                (Penalosa, Lewis)

                      Low degree of referent power (Lewis)

                                Coercive power

Son's fear of the father (Fernandez-Marina et al., Madsen)

Perpetuation: 1. Majority of boys desire to be like their father, even
                      though they fear him (Fernandez-Marina et al.)

                      2. Child as adult treats his wife and children the same
                      way his father treated him (Penalosa)

Figure 1. Mexican-American parent-child violence

In moving from these general principles to specific ethnic groups, our first step was to collect an inventory of family values and norms from the literature on each ethnic group. Family values were defined as "generally accepted aspirations and ideals which are publicly sanctioned" (Kardiner, 1963), and which are concerned with intrafamily relationships. Norms are seen as more specific rules governing behavior, arising from the values and more closely linked to violence. For example, a basic value in Mexican-American ethnic groups would be the dominance of old over young, whereas a norm would be the severity of parent-child relations.

Next, we attempted to develop hypotheses concerning causal links between the family values and the norms for violence or nonviolence. The final step was to find child-rearing norms in the literature that seem to perpetuate behavior in each ethnic group.[1]

MEXICAN-AMERICANS

Figure 1 shows how values and norms may affect the amount of family violence in the Mexican-American ethnic group. The material on family characteristics used to construct this diagram comes from the work of Carillo-Beron (1974), Fernandez-Marina, et. al. (1958), Lewis (1959, 1960, 1963), Madsen (1964), Penalosa (1968), and Ramirez (1967).

All of the basic family values in Figure 1 are concerned with the all-encompassing authoritarian role which the older male possesses in Mexican-American families.[2] The fundamental incompatibility between great authority and intimacy suggests that the four basic family values promote distant and severe father-child relations. Mirande (1977) reported that father-child relations do tend to be somewhat distant. Lewis (1960) suggested that distance may be manifested through a general lack of affective relations as fathers pay less attention to children as they grow older.

An example of severity would be that children are often severely punished for an offense such as lying (Penalosa, 1968:685). Penalosa and Lewis both report that relations between fathers and daughters tend not to be as distant or severe as father-son relations. Fathers may show a mild form of favoritism to daughters and be more protective and possessive.

Implicit in the above paragraph is the following proposition relating any one of these basic family values to more specific norms.

1. To the extent that the male possesses a great
amount of authority in family life, the more
will that culture be characterized by distant
and severe father-son relations.

An intervening variable in the relationship between the
four basic values and the distant, severe father-son
relations is the degree to which the mother supports the
father's authority. If she does support it, father-son
relations are expected to be even more distant and more
severe. The value of extreme male dominance in husband-wife
relations suggests that the mother is more likely to support
her husband's authority. Carillo-Beron (1974) found that
Mexican-American women were more likely than Anglo-American
women to support authoritarian submission, exaggerated
masculine and feminine roles, extreme discipline, and
rejection of impulsive action. On the other hand, Hawkes
and Taylor (1975) reported that the most common power
structure in Mexican-American families is egalitarian.
Attempts to link husband-wife equality to increasing
acculturation and to an increase in Mexican-American women
employed outside of the home were not successful and led
Hawkes and Taylor to conclude that the basic cultural value
of dominance and submissiveness needs more adequate
verification.

In the cultural-consistency theory for Mexican-American
families an important relationship exists between the norm
of distant, severe father-son relations and the actual use
of violence. The severe father-son relations may lead to
the son being afraid of his father; the son's fear
contributes to the father's exercising of control through
his temper and violent outbursts.

How does the son's fear of the father lead to the
display of temper and violent outbursts as a means of
control? Apparently, the presence of fear in a relationship
inhibits the degree of communication between two parties.
Possibly the distance and emotional aloofness between father
and son indicates low "referent power" and therefore the
need to use "coercive power." Referent power is the degree
to which one person's identification or oneness with another
allows the latter person to influence the former (French and
Raven, 1959:161). Coercive power does not derive from
attraction or identification but from the threat of
punishment as a means by which one person influences another
(French and Raven, 1959:157). In other words, the child
conforms to the father's wishes not because of a mutual
attraction but because of the threat of force and the high
probability of punishment. The presence of a great degree
of coercive power may contribute to the fear of the father
that Fernandez-Marina et al. (1958) and Madsen (1964)
report as prevalent in Puerto-Rican and Mexican-American
families. Madsen stated that Mexican-American college
students asked to evaluate the father's role in the Latin

family felt that it was too authoritarian. Students reported that "it is true that the children have a great respect for the father but it is a respect based on fear" and that "[the father] should be a friend to his children, not a dictator" (Madsen, 1964:52).

This fear may impair a child's understanding of the father's desires relating to a certain matter. The psychological distance and minimal communication may lead to the child acting in a way which the father feels is wrong and may increase the chance that the father will act violently.

Five propositions linking severe and distant father-son relations and the actual use of violence are implicit in the paragraphs above.

2. The more severe and distant the father-son relations, the lower the referent power in that relationship.

3. The lower the referent power, the greater the coercive power that the father needs to bring to bear on the son.

4. The greater the coercive power, the greater the son's fear of the father.

5. The more the son fears the father, the more difficult it may be for that son to understand his father's desires and the greater the chance that the son will not act according to those desires.

6. To the extent that the son does not act according to the father's desires and a coercive power relationship exists between father and son, the greater the chance that control will be based on temper and violent outbursts.

Using deductive logic, these five propositions can be merged to show the relationship between the norm of severe and distant father-son relations and the actual use of violence as follows:

Combining 2, 3, and 4:

7. The more severe and distant the father-son relationship, the greater the son's fear of the father.

Then combining the above with 5:

8. The more severe and distant the father-son relationship, the greater the chance that the son will not act according to the father's desires.

Finally, combining 7 with 6, the link between the norm for violence and the actual use of violence is made.

9. The more severe and distant the father-son relationship, the greater the chance that control will be based on temper and violent outbursts.

If deductive logic is used to combine propositions 1 and 9, the following proposition is yielded.

10. To the extent that the male possesses a great deal of authority in family life, the greater the chance that control will be based on the use of temper and violent outbursts.

Thus, according to the cultural-consistency theory, in Mexican-American ethnic groups, a value related to family life that has nothing directly to do with the use of violence acts to increase the actual level of violence. The method of linking propositions used above can be used to relate the other three family values to the actual level of family violence.

This pattern of violence is probably perpetuated through social learning processes (Bandura, 1973). Owens and Straus (1975), for example, show that the more violence experienced by a child, the greater the tendency to favor violence as an adult. Apparently the child comes to believe that the best way to have his own children act obediently is to use physical force, even if he was afraid of it as a child. Yinger's statement that individual personality has a great deal to do with the development of culture also applies here. If the child feels that the use of force is the best way of controlling other members of his family, cultural norms that may support this view are reinforced.

The discussion up to this point has centered on the formal normative system found in Mexican-American families.*3 Mirande (1977) reports that this formal structure does exist but has been interpreted both as a source of pathology and as a source of warmth and security. Mirande (1977) also suggests that while the formal structure of norms may exist, familial and sexual roles are being modified as Mexican-Americans are assimilated, in increasing numbers, into American society. Hawkes and Taylor's 1975 study of the power structure of Mexican families supports Mirande's point. Thus, it is possible that changing roles may be manifest in less support of the father's formal authority and less distant and less severe father-son

relations. As a result, the proposed link between the
formal normative structure and family violence may be weaker
than predicted above.

On the other hand, recent research on family violence
among Anglo-Americans suggests that as the traditional male
dominated power structure becomes undermined, there may be a
tendency for family violence to increase in the short run
(see Brown, Chapter 11 and Allen and Straus, Chapter 12).
This may be especially true of families which become female
centered (Straus et al., 1979).

JEWISH-AMERICANS

Jews traditionally have been characterized as having a
low rate of family violence. Most Jews would be considered
in or above the middle class today, and this status might
contribute to their low rates of family violence.*4 However,
even at the turn of the century, when most Jews were
working-class immigrants, they probably also had lower rates
of family violence than other poor ethnic groups. Jewish
family values may be related to the low level of family
violence.

Figure 2 applies the cultural-consistency theory of
family violence to Jewish-Americans.

Bernstein (1950), Gordon (1964), Shapiro and Dashefsky
(1974), Strodtbeck (1958), and Yaffe (1968) all mention that
the pursuit of knowledge is greatly stressed in Jewish
culture. Emphasis on this value could lead to a norm of
intellectuality, or rationality, which suggests less
willingness to act violently when faced with a problem.
Straus (1974a) found that to the extent that couples engaged
in rational problem-solving (measured by discussing or
trying to discuss an issue calmly, getting information to
back up one's side of an argument, or bringing in someone
else to settle things), there was a lower level of
husband-to-wife or wife-to-husband physical violence. Thus,
one who approaches a problem rationally would be more likely
to use violence only as a last resort, that is:

> 1. To the extent that intellectuality is
>   stressed, the emphasis will be on rational
>   means of solving family problems, rather than
>   on verbal or physical coercion.

A function of intellectuality in Jewish families, which
may be more closely related to nonviolence, is the fact that
norms for articulateness, argumentativeness, and
parent-child bargaining are present. These three norms
would seem to sanction conflict but to channel it off into
discussion rather than physical action. Yaffe reported

that:

> Home discipline is far less strict among Jews
> than among other groups. Jewish parents are
> naggers, screamers, nudgers—but not hitters.
> The child has to go pretty far before he'll get
> the back of his father's hand. And a lot more
> conversational freedom is tolerated. Jewish
> children are allowed to interrupt, contradict
> the grown-ups, be "fresh" (1968:312).

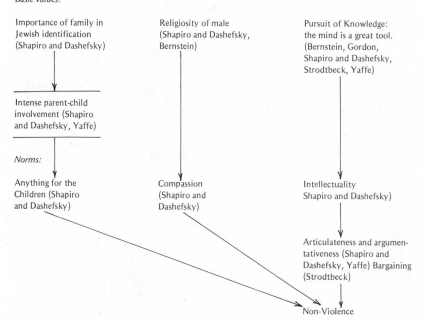

Basic values:

Importance of family in
Jewish identification
(Shapiro and Dashefsky)

Religiosity of male
(Shapiro and Dashefsky,
Bernstein)

Pursuit of Knowledge:
the mind is a great tool.
(Bernstein, Gordon,
Shapiro and Dashefsky,
Strodtbeck, Yaffe)

Intense parent-child
involvement (Shapiro
and Dashefsky, Yaffe)

Norms:

Anything for the
Children (Shapiro
and Dashefsky)

Compassion
(Shapiro and
Dashefsky)

Intellectuality
Shapiro and Dashefsky)

Articulateness and argumen-
tativeness (Shapiro and
Dashefsky, Yaffe) Bargaining
(Strodtbeck)

Non-Violence

Perpetuation: Boys perceive themselves as like their father (Shapiro and Dashefsky)

Figure 2. Jewish-American parent-child violence

Similarly, Zuk's study of 300 Jewish families (1978) found a strong current of egalitarianism running through Jewish families, particularly in more assimilated, less Orthodox ones. This feeling, combined with the channeling of aggression into verbal rather than physical expression, leads to "the high level of bickering that occurs between husband and wife, between parents and children, and between sibs.... Teasing, sarcasm and ridicule are regularly employed by parents to set limits on children's behavior." Eternally in competition, the Jewish family is a meritocracy.

Thus, it is possible that frequent conflict may be a characteristic of Jewish families. If that is the case, the frequency of conflict may be a sign that Jewish families are very stable.

> When close relationships are characterized by frequent conflicts rather than by the accumulation of hostile and ambivalent feelings, we may be justified, given that such conflicts are not likely to concern basic consensus, in taking these frequent conflicts as an index of the stability of these relationships (Coser, 1956:85).

The following proposition can be developed from the above discussion:

2. The greater the emphasis on articulateness, argumentativeness, and parent-child bargaining, the greater the chance that conflicts will be resolved through discussion rather than violent or coercive action.

Finally, the basis of a cultural-consistency analysis can be shown by combining propositions 1 and 2 to present one relationship between a basic family norm and the actual use of violent or nonviolent action to resolve a conflict.

3. The greater the extent that the pursuit of knowledge is stressed, and debate and conflict are regarded as legitimate, the greater the chance that conflicts will be resolved through discussion rather than violent or coercive action.

CONCLUSION

In this chapter we have attempted to construct a cultural-consistency theory of family violence. This theory is based on the idea that cultural values having no manifest reference to violence act either to increase or to hold down the actual level of family violence in certain ethnic groups. Values and norms were linked together, and the norms were in turn linked to the actual level of violence in an ethnic group. The perpetuation of the use of violence from generation to generation was also examined.

The Mexican-American and Jewish-American ethnic groups were used to illustrate this theory. A higher level of family violence was assumed to be present in Mexican-American than in Jewish-American families. The higher level of violence in Mexican-American families was proposed to be associated with the values of severe male dominance, strict discipline, and submission to the father. Severe and distant father-son relations were seen to be the result of these values, leading to fear of the father, poor communication, and a resulting high level of parent-child violence. Perpetuation of this subculture is accomplished through the desire for boys to be like their fathers even though they fear them, and because a child turned adult treats his wife and children the same way his father treated his family. Modifications in the formal normative structure of Mexican-American families challenging the husband-father's formal authority were noted and seen as possibly increasing family violence, at least in the short run.

Values of the Jewish ethnic group also were examined in this theoretical framework. The basic family values emphasized were the pursuit of knowledge and the use of the mind rather than the body. The value of intellectuality resulting from these values was proposed to lead to the favoring of articulateness, argumentativeness, and bargaining as a way to solve family disputes. Thus, debate and not physical coercion is used and there is less family violence. Values are perpetuated in that boys perceive themselves as like their fathers.

Finally, as noted in Chapter 1, the conclusions of this chapter, like the conclusions of the other theoretical chapters, are not put forward as established facts. Rather, they are intended as stimuli and hypotheses for empirical research.

NOTES

*A revision of a paper presented at the annual meeting of the National Council on Family Relations, August 20-23, 1975. The preparation of the chapter was supported by National Institute of Mental Health grant number 13050. I would like to thank Professor Dorothy Finnegan of Colby-Sawyer College for many helpful suggestions and comments through the development of this paper.

1. Another source of perpetuation could be feedback processes that occur in the proposed causal chain between broad family values not related to violence, norms of violence, and the actual use of violence. The use of violence to control a situation, resulting in the label of violence, might strengthen the norm of violence through a self-fulfilling prophecy. In fact, the perceived effectiveness of a norm of violence or nonviolence might even strengthen the more basic value from which the violent or nonviolent norm has originated. In other words, if the norm of violence or nonviolence is an effective means of control, then the way of life that sanctions this norm would be further reinforced.

2. The Grebler et al. (1970) study of urban Mexican-Americans found that the value placed on the man as authority figure varies by income level and neighborhood. However, nearly two-thirds of those with medium or lower income living in areas with a high percentage of Mexican-Americans felt that the husband should have complete control over the family income. This finding suggests that the value of male authority is quite strong in ethnic enclaves.

3. I would like to thank Professor Alfredo Mirande of the University of California, Riverside, for bringing to my attention a view of the Mexican-American family which differs from the view which is more prevalent in the literature. This view implies that Mexican-American families would have a lower degree of family violence than is suggested in this article.

4. Erlanger (1974), in a review of studies examining the relation between social class and family violence, reported differences between social classes, with physical punishment increasing as one goes down the status ladder. However, the differences are not as large as many would expect.

Part III Social Organization and Family Violence

Important as are the cultural norms that
make it legitimate for family members to use
physical force on each other, they do not fully
explain family violence. First, these norms are
guidelines more for culturally permissible
actions than for culturally required actions.
So the question remains as to why some families
do and others do not engage in such permissible
violence. We must also examine how or why norms
legitimizing violence within the family came
into being, and why such norms continue to
exist.

As with most aspects of society, no single
factor provides the answer to these questions.
Rather a complex interweaving of factors exists
that we are just beginning to unravel. However,
even at this early stage in the scientific study
of family violence, it is clear that many of the
threads making up the fabric of violence in the
family are those identified in Chapter 1 as
social organizational factors. A number of
these were briefly discussed in that chapter,
for example, the involuntary nature of
membership in a family, the privacy of the
family as a social institution, and assignment
of roles within the family by age and sex rather
than by interest or competence.

The chapters in Part III treat some of
these social organizational factors in detail,
indicating the types of social arrangements that
give rise to situations in which people tend to
resort to the use of violence. Since these
arrangements are regularities of social life,
most of which have been part of the structure of
the human family for perhaps thousands of years,
we can speculate that they are also at the root
of the persistence of norms that permit violence
in the family. Cultural norms tend to evolve in
a way that reflects, regularizes, and
legitimizes the typical behavior of members of a
society. In short, as was noted in Chapter 1,
culture and social organization are two facets
of a single reality. Even so, they are far from
having a fixed and immutable relationship to
each other. The emergent nature of all human
life dictates that culture and social
organization will constantly get out of line

with each other, with a resulting pressure to restore the synchronization.

The chapters in Part III have at least four things in common. First, they share what could be called an emphasis on structural conduciveness. Each chapter seeks to explain the high rate of conflict and violence in the family by focusing on some aspect of the structure of relations between family members and on how the nature of these relationships contributes to or dampens violence.

Second, each of the authors, in his or her own way, highlights the irony that the organizational structure of family life creates conditions for warmth and intimacy as well as for conflict and violence.

Third, these chapters do not present new data, but instead summarize and extend a large number of existing empirical studies and theoretical arguments. They organize and make deductions from existing theory and research on violence and family violence. Not that they feel collecting new data is unnecessary, but organizing and interpreting, from a sociological perspective, what is already known about family violence can give new insights and a sounder basis for future empirical research.

Last, possibly the most important aspect of the format of the chapters in Part III is their examination of the ways in which social variables are interrelated. For until we understand how a number of relevant variables fit together, explanations of family conflict and violence will be incomplete.

Chapter 6

Sexual Inequality and Wife Beating

Murray A. Straus

* *

This chapter describes a major aspect of the social structure underpinning husband-wife violence: the sexist organization of the family and the society in general. It argues that sexism produces violence because men use violence to maintain their position as "head of the household." More is involved in sexism than the "right" to be the head of the family as supported by cultural values and beliefs; sexism is also grounded in institutional arrangements--such as the expectation that men will marry younger women and the segregated labor market in which women's jobs are less well paid--that make male dominance a reality. A society, or groups within a society, may favor equalitarian relationships, but unless these notions go beyond beliefs and become reflected in societal arrangements, the domination of women by men is bound to continue.

Many of the issues examined in this chapter crop up again and again throughout the volume. These issues are critical in the discussion of practical steps to reduce and eventually eliminate husband-wife violence, a theme examined fully in Chapter 13.

* *

This chapter describes some of the ways in which the male-dominant power structure of the family gives rise to violence. This implies that, as our society moves toward a more egalitarian family system, both the actual levels of violence and the norms implicitly permitting such violence, will decline. Although this decrease is the likely long-term outcome, it is far from a certainty. First, many other factors affect the level of violence in the family (see especially Chapter 2). Second, as suggested earlier, and for the reasons to be discussed at the end of this chapter, one of the ironies of family life is that the immediate result of such a change could well be an increase rather than a decrease in the level of husband-wife violence.

SEXIST ORGANIZATION OF SOCIETY AND MARITAL VIOLENCE

The cultural norms and values permitting and sometimes encouraging husband-to-wife violence reflect the hierarchical and male-dominant society typical of the Western world. The right to use force exists, as Goode (1971) concludes, to provide the ultimate support for maintaining the power structure of the family, if those low in the hierarchy refuse to accept their place and roles. Nine of the specific ways in which the male-dominant structure of the society and of the family create and maintain a high level of marital violence are described below.*1

1. Defense of Male Authority. In the context of an individualistically oriented urban-industrial society, the ascription of superior authority to husbands is a potent force producing physical attacks on wives. In such a society, male-superiority norms are not clearly understood and are in the process of transition, and the presumption of male superiority must be validated by superior "resources" such as valued personal traits and material goods and services (Rodman, 1972). If every man were, in fact, superior to his wife in such resources as intelligence, knowledge, occupational prestige, and income, there would be a concordance between the authority ascribed and the individual achievements expected to accompany that authority in achievement-oriented societies. Clearly, such superiority is not always the case, despite the societal structure that gives men tremendous advantages in access to these traits and resources. Consequently, many men feel almost compelled to fall back on the "ultimate resource" of physical force to maintain their superior position (Goode, 1971; Straus, 1974b:66-67). A graphic illustration of just this process is the case of Joe and Jennifer reported by LaRossa (Chapter 10). Allen and Straus give statistical evidence in Chapter 12.

2. Compulsive Masculinity. Talcott Parsons (1947) has argued that in modern industrial societies, the separation of the male occupational role from the family and the predominance of the mother in child rearing creates a fundamental difficulty for men in respect to achieving a masculine sexual identity:

The boy has a tendency to form a direct feminine identification, since his mother is the model most readily available and significant to him.   But he is not destined to become an adult woman.   Moreover he soon discovers that in certain vital respects women are considered inferior to men, that it would hence be shameful for him to grow up to be like a woman.   Hence when boys emerge into what Freudians call the "latency period," their behavior tends to be marked by a kind of compulsive masculinity. Aggression toward women who "after all are to blame," is an essential concomitant (p.305).

Although Parsons' emphasis is on the particular family constellation just described as partial explanation for the generally high level of male aggressiveness in Western societies, it also seems likely to be part of the reason that so much male aggressiveness is directed against women, wives in particular. Similarly, Parsons' analysis also shows the origins of female aggressiveness partly in the particular structure of the family in industrial society; much of this aggressiveness is focused specifically against men, especially husbands, as the agents of women's repressed position in society.*2 This climate of mutual antagonism between the sexes provides a context that is not only conducive to attacks by husbands on wives but probably also underlies a number of other related phenomena, such as the growing evidence that in many instances, "rape is a power trip, not a passion trip" (Bart, 1975:40; Burgess and Holmstrom, 1974). Moreover, as in the typical homosexual rape in prisons (Davis, 1970), the degradation and humiliation of the victim is often a major motivating force.

3. Economic Constraints and Discrimination. The sexist economic and occupational structure of society allows women few alternatives. The jobs open to women are lower in status and, despite antidiscrimination legislation, women continue to earn less than men in the same occupations. Without access to good jobs, women are dependent on their husbands. If a divorce takes place, almost all husbands default on support payments after a short time, even assuming they could afford them in the first place. Consequently, many women continue to endure physical attacks from their husband because the alternative to divorce is poverty (Gelles, 1976).

4. Burdens of Child Care. The sexually based division of labor in society assigns child-rearing responsibility to the wife. She therefore has the problem of rearing the children, but at the same time society does not provide either economic recompense for her doing so, or child care centers that take over part of the burden so that she can earn enough to support her children. Occupational discrimination, lack of child-care facilities, inadequate

child support from either the government or the father--all
coerce women into remaining married even when they are the
victims of violence.

5. Myth of the Single-Parent Household. Another of the
cultural norms that helps to maintain the subordination of
women is the idea that children cannot be adequately brought
up by one parent. Thus, if a woman is to have children, she
must also have a man. To the limited extent that research
evidence supports this view, the situation comes about only
because of the confounding of poverty and social ostracism
with single parenthood. Although it seems likely that if
social pressure and constraints were removed, most women
would want to live with a man, an important minority does
not, and lives, in effect, in a state of forced
cohabitation. Thus, innumerable and, under present
conditions, unnecessary social and economic constraints
prevent the single-parent family from being a viable social
unit and forces many women to accept or continue a
subordinate, stressful relationship.

6. Preeminence of Wife Role for Women. Under the
present system, being a wife and mother is the most
important single role for a woman. Indeed, American
cultural norms are such that one cannot be a full woman
unless married. A man, on the other hand, has the option of
investing much or little of himself in the husband-father
role depending on his interest, ability, and circumstances.
In short, the stigma of being a divorced man is small
compared with that of being a divorced woman--to which a
special term, with overtones of immorality, has been
attached: divorcee. This forced dependence on the wife
role as the basis for a respected position in society makes
it difficult for a woman to refuse to tolerate male violence
and end the marriage.

7. Negative Self-Image. Under the present social
structure, women tend to develop negative self-images,
especially in relation to the crucial trait of achievement
(Horner, 1972; Truninger, 1971:260). As a consequence,
feelings of guilt and masochism develop, which permit women
to tolerate male aggression and violence and, in some
extreme cases, to seek it. Full sexual equality would
eliminate this as a sexually structured pattern of behavior,
even though it may remain on an individual-to-individual
basis. Only a de-emphasis on individual competitive
achievement will fully eliminate this problem.

8. Women as Children. The conception of women as the
property of men is no longer part of the legal system of
industrial countries. However, elements of this outlook
linger in the folk culture and also survive in certain
aspects of the law, such as in the statutes that declare the
husband the head of the household and give him various
rights over his wife, like the right to choose the place of

abode, to which the wife must conform.*3 In addition, there
is the related conception of women as "childlike." In
combination, these aspects of the sexist organization of
society give husbands a covert moral right to use physical
force on their wives analogous to the overt legal right of
parents to use physical force on their children (see Gelles,
1974:58).

9. Male Orientation of the Criminal Justice System.
Not only is much male violence against wives attributable to
the sexist organization of society, but the final indignity
is that the male-oriented organization of the criminal
justice system virtually guarantees that few women will be
able to secure legal relief. To begin with, the long delays
in obtaining court orders and "peace bonds" make courts
useless in securing immediate relief from the danger of
another assault. Even without these delays, many women
cannot attend court because of the lack of child-care
arrangements during the long hours of waiting for a case to
come up or because, as often happens, the case is
rescheduled. Among other impediments to securing protection
against assaults by a husband are those described in the
section of Chapter 3 on "Legitimation of Husband-Wife
Violence by the Courts and Police": immunity from suit, the
failure of police to act against husbands, the "cooling out"
by police, prosecuting attorneys, and judges of wives who
attempt to bring complaints, and the denial of compensation
by public compensation review boards.

SEXUAL LIBERATION AND THE REDUCTION OF MARITAL ASSAULT

Although Goode believes that force or its threat is
ultimately necessary for the existence of society, he also
concedes that "...the amount of force now applied in these
various areas of family life...[is not]...either necessary
or desirable" (Goode, 1971:42). One of the ways in which
the amount of force [necessary to maintain a viable pattern
of family life] can be reduced is to reduce the degree of
inequality found within the family. Children's immaturity
imposes a limit on the extent to which they can be given
equality with their parents. But the particular economic
and physical conditions that may have justified a
subordinate position for women in earlier periods of history
are clearly no longer present.

The goals of the women's movement are centered on
eliminating each of the violence-producing inequities
discussed in this chapter. Since these factors account for
the high level of physical assaults on women by their
husbands, achievement of the goals of the feminist movement
is tremendously important for any reduction of marital
assault.

In the process of advocating these fundamental structural changes the women's movement has made various short-run contributions. For example, the ideology of the feminist movement itself encourages women to resist all forms of oppression, especially physical violence. There has been an explosive growth of "battered-wife shelters," beginning in England about 1972 and in the United States about 1975. These provide immediate physical escape, particularly for those with young children who might otherwise have no alternative to being victimized by their husbands.

The women's movement has been perceptive in recognizing that superior male physical strength and skill are important parts of the process by which male dominance is maintained. This recognition partly accounts for the emphasis on karate and other self-defensive training. However, it is unlikely that karate will, in fact, protect women from assault, anymore than the ability to respond physically protects men from assault by other men. Moreover, the karate approach institutionalizes the role of physical violence in social interaction and hence increases the likelihood of further violence. Nevertheless, the emphasis on physical self-defense training is an important symbolic step towards the eventual elimination of violent repression of women. But this eventuality will only come about if the more fundamental problems of sexual inequality can be overcome. Fortunately, emphasis has shifted from training in the use of physical force to training in "assertiveness," which is an important step in the direction of sexual equality.*4

Nevertheless, the difficulties of the period of transition cannot be overlooked. The long-run consequences of a more equalitarian society may be to lessen the frequency with which wives are victims of assault by husbands. But, we suggested earlier (see also Kolb and Straus, 1974; Whitehurst, 1974), the short-run consequences may be the opposite, because a sizable number of men will not easily give up their sex-stereotyped roles. All three chapters in Part IV document this in different ways: a case study of a specific couple, logical deduction, and statistical data on a large sample of couples. Like traditionally oriented women, men are conditioned by their culture to perceive only the prerogatives and advantages of the traditional male role, and to ignore its burdens, restraints, and disadvantages. Thus, a less violent world and less violence in the family require men's as well as women's liberation.

Unfortunately, progress toward sexual equality and freedom from sexually stereotyped roles has not been as great as seemed possible in the early 1970s. At present (1978-79), there is even considerable doubt that the Equal Rights Amendment will pass. A state-by-state tally by the International Women's Year Commission found that state laws

(which govern most domestic matters) continue to give women
substantially fewer rights than their husbands in respect to
inheritance, divorce, property ownership, domestic violence,
and adultery (United Press, October 30, 1977). Many surveys
show that traditional sex roles remain entrenched, even
among the young. For example, a survey of 17-year-olds by
the National Assessment of Educational Progress found that
only half of this age group thinks all women should be free
to pursue careers outside the home (New York Times, 24 June
1977: A26; see also Reinhold, 1977).

As a recent commentator put it: "Scratch almost any
man, and you'll find wistful memories of his mother darning
socks and cooking Sunday lunch...." (Francke, 1977; see
also Stapp and Pines, 1976). The details vary, of course,
with the setting and the socioeconomic level, but the theme
of male superiority remains the same. In that same article,
Francke tells about a friend:

> ...who has made a name for herself in
> educational films in New York, had dinner in Los
> Angeles recently with another old friend, who
> has made a much bigger name for himself in
> television. Settling down over late-night
> brandies, she was stunned when he turned to her
> and said, "You know, I can't imagine being
> married to you. I'd panic and run." "Why?"
> Sally asked, hurt that their friendship which
> had never even touched on the subject of
> marriage, seemed suddenly flawed. "You're a
> star," he said. But, Sally pointed out, he was
> the one getting quoted in Time and Newsweek and
> was probably earning $100,000 a year to her
> $20,000. "Maybe so," he said declaratively,
> "but underneath it all I think you're smarter
> than I am."

> What lurking terrors possess men when their
> women achieve success on their own? The truth
> of the matter is, that in spite of Virginia
> Slims, we haven't come such a long way, babies
> (Francke, 1977:44).

NOTES

*Part of this chapter is reprinted with permission from
"Sexual Inequality, Cultural Norms, and Wife-Beating,"
Victimology, 1976, Vol, 1 (Spring):551-556, (c) 1976
Visage Press, Inc.

1. There are, of course, many other factors which contribute to the existence and maintenance of norms permitting intrafamily violence. Owens and Straus (1975), for example, present data on the correlation of childhood experiences of violence (including victimization) with proviolence attitudes and values. See also the discussion of the influence of society's positive evaluation of violence in Chapter 4; and in Straus, 1974a, 1974b.

2. See Whiting (1965:137) and the discussion of "the sex myth" in Steinmetz and Straus (1974:10-13) for other ways in which the pattern of male-female relationships built into the society helps to create antagonism between the sexes and hence strengthens the association between sexuality and violence.

3. It is pertinent that, even in a state known for its social and familial experimentation, as recently as 1971, the California State Bar Association voted _not_ to repeal this legislation (Truninger, 1971:276).

4. The combination of sexual equality, female assertiveness, and sexual liberation might also contribute to reducing rape. If women were to escape the culturally stereotyped role of disinterest in and resistance to sex, and were to take on an assertive role in expressing their own sexuality, rather than leaving such expression to the assertiveness of men, women's new status might contribute to the reduction in rape in several ways. First, many rapes are an illegitimate extension of sanctioned techniques of "overcoming" the culturally prescribed resistance of women to sex (Kirkpatrick and Kanin, 1957). Second, the confounding of sex and aggression that is built into our culture could be reduced (Steinmetz and Straus, 1974:10-13). Third, to the extent that sharply differentiated sex roles are responsible for the phenomena of "compulsive masculinity" and structured antagonism between the sexes, the elimination of sexual inequality would reduce the number of "power trip" and "degradation ceremony" motivated rapes (Brownmiller, 1975).

Chapter 7

Stress and Family Violence

Keith M. Farrington

* *

This chapter emphasizes the effect of family structural characteristics on the amount of stress experienced. Farrington suggests that compared with most other groups, the family experiences more stress and may be less capable of coping with it. The family, because of its unique structure, also may be less efficient in dealing with stressful situations.

It is interesting to contrast this sociological perspective with the implications of a "medical" model for the control of violence. "Curing" violence through drugs and surgery has a powerful appeal to laymen and scientists alike. If a day does arrive when it becomes routine to take a pill when we feel the urge to kick a co-worker or throw a punch at our mate, intrafamily violence will probably still exist. If the family runs out of nonaggression pills, one spouse could blame the other for being lax, and might feel justified in hitting the other so that he or she won't forget the next time. Or perhaps a mother will slap her child because the child refuses to swallow the nonaggression pill.

Farrington's point of view is that regardless of medical technology, the structure of relationships between family members must change if violence is to be reduced. If conflicts of interest and stress in family life are inevitable, then the family must develop a structure for resolving these conflicts nonviolently. Although Chapter 13 offers some suggestions, achieving these ends will be difficult, since, as Farrington points out, family structure works against the nonviolent resolution of stressful situations.

* *

Although social scientists have made use of the idea of
stress in investigating a wide range of phenomena, the lack
of a widely accepted, well-developed conceptual framework
has led to the concept being used in many different ways and
applied to a number of different referents. Recently,
however, investigators have attempted to develop an
integrative framework (Howard and Scott, 1965; Scott and
Howard, 1970; McGrath, 1970), demonstrating the value and
applicability of the stress concept to a wide range of
research issues. The purpose of this chapter is to apply
such a framework to the study of intrafamily violence and
aggression. Underlying this endeavor is a belief that much
family violence can be explained in terms of the "stress"
experienced by family members and family units.

A GENERAL STRESS FRAMEWORK

The concept of stress has had a history marked by
considerable conceptual ambiguity and dissension (Mechanic,
1962: Chapter 1; 1968:296-300; Lazarus, 1966:Chapter 1;
Levine and Scotch, 1967:163-165; Scott and Howard, 1970;
McGrath, 1970). Stress has been defined and studied as (1)
a threatening or disruptive stimulus (Grinker and Spiegel,
1945; Basowitz et al., 1955:7; Hill, 1958; Janis,
1958:13); (2) a particular response or pattern of responses
in the face of such a stimulus (Basowitz et al., 1955:289;
Janis, 1958:13; Mechanic, 1962:7); or (3) a state of the
organism as it is experiencing such a stimulus (Selye, 1956;
Dohrenwend, 1961; Wolff, 1968). The problems arising from
this lack of a common definition have led a number of
theorists to abandon the attempt to achieve specificity, and
instead to use the term "stress" to refer to a general field
of study that encompasses all of these more specific
phenomena (Janis, 1958:11-13; Lazarus, 1966:27; Levine and
Scotch, 1967:169; McGrath, 1970:16). This is the approach
taken in the "general stress model," according to which
family violence will be analyzed in this chapter.

Components of Stress

The phenomenon of stress can be seen as composed of
several distinct elements. Drawing from schemes developed
by Hill (1958), Dohrenwend (1961), Levine and Scotch (1967)
and McGrath (1970), the general stress model treats the
following as the component parts of any stress situation:

1. The Stressor Stimulus. This refers to any situation
or condition, encountered by an individual or group, that is
capable of producing disruption or threat for that
individual or group. When this condition occurs, it can be

said that the stimulus is imposing a "demand" on those involved, by requiring that some response be made to alleviate the stressor situation and remove the threat of danger or disruption.

Some theorists have viewed stressor stimuli as necessarily synonymous with major tragedies and catastrophes. This idea is unfortunate, for it ignores the subtle effects of less dramatic stimuli. As Scott and Howard note:

> The concept of stress has been too closely equated with extreme trauma and duress. This association has had the effect of diverting attention away from the study of stimuli that are wearing to the organism, and that have important physiological and psychological consequences for it, but which are neither dramatic or especially unusual...both traumatic and nontraumatic but wearing events are stressful in the sense that they both produce the same types of physiological and psychological responses (1970:266-267).

In fact, it is not even necessary that the stimulus be viewed in negative terms. Many neutrally or even positively defined stimuli are capable of placing great demands upon those experiencing them (Holmes and Rahe, 1967). Because people respond as much to their perception of a situation as to the actual situation, virtually all stimuli in man's social environment have the potential to produce stress for some individuals.

     2. Objective Demand. This refers to the "objective reality" of a given situation. To the extent that a stressor stimulus poses demands that are independent of the cognitive processes of definition and perception, the individual or group involved can be said to be experiencing objective demand. While perhaps quite common at the physiological or biochemical levels of human existence, stressors that completely bypass cognitive awareness and evaluation are probably somewhat rare at the social level. However, this is not meant to imply that objective demand is never an important aspect of "sociological" stress situations. For example, facing the thought of parachuting from a plane, or being confronted by what appears to be an armed criminal, are situations that pose a very real threat to the unfortunate victim, independent of that person's specific evaluation and definition of the situation.

     3. Subjective Demand. Appley and Trumbull have observed that, "With the exception of extreme and sudden life-threatening situations, it is reasonable to say that no stimulus is a stressor to all individuals exposed to it" (1967:7). This variation in what is viewed as stressful is

due to individual differences in learning and experience.
As Wolff has aptly noted, "Man is vulnerable [to stress]
because he reacts not only to the actual existence of
danger, but to threats and symbols of danger experienced in
the past" (1968:3). Therefore, it frequently happens that a
stimulus posing no real "objective" danger is nonetheless
perceived and defined as problematic. In such an instance,
it makes little difference how much objective demand
actually exists; what is important is that the definition
of danger or threat has been made, and the individual(s)
involved will be acting in accordance with this definition.
Within the terminology of the general stress model, this can
be referred to as "subjective" demand.

     4. Response Capabilities. This category includes all
of the skills, attributes, and resources that an individual
or group has at its disposal in dealing with stressor
stimuli. Although the list of possible response
capabilities is endless, some of the more important ones
would include past experience in dealing with similar
problems, various skills that have been learned or acquired,
intelligence and creativity, the motivation to deal with the
situation, support and encouragement from others in the
social system, the amount of energy available, and the
ability to control one's emotional state. All of these
diverse elements are viewed by the general stress model as
combining to form a reservoir of possible responses to
stressful stimuli.

     5. Choice of Response. When an individual or group is
confronted by a stressor stimulus, one or more responses
will be selected from those available and applied toward
this stressor. Obviously, just as individuals and groups
vary substantially with regard to what they see as posing a
threat or problem, so also will they vary in their capacity
to deal with various situations and in the reponses that
they will make in a given situation. However, it seems
reasonable to assume that, in the great majority of cases,
the effort will be made to meet the impending demands to the
greatest degree possible. This does not imply that the best
choice will always be made, but it does assume that the
individual or group will be motivated to act in its best
interest by making what it believes to be an appropriate
response.

     6. Stress Level. If the response made to a stressor
stimulus is sufficient to meet and eliminate the demands
being posed by that stimulus, it can be said that mastery,
or successful resolution of the problem, has taken place.
Under these circumstances, the stressor situation should no
longer be problematic. In fact, the individual or group
will probably be more effective in dealing with similar
problems in the future because of this experience (Scott and
Howard, 1970:272). In this sense, it can be argued that
stress has certain positive consequences, provided it

remains within reasonable limits.

However, the response made to a stressor stimulus does not guarantee that demand will be eliminated. In many instances, the response(s) will be insufficient or inappropriate, and mastery will not occur. The result of such failure on the part of response capabilities is, according to the general stress model, an increase in the "stress level" of those involved.

Viewing "stress" as the discrepancy between demand and response capabilities is not a new idea; such a conceptualization is suggested by Mechanic (1962: 220-221; 1968:301) and McGrath (1970:17-21), and is implicit in Scott and Howard's "problem-solving" stress model (1970; Howard and Scott, 1965). According to this view, the greater the discrepancy between impending demands and existing response capabilities, the greater the stress level of the individual or group in question. In using the term "stress level," rather than simply "stress," the general stress model assumes that man and the groups he forms are in a continual state of stress, and that a complete congruence between demands and response capabilities for any individual or group is impossible.

In accordance with this view that stress is a "constant" in human experience, the general stress model suggests that individuals and groups adapt to this fact of life by developing a stress level at which they feel most comfortable and function most effectively. These "optimum" stress levels develop over time, and they represent the combined product of a number of social, psychological, and structural factors. Scott and Howard suggest that there are wide individual variations in these optimum stress levels, with some persons and groups demanding more congruence than others:

> The nature of this level varies tremendously among individuals: There are persons who require high and sustained levels of stimulation in order to feel comfortable and satified; there are others who require comparatively low levels of stimulation, and who feel most comfortable when demands made on them are tightly dispersed around very low activity levels (1970:270).

In addition to purely individual differences in optimum stress level, substantial macroscopic variation between and among societies is also likely, with some groups accustomed to a much higher level of stress than others.

Because these optimum stress levels are, in effect, the cumulative product of all past experience, they are likely to be firmly entrenched and quite resistant to rapid or severe change. On the other hand, an individual or group's current actual stress level is likely to be subject to continuous fluctuation, depending on the particular stimuli encountered. For the most part, these changes should be relatively minor, allowing the stress level to remain within comfortable, or at least tolerable, limits. In those instances in which changes are not minor, where stress level limits are exceeded, the situation becomes problematic.

According to the general stress model, changes in stress level occur whether the discrepancy between demands and response capabilities is "positive" or "negative" in direction. Just as the demands being placed on an individual or group may be too great, so too can they be too low. McGrath uses the terms "overload" and "underload" to speak of this distinction, and states:

> There is now a substantial body of literature...which suggests that stress-like effects may result from an environment that places too little demand on...the focal organism (1970:18).

Recent works such as Palmer's theory linking "tension" and violence (1970; 1972), Klausner's studies of stress-seeking (1968), Heron's investigation of the "pathology of boredom" (1957), and Seidenberg's clinical description of the "trauma of eventlessness" (1972) seem to support the contention that too little demand can be just as dangerous as too much.

To summarize the notion of stress level, it can be said that, "Stress not only involves a 'state' of the focal organism and a 'state' of the environment, but also involves a relationship between the two" (McGrath, 1970:16). The greater the discrepancy between existing demands and available response capabilities, the greater will be the stress level of that individual or group. To the extent that this imbalance is not presently, and does not suddenly become, too great; as long as most existing demands can be met satisfactorily from within these response capabilities; and as long as enough demand exists to challenge the individual or group sufficiently, the stress level can be said to be at a minimal, nonproblematic level. However, if an increase in the actual stress level of an individual or group is a significant departure from the optimum stress level of that individual or group, this change is likely to have overall negative consequences for those involved.

Unresolved Stress Situations

In the discussion thus far, it has been argued that two variables interact to determine an individual's or group's stress level. From this proposition, it follows that any failure to achieve mastery over a particular stressor stimulus can be attributed to (1) the nature of the stressor situation, and/or (2) the response(s) made by those experiencing this stressor situation. As we shall see, characteristics of each of these elements of the stress experience can preclude successful resolution of the problem at hand.

First, in considering stressor stimuli, it is obvious that problems vary in terms of their potential for resolution. Some problems have a solution; others don't. Certainly, if a problem is unsolvable, those facing that problem will be unable to come up with a successful response, no matter what they attempt. Scott and Howard (1970:271; Howard and Scott, 1965:146-147) have identified three types of problem situations that prelude successful mastery: (1) problems that pose demands in excess of the organism's reponse capabilities, (2) problems that have no possible resolution, and (3) problems in which contradictory demands exist, so that it is impossible to meet both successfully. In any of these situations, no matter what response(s) are chosen, they simply will not be sufficient to achieve mastery over the stressor stimulus.

Concerning the responses made to stress situations, Scott and Howard (1970:272; Howard and Scott, 1965:147-148) have nicely delineated a typology of possible responses. These include (a) the assertive response, in which those involved meet the problem "head-on," and attempt to solve it in a direct and meaningful fashion, (b) the divergent response, in which resources and energy are applied to the problem but are misdirected, thus leaving the actual problem virtually untouched, and (c) the inert response, in effect, a "non-response," in which there is no meaningful attempt made to resolve the problem at hand.

Even in stress situations in which an individual or group faces a stressor stimulus that is potentially solvable--in that they possess response capabilities sufficient to meet its demands--only by choosing an assertive response will they actually achieve mastery. Divergent or inert responses are not actually directed at the problem in question; thus, these responses are unable to contribute directly to a resolution of that problem.

Consequences of the Failure to Achieve Mastery

For the above reasons, there are numerous stress
situations in which the demands posed by a stressor stimulus
will not be met successfully. Responses to these stressors
may be made, yet mastery of the situation does not result.
As explained earlier, this discrepancy between demand and
response capabilities represents the stress level of the
individual or group in question. And, to the extent that
this discrepancy represents a drastic or major change in
one's stress level--in the direction away from one's optimal
stress level--it is to be expected that this unresolved
stress situation may become even more problematic over time.

For example, the continued presence of the still unmet
demands may have a serious impact upon those involved. For
example, the failure to resolve a problem of faulty
communication between a husband and wife can easily lead to
further, more serious, marital problems.

A second possible consequence of an ineffective
response to stress may be that, not only has this response
failed to deal with the original problem, but it may have
inadvertently introduced new stressor stimuli. As Wolff
(1968:3) suggests, the consequences of a response made to a
stress situation may turn out to be more damaging than the
effects of the stress situation itself. For example,
whereas a husband hitting his wife might appear to terminate
effectively a current marital argument, this divergent
response could, on a long-term basis, cause resentment and
hostility to build up within the wife, thus posing an even
more serious problem for the future.

Also, there is what Scott and Howard have termed the
"second order problem" of handling the unresolved tensions
that have arisen during the attempt to resolve the current
stress situation. These "tensions" refer to a state of
energy arousal within the individual. In the words of Scott
and Howard:

> ...even when problems are successfully solved, a
> time gap exists between the initial provocation
> and the ultimate resolution. During the time in
> which the problem is being dealt with, the
> organism is in a state of greater or lesser
> mobilization, a state in which energy and
> resources are bound up so that the organism
> experiences tension. In cases of successful
> problem solving, tensions are eventually
> dissipated and the organism returns to its usual
> level of functioning. When problems are not
> solved, however, tensions persist until
> mechanisms are found to cope with them. The
> failure to master threats therefore gives rise
> to a second-order problem;...that of dealing

with unresolved tensions. In effect, failure in
mastery requires the organism to use an excess
of energy and resources in maintenance
activities over what would have been required
had mastery been achieved, and the necessity of
excessive maintenance activity involves the
organism in a state of continuous mobilization
or tension (1970:272-273).

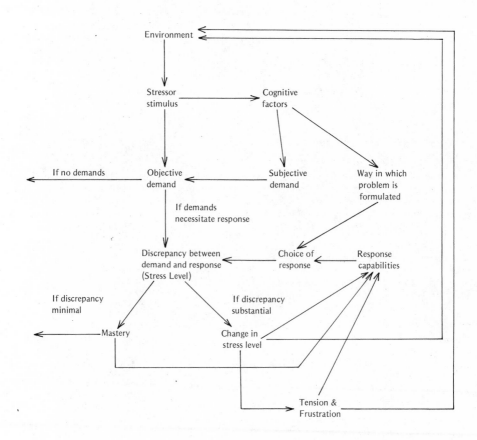

Figure 1. Stress model

Thus, to summarize the general stress model
(represented diagrammatically in Figure 1), as stressor
situations present themselves to an individual or group,
response(s) will be made. Sometimes these responses will
produce mastery of the stressor; in such instances, the
stressor should present no further difficulty. However, in
many instances, the stressor situation will not be resolved
by the responses made. In these situations, the discrepancy
between demand and response capabilities represents an
increase in stress level. This increase in stress level has
the potential to produce additional problems for those
involved. Let us now apply this framework to the study of
family violence.

APPLYING THE GENERAL STRESS MODEL
TO INTRAFAMILY VIOLENCE

Stress and the Family

A number of theorists have already begun to indicate
the importance of "stress" for explaining a major portion of
intrafamily violence, especially in the area of child abuse.
For example, Blumberg (1964-1965) views overzealous physical
punishment of children by parents as being as much a result
of the various stresses experienced by the child's parents
as it is a result of the actual desire or need to control
the child's behavior. In Blumberg's words, "When everything
is getting on top of a mother she smacks more"
(1964-1965:149). Gil (1971) explains socioeconomic
differences in child abuse as resulting at least partially
from the differential number and severity of stressful
experiences characterizing family life at different social
class levels. In explaining violence directed toward
children, Gelles' "social psychological" model of child
abuse (1973) attributes primacy to a variety of "situational
stresses."

The common thread running through these statements is
that any theory that attempts to explain intrafamily
violence must give primary consideration to the structural
variables likely to determine a family's predisposition to
violence. This is precisely what the stress framework
allows us to do, since it views these structural variables
as stressor stimuli that impose demands on individuals and
families, and to which some response must be made if stress
levels are to remain within tolerable limits.

There can be little doubt that the modern family, both
as a social unit and through its individual members,
encounters numerous stressor stimuli in the course of its
day-to-day existence. As Campbell states,

[Modern] changes [in family solidarity] do not
necessarily signify a decline in the importance
of the family. They do reflect the increasing
pressures which the family is under--but these
stresses frequently stem precisely from the fact
that more is being demanded of family life than
ever before (1969:251).

The stressor stimuli that confront families and their
members stem from many different sources. For example, some
are related to the functions that the family is "entrusted"
with performing, both with regard to its individual members
and to the larger social structure. Others are the result
of particular characteristics of individual family units,
such as their status in the social stratification system and
their present position in the "family life cycle." However,
regardless of the specific origins of the stressor stimuli
that confront any particular family, the point to be made
here is that these confrontations are facts of family
life--not isolated and out-of-the-ordinary occurrences.

In addition to these external stresses, the family
itself is often a source of stress, in that many problems
can be traced back to particular family situations or
structures. For example, Croog (1970) notes that such
problems as intrafamily value conflicts, the particular
characteristics of the various stages of the family life
cycle, and problems of role conflict are potential sources
of stress that arise from directly within the family unit.
In addition to those stresses that emanate from within the
family are numerous events experienced by individual members
in the "external world," which are then brought back into
the family setting. Although the family is commonly thought
of as a place which family members can bring these external
pressures and "let off steam," this action may have overall
negative consequences for the family as a whole. As Croog
states, "The release of these emotions may in themselves
create tension situations that have the effects of stressors
as far as other family members are concerned" (1970:46).
Even in situations in which the family itself is not the
source of a particular problem, the family may nevertheless
amplify the effects of that problem on its members, by
operating as a "crystalizing entity within which these
stressors emerge and exert their impact" (Croog, 1970:25).

Violence as a Response to Stress

If the family does experience numerous stressor
situations, it follows that individual family members, and
families as social units, often will be called on to attempt
to meet and eliminate the demands posed by various
stressors. And, as discussed earlier, when confronted with
a stressful situation, these people will look to their
repertoires of response capabilities as they try to come up

with a response that produces mastery.

Clearly, as Goode (1971:624) has suggested in his "resource theory" of family violence, the potential to use violence can be regarded as an important resource of individuals or groups. Put into the terms of the general stress model, the capacity for violence represents a portion of an individual's or group's response capabilities that can be applied to the solution of various problems.

Not only is violence a possible response to stressful situations; in our society, it often represents an acceptable response. As Steinmetz and Straus note, "Americans have always had a propensity to use violence to achieve national and personal goals" (1974:141). A major reason for the prevalence of violence throughout our society's history has been that our social norms and cultural values actually sanction and legitimize the use of violence as appropriate behavior in many situations (see Chapter 3). This normative approval of violence seems to be especially true within the context of the family, where, for example, it is acceptable, or at least permissible, to spank a misbehaving child or slap a nagging wife when circumstances "call for" such behavior.

When Is Violence Used as a Response to Stress?

The use of violence as a possible response to stress situations represents an interesting paradox. The availability of most resources for any particular individual or family is likely to depend on a number of structural and personal features, including socioeconomic status, age, and sex. However, virtually everyone possesses the resource of potential violence. It is true that different individuals will require vastly different situations to provoke them to the extent that they will commit an act of violence or aggression. Also, the actual means of expressing violence, and the resulting "success" of the act, will vary greatly. However, the point to be made here is that, whereas the possession of most other resources varies from person to person and family to family, the potential for violence is a "constant" part of all individual and family response capabilities, no matter how extensive or how minimal the remainder of the response capabilities.

On the other hand, although everyone can use violence, not everyone does. Violence is not always the response chosen to a stressful situation. In fact, it is used relatively infrequently. Thus, one question of major importance concerns the issue of when violence is used as an assertive response to a stress situation, and why it is used in those instances.

The Availability of Alternative Responses to Stress

One of the most important considerations in answering this question concerns the nature of the other response capabilities. As Bettelheim suggests, "Whether or not we will use violence or avoid it depends entirely on what alternative solutions are known to a person facing a problem" (1967:301). Similarly, Steinmetz and Straus argue:

> We believe that the willingness and ability to use physical violence is a 'resource'.... A family member can use this resource to compensate for lack of other such resources as money, knowledge, and respect (1974:9).

Goode has developed this general idea in his resource theory of family violence (1971). Goode identifies "force and its threat" as one of four major sets of resources that an individual can use in attempting to achieve desired ends. Violence can be used as a resource when other alternative resources, i.e., economic, prestige, and trait resources, are unavailable or have proved ineffective. However, Goode emphasizes that the actual use of violence is likely to be dependent upon the state of the individual's total resources. Thus, if other appropriate resources do exist, it is likely that one or more of these will be tried as a solution to the problem instead of violence. As Goode states:

> Most people do not willingly choose overt violence when they command other means because the costs of using force are high in any social system, but especially in the family.... Consequently, it is a general rule that the greater the other resources an individual can command, the more force he can muster, but the less he will actually deploy or use force in an overt manner (1971:628).

Thus, we see that violence and aggression are "substituted" for other types of resources when these other resources are not a part of existing response capabilities.

Subcultural or Family Norms Regarding Violence

On the one hand, it has been argued that our society has norms and values that positively sanction the use of violence in the family setting. And this legitimization of aggressive behavior is likely to increase the extent to which violence is actually used as a "problem-solving technique" within the family.

However, as Wolfgang and Ferracuti suggest in their "subculture of violence" theory (1967), it is also likely that the norms governing the appropriateness of the use of violence will also vary somewhat within society. Thus, in some segments of society, violence may be regarded as more culturally acceptable than it is in other portions of society. As this legitimation of violence varies, the predisposition to use violence as a response to stress situations should vary accordingly. Thus, in those "subcultures," and in those particular family units, where existing norms most explicitly sanction violence and aggression, we should most often expect responses of a violent nature.

Past Experience with Violence

According to a "social learning theory" view of violent behavior (Bandura and Walters, 1963; Bandura, 1973: Gelles and Straus, 1978), violence and aggression are learned via the same basic learning processes as any other type of behavior. Thus, another factor likely to be of major importance in determining whether people will respond to a stressor with violence is their past exposure to violence. If family members have used violence as a means of coping with problems in the past, or have seen others use violence for this purpose, and this experience has caused them to believe that the response successfully resolves the problems, then the likelihood increases that these people will apply violence to similar stress situations in the future.

Empirical evidence suggests that persons who behave aggressively within their families tend to have family backgrounds of violence (Kempe et al., 1962; Steele and Pollock, 1968; Gil, 1971). This suggests that, not only is violence a learned behavior, but in addition, is taught and transmitted by the family as part of the socialization process. Thus, it can be argued that the family operates as a "training ground" for violence (Steinmetz and Straus, 1974: Part IV; Gelles and Straus, 1978).

Violence, Tension, and Frustration

Thus far, discussion has centered on the use of violence as an assertive response to a stressor stimulus. The implication has been that violence, when used in this fashion, represents a rational attempt on the part of a person to deal with a problematic situation in what that person believes is an appropriate and effective manner to achieve a desired end. This conception of stress-induced violence seems comparable to what Gelles and Straus have termed instrumental violence--"the use of pain or injury as a punishment to induce another person to carry out some act or refrain from an act" (1978).

However, there is another place in the general stress model where violence is expected to occur—as a consequence of the second-order problems of tension and frustration that can result from unresolved stress situations. In fact, it is here that intrafamily violence is likely to occur most often—not as an assertive, problem-oriented attempt to achieve mastery of a situation, but rather as an "irrational," lashing-out behavior spawned by seemingly unresolvable problems. And, just as the concept of stress-induced violence appears to correspond closely to Gelles and Straus' definition of "instrumental" violence, so does the idea of violence as a reaction to frustration and tension seem roughly comparable to "expressive" violence as defined by these authors—"the use of physical force to cause pain or injury as an end itself" (Gelles and Straus, 1978).

Frustration and Stress

As used by social scientists, the concept of frustration seems to refer most often to an emotional state, accompanied frequently by anger and anxiety, that may arise when an individual is prevented from attaining a desired goal. We suggest that this affective state of frustration can, like tension, be viewed as a "second-order problem" springing from the failure to satisfactorily resolve a stress situation—in effect, an "emotional counterpart" to the unexpended energy that Scott and Howard term "tension."

The incorporation of stress-produced "frustration" into the general stress model appears to be consistent with the rest of the framework. Implicit in this treatment of frustration are all of the necessary elements of a stress situation discussed earlier: (a) a stressor stimulus, in the form of a desired goal, and pressures, both internal and external, to attain that goal; (b) objective and/or subjective demand to achieve that goal; (c) the response capabilities of the person from which an assertive, a divergent, or an inert response, will be chosen; and (d) a discrepancy between demand and response, implying that, for one reason or another, the desired goal has not been attained.

Viewing frustration in this manner, the general stress model is able to treat a wide range of specific situations and conditions as "frustrating." For example, a mother may become "frustrated" by the fact that her young child continually cries and misbehaves. A husband and father whose racial and educational background prevents him from obtaining a stable job through which he can support his family may well be "frustrated" by this situation. A woman may find the housewife-mother role "frustrating" in terms of

the personal fulfillment and satisfaction that it provides.
A man who would like to leave his wife for another woman may
be "frustrated" by the strong social, legal, and economic
commitments tying him to his marriage.

The general stress model would not deny the important
qualitative differences in the "frustration" produced in
these different instances. However, it would argue that, in
each case, the resulting affective state of frustration can
be seen as arising from an unresolved stress situation.
Thus, the general stress model sees all frustration as
implying the existence of stress, in that it ultimately
stems from the discrepancy between a desired goal and the
ability to achieve that goal.

Frustration and the Family

A number of investigators have linked frustration with
intrafamily violence. For example, Gil's theory of child
abuse (1971) holds that the poverty existing in the lower
socioeconomic levels of society creates frustrations
released in child abuse. O'Brien explains violence between
husbands and wives by suggesting that the inability to
achieve adequate economic rewards might result in "family
centered venting of the aggressiveness on the part of the
husband which had its antecedence in frustrations
encountered in the larger structures of the social and
economic world" (1971:696). Whitehurst (1974) predicts that
the trend toward greater equality for women may well pose a
major source of frustration, and hence of violence, for men
who cannot cope with their new status.

But what is it about the family that has prompted these
and other frustration-based theories of family violence? Is
there a special connection between frustration and the
family? Is the family a more likely setting than other
social groups for the generation, and acting out, of
frustration?

The family can be regarded as a unique social entity in
terms of its potential for frustration. Part of the reason
for this special position, as discussed earlier, is that the
family routinely encounters numerous stressor stimuli in the
course of its daily existence. The sheer number of stresses
faced probably ensures that at least some of these cannot be
resolved.

In addition, the family owing to its position in
society and the mechanics of its internal structure, is
likely to be confronted with a number of stressors that have
a low probability of successful resolution and hence a high
potential for generating frustration. Some of the more
common "insoluble" demands families often face include the
simultaneous satisfaction of its members' emotional needs,

the successful regulation of the conflicts that so often
occur among intimates, and the supervision of the activities
of all family members in the external world.

Thus, the family seems to engender frustration because,
both quantitatively and qualitatively, it faces serious
problems in trying to counter stressor stimuli. In fact,
Gelles and Straus probably do not overstate the case in
saying that "the family, by virtue of its structure and
functions, can be viewed as an inherently frustrating
institution for its members" (1978:28).

Response Capabilities of Families

However, the large number and wide variety of difficult
stress experiences are only part of the reason that
frustration is typical of families. Another set of factors
increases the likelihood of frustration within the family.
These factors derive from the ability of families to manage
the stresses they do face.

Although the family may be relatively "stress-prone,"
it does not necessarily follow that the family is
well-equipped to cope with these stressors and the demands
that they impose. On the contrary, apparently the modern
urban family is "a less than successful group dealing with
stresses and problems" (Gelles and Straus, 1978).

There are many reasons for this inadequacy. For
example, the status positions represented within the family
generate diverse, often conflicting, interests, and these
conflicts may interfere with optimal decision-making. Also,
because the typical modern family is relatively small, a
limited number of people can be used as resources in
attempting to cope with a difficult situation. In addition,
the intimate and intense nature of family relationships
often means that decisions are made emotionally rather than
rationally.

These and other structural characteristics are likely
to render the family a relatively inefficient social unit,
with regard to both the decision-making and the performing
of tasks based upon these decisions. This inefficiency
often makes it difficult to meet the demands of such basic
family responsibilities as socialization of the young and
fulfillment of the emotional needs of all family members, to
say nothing of the more dramatic crises that frequently
befall individual families.

The resulting picture of the family is that of a social
group that encounters numerous and diverse stressor stimuli,
many of which are difficult--perhaps impossible--to resolve.
In addition, this social group has structural
characteristics that make it particularly vulnerable to the

demands posed by these stimuli. And, according to the
general stress model, the result of this unfortunate
combination of qualities within the family is a high
potential for the generation of frustration.

Violence as a Reaction to Frustration and Tension

Even if we agree that the likelihood of frustration
occurring in the family is high, the eruption of violence is
not explained. A causal linkage is necessary to determine
exactly how frustration in the family translates into
aggressive behavior.

Because the general stress model equates the
occurrences of tension and frustration, it is useful to
return to Scott and Howard's treatment of tension
(1970:272-273) in attempting to determine the relationship
between frustration and violence. These authors argue that,
when an individual is faced with the "second-order problem"
of attempting to resolve the tension created by a failure at
mastery, the only real course of action available is to
dissipate this accumulated tension through some mechanism of
release. That such a line of reasoning is applicable to the
emotional state of frustration is shown by what Bandura
(1973:31-39) has referred to as the "aggressive drive
theories" of violent behavior, most notable of which is
Dollard et al.'s "frustration-aggression hypothesis" (1939).

Whether one prefers to attribute this behavior to
processes of social learning (Bandura and Walters, 1963;
Bandura, 1973; Steinmetz and Straus, 1974) or to innate
biological potential (Dollard et al., 1939; Ardrey, 1966;
Lorenz, 1966), there can be little denying that violence is
certainly one of the more popular means of "blowing off
steam" in our society. Not only is violence a frequent
mechanism of tension release, but, at least in America,
"aggression is defined as a normal response to frustration"
(Steinmetz and Straus, 1974:9). Thus, to the extent that
the family has an "inherently frustrating" character,
expressive violence should be expected to occur often within
the family setting.

It should be emphasized that a distinct, qualitative
difference exists between violence that is an assertive,
instrumental reponse to a stressor situation, and violence
that is an expressive reaction to frustration and tension.
This difference holds even though the same stressor
situation can be the source of violence in both cases, and
even though these two types of violence can be outwardly
indistinguishable.

The reason for making this distinction is that very
different cognitive processes appear to be involved in these
two types of violent act. On the one hand, stress-induced,

instrumental violence is problem-oriented and goal-directed--an attempt to directly meet and resolve the demands posed by a stressor stimulus.

On the other hand, frustration-produced, expressive violence lacks this rational, problem-solving dimension. It is not an assertive response, and it is not really directed toward the solution of a problem. Although this kind of violent behavior is governed, at least to some extent, by internalized norms that specify appropriate types of conduct in given situations (Gelles and Straus, 1978:21)--and thus is not really "unconscious" or "beyond the control" of the actor--the fact remains that expressive violence does not represent the rational, carefully chosen response to a stressor situation that instrumental violence does.

Expressive Violence and Catharsis

The general stress model's treatment of expressive violence does not imply adherence to what Steinmetz and Straus have termed the "catharsis myth" (1974:14-16; Straus, 1974). Proponents of the catharsis viewpoint (Dollard et al., 1939; Bettelheim, 1967; Bach and Wyden, 1968) have argued that the expression of a limited amount of violence tends to prevent a "build-up" of aggressive feelings to the point where more serious aggression results; hence, they regard the limited expression of aggression as desirable and beneficial. However, the general stress model does not consider frustration-produced violence in such functionalist terms; rather, it expresses an empirical fact regarding intrafamily violence--that it is often a consequence of unresolved stress situations, and that the "intervening" process is frustration.

Possibly, expressive violence does improve a stress situation temporarily. Even Straus, a severe critic of the catharsis viewpoint, concedes, "There can be little doubt that an outburst of aggressive activity is often followed by a sharp reduction in tension, an emotional release, and even a feeling of quiescence. Thus, there is often an immediate cathartic effect" (1974a:25). However, even if violence does dissipate accumulated frustration and tension, these outcomes are probably only temporary and superficial. From a long-term viewpoint, it is doubtful that frustration-caused violence will have any meaningful, positive effect on a problem: Expressive violence rarely is directed at the genuine causes of a problem. Therefore, it is unlikely to change the conditions that caused the tension and frustration in the first place. In fact, because of its potential for reinforcing future violent behavior (Feshbach, 1970; Bandura, 1973:31-39; Steinmetz and Straus, 1974:14-16), expressive violence not only fails to improve a present troublesome family situation, but also can cause unintended and undesirable long-term consequences.

"Overload" versus "Underload" Stress Situations

A source of some difficulty in the scheme proposed here is whether any qualitative differences exist between "overload" and "underload" stress situations in their potential for generating expressive violence. As discussed earlier, the general stress model defines stress as any significant discrepancy between demand and response capabilities, whether demand exceeds response capabilities or vice versa. The connections between stress, frustration, and violence may be fairly clear in the case of "overload" stress situations; what about the connections between expressive violence and "underload" stress situations marked by excessive routine, lack of challenge, and a general absence of stimulation?

Regarding the comparative effects of "overload" versus "underload" stress situations as causes of violence and aggression, the present inclination of the general stress model is to assume that they are, in effect, the same. This is consistent with the "Clockwork Orange" theory of family violence (Gelles and Straus, 1978:30-32), which suggests that aggressive behavior often occurs in situations where "the glove fits too smoothly and family members try to 'stir things up' just to make things interesting." On the strength of this theory, then, one would expect persons to attack others when their lives are marked by boredom and lack of excitement, just as they do when faced by unsolvable problems. However, there are those who would probably question this assumption (Palmer, 1970; 1972; Gelles and Straus, 1978:31), suggesting that this aspect of the relationship between stress and violence needs much investigation before this question can be resolved.

CONCLUSIONS

This chapter has argued that the family is a unique social group in terms of its potential for violence and, furthermore, that much of the violence occurring in the family setting can be attributed to various stresses operating within the family environment. Building on these two basic premises, this chapter has presented a "general stress model" of behavior, which attempts to help explain intrafamily violence. According to this theoretical framework, violence occurs so often in the family setting because (1) the family encounters a high amount of stress, (2) it tends to be poorly equipped to handle stress, and (3) there is thus a great potential for frustration within the family. These characteristics increase the likelihood of both instrumental and expressive intrafamily violence.

If sound, the general stress model would seem to be in a strong position to contribute substantially toward an integrated theory of family violence. It allows for the incorporation of elements from several important social-psychological approaches to family violence, for example, frustration-aggression theory and social learning theory. At the same time, the general stress model takes into account the various structural factors that determine which families will be most likely to experience stress, what resources they will have at their disposal to deal with stress, and, most important of all, the likelihood that stress will result in violence (Farrington, 1975:37-45).

NOTE

*Portions of sections of this paper appear in "Toward a General Theory of Stress and Family Violence," by Keith Farrington, a paper presented at the 1975 annual meeting of the National Council on Family Relations.

Chapter 8

The Paradoxical Nature of Family Relationships and Family Conflict

Joyce E. Foss

* *

Not all violence between family members is
the result of a conflict. And not all conflicts
end in violence. Whether or not the inevitable
conflicts of family life eventuate in violence
depends partly on whether there are alternative
methods for resolving the conflict. However, in
Chapter 7 Farrington proposed that families may
be structured in a way that adversely affects
their capabilities for resolving conflicts. In
this chapter, Foss examines this contention in
more detail and also concludes that in intimate
groups like the family, structural constraints
work against effective conflict resolution.

Among the factors working against families'
using conflict resolution techniques that have a
low probability of producing violence are the
high emotional investment between family
members, their total personality involvement,
and the knowledge that members cannot simply
pick up and leave when a conflict develops.
Simple avoidance is a widely used technique to
prevent an escalation into violent encounters,
but it is a very difficult strategy in groups
that are structured to generate high levels of
interaction, economic interdependence, and
emotional commitment. Besides, as Foss notes,
the avoidance of conflict in intimate groups
will lead only to more conflict.

* *

This chapter examines how certain structural features
of family relationships affect strategies for dealing with
conflict of interest and, as a result, affect the level of

interpersonal violence and aggression. The issue of the
relationship between family structure and conflict and
violence is important for several reasons. First, neither
family sociologists nor conflict theorists generally have
taken full advantage of the family arena as one in which a
conflict approach might be usefully applied (Farrington and
Foss, 1977; Skolnick, 1973; Sprey, 1969). Second, more
specifically, conflict theory has been identified as a
potentially fruitful approach to the study of violence in
families (Gelles and Straus, 1974; Steinmetz and Straus,
1974:5-6). Further, several other frameworks identified as
valuable in the area, such as resource, structural,
exchange, and frustration-aggression theories (Gelles and
Straus, 1974), also include conflict as a central concept.
Yet, though conflict often is presented as central to, or a
precondition for, violence, a specific theory of how
conflict processes and violence are related has not been
adequately delineated.

Lewis Coser's work on conflict provides a foundation
for this analysis; his extensive attention to intimate
groups makes his work readily applicable to the family.
This chapter presents a number of propositions concerning
family conflict and violence and summarizes the formulation
in diagrammatic form. A major emphasis in the chapter is
careful specification of key concepts in the area.

THE FAMILY AS A STRUCTURAL PARADOX

Coser's analysis of conflict in intimate groups hinges
on a recognition of the paradoxical nature of their
structure. Intimate groups are paradoxical in that the same
structural elements that make hostility likely also create a
high probability that hostility will be suppressed. The two
key characteristics of intimate groups are the high
frequency of interaction and the total personality
involvement among group members. The following propositions
illustrate the paradoxical relationship of these structural
features with hostility and the suppression of hostility.

Two focal variables in this part of the analysis are
conflict of interest and hostility, which are defined as
follows:

> Conflict of interest: An "objective" situation
> in which two or more parties hold
> contradictory values and claims over scarce
> status, power, and resources.

> Hostility: A feeling of opposition (enmity, ill
> will, etc.).

This definition of conflict of interest concurs with Coser's use of phrases like "conflict situation" or "occasions for conflict" to refer to a situation in which the interests of the participants are objectively at odds. Coser sharply distinguishes between such a situation and conflict itself, which refers to a particular kind of action or behavioral strategy. This distinction will be further explored when conflict itself is discussed. Hostility also is not a behavior or action, but is a subjective feeling of opposition, that may or may not occur when people have conflicting interests.

Family Structure and Hostility

Intimate groups are by definition characterized by total, rather than segmented, personality involvement and by a high frequency of interaction (Coser, 1956:64). Following the work of Simmel and Freud, Coser argues that habitual or intense interaction "furnishes frequent occasions for conflict" (1956:62)--or frequent conflicts of interest, in terms of the present argument. In relationships with a high frequency of interaction, conflicts of interest will be varied and numerous. In other words, frequent interaction produces both a high number or variety of conflicting interests and a high frequency with which those conflicts of interest will arise.

The relationship between degree of personality involvement and conflict of interest is similar. "The more the relationship is based on the participation of the total personality--as distinct from segmental participation" (Coser, 1956:62), or the more bases on which persons are interacting with one another, the greater the variety and frequency of the conflicts of interest that arise. Two propositions can then be stated:

> Proposition 1. The more frequent the interaction, the more frequent and varied are conflicts of interest.

> Proposition 2. The more total the personality involvement in a relationship, the more frequent and varied are conflicts of interest.

Coser further asserts (1956:62):

> Proposition 3. Conflicts of interest tend to produce hostility.

This proposition states that when people are faced with conflicts of interest, subjective feelings of ill will or opposition are likely to arise. However, this rule is not without exception. For example, subjective hostility may

not occur when the participants define as legitimate an
"objectively" unequal distribution of resources. Yet even
though conflicts of interest do not always lead to
hostility, it is appropriate to state proposition 3 as a
general tendency.

Connecting Propositions 1, 2, and 3, we can state:

Proposition 4. Frequent interaction tends to
create hostility.

Proposition 5. Total personality involvement
tends to create hostility.

To further summarize the argument thus far, if intimate
groups are those characterized by frequent interaction and
total personality involvement, then:

Proposition 6. Intimate relationships tend to
create hostility.

Family Structure and Suppression of Hostility

Intimate relationships tend not only to cause
hostility, but also to cause a high affective or expressive
investment in the relationship that in turn generates
efforts to suppress hostility (Coser, 1956:60-65).
Affective investment seems to involve two elements: a
positive liking or attraction to the relationship, and low
replaceability of the members of the relationship*1. These
two concepts are roughly equivalent to the concepts of
Comparison Level and Comparison Level of Alternatives in
Thibaut and Kelley's exchange theory (1959).

In accordance with Homans' hypothesis that increased
interaction is related to "mutual sentiments of liking,"
Coser suggests (1956:62):

Proposition 7. The more frequent the
interaction, the greater the positive affect
among group members.

The specific effects of personality involvement are not
entirely clear in Coser's discussion, but it seems
reasonable to posit that total personality involvement does
not have an important direct effect on positive affect, but
influences the perception of the replaceability of group
members. A relationship characterized by total personality
involvement is largely built on the unique contributions of
each personality. As Simmel points out, this is especially
true in dyadic relationships like marriage (1950:122-132).
When this occurs, the replacement of one group member will
at the very least seriously alter the quality of group
relationships. Thus:

Proposition 8. The more total the personality
involvement in a relationship, the lower the
replaceability of group members.

As suggested above, positive affect and low
replaceability of group members can be further related in a
connecting proposition.

Proposition 9. The greater the positive affect
and the lower the replaceability of group
members, the greater the affective or
expressive investment in the group.

Coser further suggests (1956, 1962, 1968):

Proposition 10. The greater the affective
investment in a relationship, the greater the
fear of dissolution of the relationship.

Proposition 11. The greater the fear of
dissolution of a relationship, the greater
the tendency to suppress hostility.

And finally, to summarize, we can state:

Proposition 12. Intimate relationships tend to
produce suppression of hostility.

Instrumental Dependency and Suppression of Hostility

The preceding discussion treats only the high affective
investment in intimate groups and its subsequent effect on
suppression of hostility. There are also significant
instrumental investments in relationships. Coser's emphasis
on intimate groups that are based on voluntary association
may have influenced his lack of attention to the
instrumental aspects of intimate relationships. This is not
to say that voluntary relationships are never based at least
partially on instrumental concerns. Rather, we suggest that
when relationships are nonvoluntary their instrumental bases
become more important and more apparent. This seems to be
the case with the family.

As Sprey points out, "participation in the family is
not a truly voluntary matter" (1969:702). In the first
place, children have no choice in participating in family
relationships. Second, for adults, marriage is essentially
nonvoluntary in that there is "no real alternative...to the
married state as a life career" (Sprey, 1969:702). Sprey
argues that individuals have little or no choice as to
whether to enter family relationships in general. Yet, the
instrumental dependencies in family relationships are
well-recognized (see Scanzoni, 1970; 1972:62-66): having
once entered a particular family relationship, it is at best

difficult to leave it. Thus, family relationships are also
relatively nonvoluntary or coercive at this level. The
difficulty in leaving family relationships may be due partly
to the affective investment in intimate groups discussed by
Coser, but it is also due to the instrumental investments or
dependencies of family members.

That the high instrumental investment in families
suppresses hostility may actually be contradictory. Like
affective investment, high instrumental investment in a
relationship may increase fear of the relationship's
dissolving, and in turn produce attempts to suppress
hostility. Thus, we state a parallel to Proposition 10:

> Proposition 13. The higher the instrumental
> investment in a relationship, the higher the
> fear of dissolution of the relationship.

Since Proposition 11 further asserts that fear of
dissolution produces suppression of hostility, we can then
suggest that the greater the instrumental investment in a
relationship, the greater the suppression of hostility.

On the other hand, a family member may be aware of the
instrumental dependence of the other on the relationship and
thus may recognize the low probability of the other's
leaving. The person may then have less fear of the
relationship's terminating (perhaps rightly so) and may
therefore be less likely to suppress hostility. Three
factors mitigate against this possibility. First,
instrumental investment may increase the fear of dissolution
indirectly, by increasing affective investment. This is
suggested in Scanzoni's exchange model of marriage
(1970:16-25). Second, family members may not recognize the
instrumental bases of their relationships. This
nonrecognition may even be the norm for marital
relationships in which cultural emphasis on romantic love as
the basis for the relationship may obscure the instrumental
aspects. Third, even when the person does recognize the
instrumental bases of the relationship, a partner would
probably recognize his or her own dependencies before those
of the other, if only because one is more sensitive to and
familiar with one's own predicament. Consider the position
of a young woman with several young children and few skills
relevant to employment outside the home. Her own
instrumental dependencies on the marital relationship seem
so obvious and extreme that she may not realize that her
husband's dependency may be equal to hers. Perceiving
herself as having the most to lose should the marriage break
up, she will fear its dissolution and therefore attempt to
suppress hostility.*2

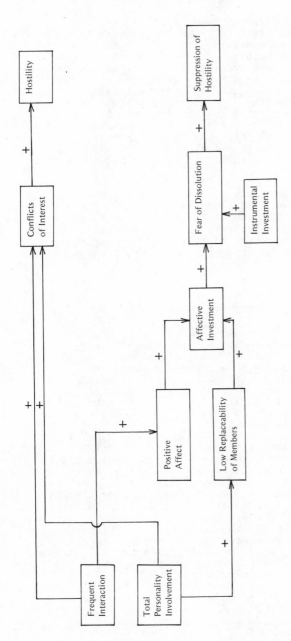

Figure 1. The family as a structural paradox

Thus, to the extent that both (or all) members of a group have an instrumental investment, each has something to lose if the group dissolves and so each may be fearful of expressing hostility. For the above reasons, Proposition 13, that instrumental investment increases fear of dissolution, stands--at least for the present. One further comment is in order. Propositions 10 and 13 suggest that both affective and instrumental investments in a relationship lead group members to fear the dissolution of the relationship. Yet, objectively speaking, it is possible to argue that those very investments that lead group members to fear dissolution of the group are indeed the strengths of that relationship--a curious contradiction in the life of intimate groups.

Figure 1 summarizes in diagrammatic form the main outlines of the model presented thus far. Intimate groups, characterized by frequent interaction and total personality involvement, are paradoxical in structure, in that they promote both subjective hostility and attempts to suppress hostility. The instrumental investments which characterize family relationships also contribute to the suppression of hostility.

AVOIDANCE AND FORMS OF CONFLICT

The processes in intimate groups considered thus far place the actor in a state of ambivalence. On the one hand, he or she is faced with a number of conflicts of interest and feels resulting hostility toward another. On the other hand, he fears the relationship's dissolution and attempts to suppress hostility. The intimate group represents a paradoxical structure likely to produce subjective ambivalence or tension.

At this point it is appropriate to shift our focus from causal chains to the options or choices available and the conditions influencing these choices. The three behavioral options examined are avoidance and expressive and instrumental conflict. Coser does not as clearly present this stage in the conflict process as a decision point at which a number of options are open to group members. Rather, his analysis implies an almost inevitable progression toward expressive conflict in intimate groups. Further, Coser does not explicitly include avoidance as a possible choice, although he does suggest some possible consequences of avoidance strategies.

Forms of Conflict

Before examining the conditions influencing the choice of strategy, we need to consider the meaning of some key concepts. Conflicts of interest were defined earlier as an objective __situation__ in which the participants hold contradictory values and claims, and we noted that Coser carefully distinguishes between such an objective situation and behavioral strategies like conflict. This distinction is maintained here.

> __Conflict__: Active opposition between parties holding contradictory values and claims over scarce status, power, and resources.

This definition underscores the very real possibility that persons with objectively antagonistic interests do not necessarily engage in antagonistic behavior. It must be stressed that the term conflict refers to the actual __behavior__ of group members. No matter how serious the conflicts of interest among group members appear to be, conflict itself has not occurred unless the participants actually engage in some form of antagonistic behavior.

This definition of conflict is equivalent to that of Coser, as a "struggle over values and claims to scarce status, power, and resources" (1956:8). However, we distinguish between two forms of conflict.

> __Instrumental conflict__: Task-oriented conflict.

> __Expressive conflict__: Conflict oriented toward the expression or release of hostility.

The distinction between expressive and instrumental conflict is based on Coser's modification during the course of his analysis of key concepts and definitions. Most important is his discussion of "realistic" and "non-realistic" conflict:

> Conflicts which arise from frustration of specific demands within the relationship and from estimates of gains of the participants, and which are directed at the presumed frustrating object, can be called __realistic conflicts__ insofar as they are means toward a specific result. __Non-realistic conflicts__... are not occasioned by the rival ends of the antagonists, but by the need for tension release of at least one of them (1956:49).

Coser goes on to state that "henceforth, the term 'conflict' will apply to realistic conflict only" (1956:60).

To the extent that Coser distinguishes between task-oriented behavior and behavior oriented toward release of hostility, his concepts are equivalent to instrumental and expressive conflict. However, the present terminology is preferable for several reasons. First, Coser's terms imply that expressive behavior is somehow either less "real" or less "realistic" than instrumental behavior. On the contrary, not only is expressive conflict real, it may also be realistic behavior under circumstances where task-oriented conflict is precluded. Second, Coser's discussion unfortunately suggests that "nonrealistic" (expressive) conflict arises not out of the real, objectively conflicting interests of the participants, but out of the psychological needs of group members. In contrast, we argue that expressive conflict, just as instrumental conflict, originates in conflicts of interest, although the two forms of conflict are facilitated by somewhat different conditions. Finally, since Coser's decision to use the single term conflict to refer to "realistic" (instrumental) conflict invites confusion, we prefer the compound terms "expressive conflict" and "instrumental conflict."

Two additional definitions are:

Aggression: A specific strategy with the intent or goal of injuring the other.

Violence: Specifically physical aggression.

Consistent with the theories of Steinmetz and Straus (1974:4) and Coser (1956:50-51), aggression can be a substrategy of either instrumental or expressive conflict. In other words, aggression itself can be characterized as instrumental or expressive.

Distinguishing Instrumental and Expressive Conflict

Instrumental and expressive conflict are pure types that, in reality, often are mixed in the same act (Coser, 1956:53-54). Still, criteria by which we should distinguish these two forms of conflict need examining. Coser is not altogether consistent on this matter. On the one hand, he argues that expressive and instrumental conflict can be distinguished in terms of their consequences: "Whereas [instrumental] conflict necessarily changes the previous terms of the relationship of the participants, mere hostility [expressive conflict] has no such necessary effects and may leave the terms of the relationship unchanged" (1956:40).

The flaw in this analysis is that instrumental conflict is essentially defined as that kind of behavioral expression of hostility that results in change or is instrumentally successful. One · difficulty is that whether a strategy was indeed instrumental or expressive conflict must be empirically assessed ex post facto as to whether it was successful (for a discussion of problems with ex post facto analyses in a related connection, see Skinner, 1953:31-35; Underwood, 1957:195-233). Second, the analysis implies that whenever an instrumental strategy is used, a successful outcome is inevitable. This contradicts Coser's own recognition that even when an instrumental conflict stategy is used, the specific means adopted are not necessarily adequate for reaching the intended goal (1956:54). Third, this approach implies that expressive conflict is never successful in fostering the attainment of instrumental goals. Finally, confounding the potential consequences of a behavioral strategy with the very definition of the strategy precludes empirically examining relationships between various strategies and outcomes.

A second possibility for distinguishing between instrumental and expressive conflict is to examine the quality of the acts performed. The major difficulty with this possibility has already been suggested: that particular strategies can often be used in both instrumental or expressive conflict. For example, aggression is probably most often indicative of purely expressive behavior, but can be a rational choice of behavior in pursuit of some instrumental goal. Thus, the aggressive quality of an act is not sufficient evidence that the act necessarily falls into one or the other types of conflict.

The third approach, used here, is to differentiate instrumental and expressive conflict according to the intent or goals of the participants. This approach is consistent with the portions of Coser's analysis that do not base the distinction on success or outcome, as in: "...conflict is viewed by the participants as a means toward the achievement of realistic ends, a means which might be abandoned if other means appear to be more effective for reaching the same end" (1956:54). In contrast, expressive conflict has as its goal "the mere expression of diffuse hostilities" (1956:51). The same approach is also used here in defining aggression in terms of one party's goal of inflicting some injury on the other. This goal can in turn be a means toward achieving a more general instrumental or expressive goal.

The use of goals is itself a rather shaky basis for these important distinctions. Still, it is consistent with one of Coser's approaches and avoids the problems of his other, outcome-based, approach. Finally, using goals in defining aggression is internally consistent with our approach to instrumental and expressive conflict, and is compatible with current literature on family violence.*3

AVOIDANCE AS A BEHAVIORAL OUTCOME

After this rather long foray into matters of terminology, we can now return to the question at hand: conditions influencing conflict strategies in intimate groups. A central concern of this analysis is whether subjective hostility outweighs the tendency to suppress hostility. If not--if the fear of dissolution of the relationship and the consequent desire to suppress hostility outweighs feelings of hostility--then the most probable outcome is an avoidance strategy. Whether subjective hostility outweighs suppression of hostility would be difficult to assess empirically. Yet the balance between these two subjective tendencies is central to Coser's discussion, and it seems legitimate to include this as a theoretical link in the conflict process. Thus we can state:

> Proposition 14. If the tendency toward hostility does not outweigh the tendency toward suppression of hostility, avoidance is the most likely outcome.

Avoidance may be defined as:

> Avoidance: Any tactic oriented toward nonengagement or disengagement, including physical, emotional, and intellectual nonengagement or withdrawal (adapted from Hotaling in Chapter 9).

Coser suggests that in intimate groups a strategy of avoidance in conflicts of interest is destined to fail (1956:62). In the first place, if no attempt is made to deal with contradictory interests, the original conflict will remain unresolved. At the same time, new conflicts of interest will arise out of the structure of the relationship. Thus,

> Proposition 15. When an avoidance strategy is used, conflicts of interest will accumulate.

Further, since Proposition 3 suggested that conflicts of interest create hostility, we can state that the accumulation of conflicts of interest indicated in Proposition 15 will cause further hostility. Combining the two propositions, we can state in summary:

> Proposition 16. When an avoidance strategy is used, hostility increases.

As this strategy of avoidance continues, and hostility increases, subjective hostility will eventually be too great to be suppressed, and a more active conflict strategy will be used.

> Proposition 17. The greater the hostility, the
> more likely is hostility to outweigh
> suppression of hostility.

And, the corollary of Proposition 14, which stated that
if hostility does not outweigh suppression of hostility then
avoidance is the outcome, follows:

> Proposition 18. If hostility outweighs the
> suppression of hostility, conflict--either
> expressive or instrumental--is the most
> likely outcome.

The logic of Coser's analysis suggests that any kind of
avoidance in an intimate relationship will eventually fail
in this manner. However, in contrast to Coser, some kinds
of avoidance may actually provide a fairly stable resolution
of conflicts of interest, under certain circumstances.
Avoidance can simply mean avoiding recognition or discussion
of the specific conflicting interests that have created
hostility. Or avoidance can involve more general strategies
of reducing the amount of interaction or personality
involvement in the relationship.

Resolving Conflicts of Interest Through Avoidance

Reducing the amount of personality involvement and/or
interaction in a relationship may resolve a specific
conflict of interest; perhaps more important, if we accept
Propositions 1 and 2 that frequent interaction and total
personality involvement engender conflicts of interest, then
reducing the level these two elements should lower the
possibility that new conflicts of interest will develop.

Even though the family tends to be a coercive
institution in that it is relatively difficult to "leave the
field," regular family patterns do provide for a certain
amount of interpersonal withdrawal. For example, one spouse
may become immersed in work or in child care, thereby
lessening interaction and involvement with the other. Such
accommodations involving personal withdrawal are represented
in Cuber and Haroff's (1965) typology of marriages. In the
"devitalized marriage" couples gradually drift away from
their initial closeness, and in the "passive-congenial
marriage" the couple views their marriage as a "convenient
and comfortable way to live while directing one's true
interests and creative energies elsewhere" (Skolnick,
1973:239). In general, marriages that have an openly
recognized instrumental rather than expressive emphasis show
less intense patterns of involvement.

Whether such marriages always result from an avoidance strategy in conflicts of interest is not the point. Rather, we simply wish to note that family patterns commonly exist that allow for reducing the intensity of interaction and therefore lowering conflicts of interest and hostility. Still, certain conditions need to be met if an avoidance strategy is to actually reduce, or at least not exacerbate, conflicts of interest and hostility. First:

> Proposition 19. If a strategy is considered illegitimate, then the strategy itself will become an issue, thereby increasing conflicts of interest.*4

This proposition is relevant both to the general strategies of withdrawal just discussed and to a more specific avoidance of particular issues that does not involve general interpersonal withdrawal. When considered legitimate, this specific kind of avoidance may take the form of "agreeing to disagree." As Sprey points out, "families may live together in mutual respect in the face of great differences in beliefs or values" (1969:704).

However, whether avoidance of specific issues or avoidance in the form of general interpersonal withdrawal resolves or reduces conflicts of interest also depends on whether that avoidance occurs specifically in the areas where conflicting interests arise. The avoidance must be "on target" if it is to have such a dampening effect. For example, avoiding discussions of politics will make little difference if the conflict is over child-rearing practices. Similarly, decreased interaction and/or personality involvement will not help if most conflicts involve one's instrumental contributions to the group (except insofar as decreasing "expressive" involvement in the group allows greater effort in the instrumental area). Given these considerations, we can tentatively state:

> Proposition 20. If an avoidance strategy is considered legitimate and if it actually reduces involvement in areas where conflicts of interest tend to develop, then the number of conflicts of interest will decrease.

The basic argument is that although families in general may be intimate environments, some families are more intimate than others. Moreover, in some patterns of family life legitimacy is conferred on less intimate or intense involvement, such as the American marriages identified by Cuber and Haroff, and many of the English working and middle-class couples Bott studied (1957).*5 To the extent that an intimate relationship becomes legitimately less intimate, then the pressures toward hostility inherent in intimate relationships are lessened.

However, we reemphasized that, as Propositions 14 and 15 suggest, an avoidance strategy in intimate family relationships in general will not resolve existing conflicts of interest, and conflicts of interest and hostility will accumulate. In addition, avoidance strategies, even under conditions of legitimacy and specificity, may have only limited usefulness in resolving conflicts of interest and may exacerbate problems over the long run. In the first place, avoidance used repeatedly and indiscriminately may lead to the "corrosion" of relationships described by Blood and Wolfe (1960:87-88). Second, avoidance used frequently may become the characteristic style for dealing with any conflict of interest. Thus, when important issues come up for which one or more parties consider avoidance an illegitimate strategy, continued avoidance will lead to the general accumulation of hostility described above. Perhaps as important, the lack of previous practice in working out minor issues will make attempts to deal directly with the current ones more difficult.

ACTIVE ANTAGONISM: EXPRESSIVE ANTAGONISM AND CONFLICT

The preceding discussion suggests that while avoidance may be the most probable initial strategy in intimate groups, it is usually ineffective in resolving conflicts of interest and eventually leads to greater hostility. In the long run, avoidance is the least probable outcome. As Proposition 18 suggests, when subjective hostility outweighs the tendency to suppress hostility, the behavioral option of conflict in either the expressive or the instrumental form will be employed. Coser's analysis further suggests that, of the two kinds of conflict, expressive conflict is by far the more probable. Again, the structural features of intimate groups affect the outcome.

To the extent that personality involvement in a relationship is total, expressive antagonism is likely to occur, partly because greater knowledge of the other makes using personal attack possible. As Hotaling pointed out, "...intimates know how to support the identities of each other because each knows about the things that matter or are important to the other. While this extensive knowledge can be used to support and enhance identities, at the same time it can be used to damage the identity...." (see Chapter 9).

Also, where ties are "diffuse and affective" (Coser, 1956:68)--as when there is total personality involvement--it is difficult to divorce the personality of a partner from the objective issues involved in a conflict of interest. To use a common example, one cannot easily distinguish between an action being "a mean thing to do" and the actor being "a mean person," when there is total personality involvement. In another sense, the expressive and instrumental aspects of the relationship are so intertwined that they are difficult to separate. Thus, for example, raising the issue of reassigning instrumental responsibilities may be interpreted by the other as an accusation of laziness. Based on these considerations:

>   Proposition 21. The greater the personality
>   involvement, the more likely is conflict to
>   take the form of expressive conflict.

Second, if much hostility has accumulated, conflict is more likely to be expressive. Proposition 16 in the discussion of avoidance suggests that hostility is likely to accumulate in intimate groups. Increased hostility, like great personality involvement, may make it difficult to examine issues on their merits. Thus,

>   Proposition 22. The greater the accumulation of
>   hostility, the more likely is conflict to
>   take the expressive form.

Effects of Expressive and Instrumental Conflict

Certain effects of an avoidance outcome have already been considered. To summarize, unless an avoidance strategy is used in actual areas of conflicting interests and is viewed as legitimate, it will fail to resolve the initial conflicts of interest; this failure of resolution, combined with the addition of the avoidance itself as an issue and with the inevitable occurrence of new issues, will cause an accumulation of conflicts of interest and an increase in hostility. The implications for success of expressive and instrumental conflict need similar consideration.

Aggression and Successful Resolution. The preceding discussion suggests that certain features of intimate groups make expressive conflict more probable than instrumental conflict. Unfortunately, as Coser argues, the use of expressive conflict lessens the likelihood that the original conflicts of interest will be resolved. First, Coser suggests that expressive conflict tends to increase the intensity of the encounter. Although Coser does not explicitly define "intensity," it seems roughly equivalent to aggression and/or violence (1956:69). Aggression has been defined here as "a specific strategy with the intent or goal of injuring the other," and violence is a subtype of aggression. In line with Coser's discussion of expressive conflict and intensity, it is suggested that:

>   Proposition 23. Expressive conflict tends to
>   increase aggression.*6

Coser further suggests that when aggression is used, the likelihood decreases that conflicts of interest will be successfully resolved. The "aggressive overtones" of an encounter interfere with the participants' ability to consider the original claims of conflicting interest (1956:59).

>   Proposition 24. Aggression tends to reduce the
>   likelihood of successful resolution of
>   conflicts of interest.

By combining Propositions 23 and 24, it can be further argued that expressive conflict tends to reduce the likelihood that conflicts will be resolved successfully. The converse should also be noted, that instrumental conflict tends to increase the likelihood of successful conflict resolution.

Legitimacy and Conflict Resolution. Proposition 19 asserts that if a strategy is considered illegitimate, the strategy will become a new issue, thereby increasing conflicts of interest and hostility. This proposition was advanced in reference to avoidance, but it seems equally applicable to instrumental and expressive conflict strategies. Expressive conflict seems more likely to be considered illegitimate than instrumental conflict, and thus more likely to increase conflicts of interest. However, as Straus points out (1974a:442), the participants may view as legitimate expressive conflict that militates against increasing conflicts of interest, or may see instrumental conflict as illegitimate, in which case instrumental conflict would increase conflicts of interest.

Yet even if expressive conflict is considered legitimate and does not add to future conflicts of interest, it may still be relatively ineffective in resolving present conflicts of interest. As Propositions 23 and 24 suggest, expressive conflict introduces elements into an encounter that interfere with facing the initial conflicts of interest. Put another way, expressive conflict interferes with the possibility of task-oriented conflict occurring.

Under most circumstances, instrumental conflict is most likely to resolve conflicts of interest, while expressive conflict and avoidance are generally less effective. However, any of the three strategies could be effective under certain conditions. The final proposition asserts that regardless of the strategy used, if conflict is resolved successfully, then the strategy employed will be reinforced.

>   Proposition 25. Successful resolution of
>   initial conflicts of interest reinforces the
>   strategy used.

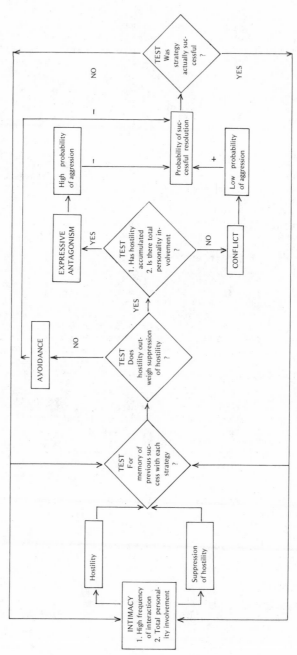

Figure 2. Strategies of conflict resolution in intimate groups

Figure 2 summarizes in diagrammatic form the overall model.*7 Intimate groups, like the family, characterized by frequent interaction and total personality involvement are paradoxical in structure in that they promote both hostility and the suppression of hostility. If the tendency toward hostility does not outweigh the tendency to suppress hostility, then the most probable outcome is avoidance. In general, avoidance is not an effective means of conflict resolution and is likely to increase hostility. If hostility outweighs the tendency to suppress hostility, the outcome will be one of two forms of conflict. Of these, expressive conflict is more likely than instrumental conflict. However, expressive conflict is more likely to produce aggression and as a result is less likely to resolve initial conflicts of interest than is instrumental conflict. Finally, regardless of the strategy used, if the strategy is considered illegitimate, it will increase conflicts of interest, and if the strategy is successful, it will be reinforced.

CONCLUSIONS

In this chapter we have examined how certain characteristics of intimate groups affect strategies for dealing with conflicts of interest. It seems worthwhile in closing to briefly discuss other elements and approaches important to such processes, as well as some implications of the model offered here. Additional features of intimate groups should be included; for example, the effect of a third party or mediator on conflict processes, an important element in Coser's analysis (1956:59-60) and in recent work on family violence (Hotaling in Chapter 9; Whitehurst, 1974). Further, exchange processes, power relations, and processes working for and against dissolution of relationships all are inextricably linked to the strategies considered here and contribute to a fuller understanding of conflict and violence in the family.

Relevant to the present discussion is the often cited basic tenet and contribution of conflict theory; that conflict is an integral, inevitable part of all social life. Examination of this assertion requires returning to the distinction between conflicts of interest and conflict. It seems quite reasonable to assert that conflicts of interest, in the sense of occasions generating contradictory claims, are inevitable. Yet conflict, especially task-oriented or instrumental conflict, is certainly not inevitable. In fact, the thrust of this chapter is that in intimate groups like the family, conflict in this specific sense is very difficult to carry out and is thus highly likely to be absent.

Finally, we trust the attention to terminology has helped keep conflict and violence conceptually distinct. Popular conceptions often seem to equate

conflict and violence, or to view conflict as producing

violence. In contrast to such a view, we argue that it is the absence of specifically instrumental conflict in families that leads to a high level of interpersonal violence and aggression.

NOTES

*I would like to especially thank Dennis Foss and Gerald Hotaling for their comment on earlier drafts of this chapter.

1. Personality involvement and affective investment may be related (see Propositions 8 and 9), but they are conceptually distinct. The important feature of personality involvement is its totality. Affective investment involves both the strength of attraction or liking and low replaceability of members.

2. This is not an entirely satisfactory resolution of the contradiction, particularly since it ignores unequal exchange. Yet to resolve this question fully would require an intricate series of propositions about exchange processes, which would take us far afield and would be well beyond the scope and focus of this chapter.

3. Hotaling defines aggression as "a physical or psychological act or acts, occurring in an interpersonal situation, which are judged to be intentionally harm-producing" (Chapter 9). Since he focuses on attribution of aggressive intent in families, the emphasis in definition is on the perception by others of the person's intent. While the focus here is not on perceptions by others, we suggest that these approaches to defining aggression are similar in emphasizing intent or goals of the actors. The possibility of using intent or goals as a definitional basis is also recognized in the suggestion that "...to the extent that actors define such behaviors as normal and not intended to injure, they are not aggressive acts..." (Straus, 1974a:442).

4. This proposition is stated in general terms, since it applies not only to avoidance, but also to expressive and instrumental conflict, which will be discussed later.

5. While we are not primarily concerned here with conflict in extended families, such families in general may be considered less intense or intimate and thus much of this particular discussion may be applicable. Indeed, many of the formal rules of etiquette between husbands and wives in traditional extended (especially patriarchal) families may be seen also as providing legitimized patterns of avoidance. Such patterns may have the effect of lessening intimacy as well as interaction in areas of potential conflicts of interest.

6. This proposition is stated in terms of aggression in general rather than in terms of specific subtypes like verbal aggression and physical violence. Straus' discussion of the relationships between verbal and physical aggression (1974a) could be relevant here.

7. For the sake of clarity the diagram includes only the main lines of argument. Thus, most propositions already included in Figure 1, and those propositions that served to specify major propositions, are generally excluded.

Chapter 9

Attribution Processes
in Husband-Wife Violence

Gerald T. Hotaling

* *

A central tenet of this chapter is that
"intent" is imputed rather than observed.
Therefore, an action is intentionally aggressive
or violent only when the imputation is made.
Attribution theory alerts us to the importance
of understanding why, and under what conditions,
one perceives an action as aggressive rather
than as unintentional or accidental.

The chapter attempts to show that certain
structural characteristics of the family produce
conditions that increase the probability that a
family member will attribute malevolent intent
to the acts of another family member. The acts
we refer to are those that violate family rules.
Hotaling points to what he feels is a central
irony in family life: the factors that
contribute to the warmth and intimacy of family
relationships, such as the sharing of secrets
and personal information, also facilitate
perceiving rule violations as intentionally
malevolent.

A final section of the chapter examines the
way in which attribution of aggression or
violence serves to stabilize violence as a
regular feature of family life.

* *

Violent behavior results from a process that its
participants construct within a situation. Structural
theories of violence have tended to neglect the
interpersonal development of violent behavior and focus

instead on such variables as subcultural norms (Coser, 1967; Wolfgang and Ferracuti, 1967; Carroll, Chapter 5), social class (Kohn, 1969; Levinger, 1966), and resources (Goode, 1971; O'Brien, 1971; Allen and Straus, Chapter 12) as determinants of physical violence. Such theories, while specifying populations and their prevalence to use violence, do not account for the large amount of variation among actors and between situations.

Since the majority of acts of violence occur between friends and family members and begin with an altercation over relatively "trivial" matters (Hepburn, 1971; 1973), this chapter will focus on the processes by which seemingly minor issues between husbands and wives escalate into episodes of violent behavior.

The transformation of "trivial" into "serious" matters in intimate relationships, like the family, is seen as being facilitated by certain organizational or structural features of the marital bond.

A logical starting point in this kind of social psychological analysis is the examination of the contention that the "meaning" of aggression*1 and violence is problematic. The perception of an act as intentional aggression or as accidental harm-doing is an important distinction in analyzing violence (e.g., Tedeschi, et al., 1974).

In many instances, the perception of aggressive actions is nonproblematic. Cultural values and beliefs greatly assist the identification of aggressive acts. High-intensity, offensive, and pain-producing actions are usually taken for granted as signs of aggression or violence. But human aggression need not take the form of overt physical damage; aggression can be manifest in verbal, indirect, passive, and subtle forms of psychological harm. It is especially when harm-doing actions take these forms that judgmental controversies are likely to arise. Much human aggression is of this type and there are good reasons why this is so. As Bandura (1973:9) states:

> People ordinarily refrain from direct personal assaults because such obvious actions carry high risks of retaliation. Rather, they favor disguised modes of aggression that, being difficult to interpret or to consider blameworthy, afford protection against counterattack.

A major focus of this chapter will be on the imputational processes people use in discriminating between aggressive and nonaggressive actions. To this end, husband-wife violence will be examined within the context of attribution theory.

ATTRIBUTION THEORY

In its simplest form, attribution theory describes the process by which people attempt to explain and predict human behavior. In other words, it investigates people's search for the meaning of behavior.

As Kelley and Thibaut (1969) have defined it:

> Attribution refers to the process of inferring or perceiving the dispositional properties of entities....Attribution theory describes the process by which the individual seeks and attains conceptions of the stable dispositions or attributes (p.7).

While there are at least three distinct attribution approaches (see Heider, 1958; Jones and Davis, 1965; and H. H. Kelley, 1967, 1971), all three perspectives have common elements. Shaver (1975) has identified some of the commonalities of the above theorists in terms of three stages in the attribution process. The first stage involves the observation of an action, either directly or indirectly through the reports of others. The second stage, and the one that is important to the theme of this chapter, involves the attribution of intention. One attempts to interpret the actions of others as intentional and goal-directed or as the result of accident, reflex, or habit. The final stage concerns the imputation a "cause" and searches for the answer to "why the person acted as he/she did." The answer usually takes one of two forms: the action is attributed to causes in the environment or the situation ("He's under a lot of pressure lately") or to the underlying disposition of the person ("He's just an aggressive person"). This sequence of events may require only seconds to complete or in some cases, such as jury deliberations, several days or weeks.

The concern with attributional processes, especially the attribution of intention, has been evident in the work of psychologists in work on aggression and violence. Over the years, researchers have argued about how they would decide when to label a response or set of responses as aggressive or violent (Buss, 1971; Bandura, 1973; and Tedeschi, et al., 1974). The emphasis in these writings is on the experimenter-subject relationship, i.e., what criteria an experimenter would use to characterize subject responses as aggressive. Unfortunately, the question of how a person imputes intentional aggressiveness in a variety of relational contexts has not been fully investigated.

In this chapter, the attribution of aggression and its role in the production of family violence will be examined via the rule system and structure of the husband-wife

relationship. A major question will be: are there
organizational features peculiar to the husband-wife
relationship that facilitate the attribution of malevolent
intent?

THE NATURE OF RELATIONAL RULES

All enduring social groups have rules and regulations,
but show considerable variation in the extent to which
behavior is controlled by rules. In other words, groups
differ in the scope of their rules: (1) their substantive
range, that is, how much behavior they control; and (2)
their spatiotemporal range, that is, where and when they
control behavior. As an example, workers in a steel plant
have rules for when to show up for work, when to go home,
how much work to get done, and how to get the work done.
Similarly, in graduate school departments, rules (at times
implicit) concern the appropriate amount of work to be done
within given periods. These sorts of rules are of limited
substantive and spatiotemporal range, in that they are
concerned primarily with instrumental behavior and are
applicable only during specified times and in specified
places. Their scope is not all-embracing.

In the husband-wife relationship, rules are of broad
substantive scope. Here, rules are designed to control both
instrumental and expressive behavior. Furthermore, they
have a wide spatiotemporal range: they are applicable
across situations and in and out of one another's presence.
Opinions differ as to why relational rules are of such broad
scope, but various authors agree that these rules attempt to
control a large amount of behavior.

Both D. Cooper (1971) and R. D. Laing (1972) have
addressed the nature of relational rules in families and
their import for individual members. These authors
emphasize the political nature of family rules; holding
that the family as an extension of capitalist society
creates rules through which "dehumanization" of the
individual takes place. From their perspective, family
rules are all-inclusive and restrict individual growth and
development. Through rules, family members are forced into
roles in which a major portion of reality is kept beyond
everyday experience. While their ideological orientation
may differ, these authors both highlight the fact that the
family attempts to control a wide range of behavior.

From a somewhat different perspective, Denzin (1970)
and Turner (1968) outline a set of rules, applicable to the
husband-wife relationship, whose function it is to protect
and enhance individual identities.*2 Denzin argues that
"rules of relationship" are generated in intimate relations
in which the self of each actor is defined and acted upon.

These rules are: (1) task rules, to specify who does what,
when, and with whom;   (2) rules specifying deference and
demeanor;   (3) rules for regulating knowledge, secrecy, and
personal problems; and (4) rules specifying proper conduct
of ego and other when not in each other's presence.
Similarly, Turner (1968) suggests two rules that will be
developed between intimates to protect the identities of one
another.   They are: (1) the avoidance of one another's
sensitive zones; and (2) the declaration by the winner that
his/her victory is attributable to luck or experience rather
than the ineptness of the vanquished.

Taking Denzin and Turner together, we could say that
relational rules are agreements between intimates that each
will avoid behavior that threatens the situated identities*3
of each.   These rules are necessary because each has
revealed to the other intimate knowledge, secrets, desires
and personal problems, important to identity, that are not
available to the public at large.

To summarize the discussion thus far we can conceive of
relational rules as being somewhat ironic. For people to
remain in physical and emotional proximity, rules must be
developed that protect and enhance situated identities, and
that at the same time restrict and control behavior.

THE NATURE OF RELATIONAL RULE VIOLATIONS

Most relational rules between intimates are undefined,
implicit, and ambiguous. In addition, they are constantly
being modified according to different situational demands.
For example, one spouse may begin to interpret rules
differently without informing the other of the changed
perspective.   In such a situation, violations of rules are
easier since the boundaries between rule conformity and
violation become quite precarious. For example, a husband
talking to another woman at a party may be considered a rule
violator by his wife according to his distance from the
woman, the expression on his face, and the content of the
conversation.   This may be so even though the husband never
intended a violation of relational rules. The point is that
the ambiguous, undefined and implicit nature of relational
rules raises the probability that rule violations will
occur.

Since rule violations may be either intentional or
accidental, the meaning of the violation that the other
attributes to the violating actor is significant (Scott and
Lyman, 1970).   The violation of relational rules leads
intimates to feel embarrassment, irritation, annoyance, and,
at the extreme, self-threat and publicly designated deviance
(Denzin, 1970).

The manner in which a violaticn is perceived has import
for the consequences.   A person will give the response
appropropriate to a viclation, according to his/her
perception of the violation as "accidental" harm-doing or as
aggression. Most interaction between family members is
harmonious and cooperative.   Indeed, most rule violations
are not seen as aggressive, but rather as accidents, as
responses to situational demands, or as responses to
extraneous influences, such as alcohol or drugs.   Actually,
relative to the rate of relational rule violations perceived
as aggressive, most rule violations are denied or dismissed.
If this were not so, intimate relationships would be very
difficult to maintain.

THE RELATION BETWEEN THE ATTRIBUTION OF RULE VIOLATIONS AS AGGRESSIVE AND INTERPERSONAL VIOLENCE

As mentioned previously, the attribution of rule
violations as intentionally aggressive is an important step
in the occurrence of interpersonal violence.   As Turner
(1968) puts it:

> When ego perceives that alter is attempting to
> negatively affect his interests...the character
> of the interaction is pervasively altered by
> heightened preoccupation with self-images,
> increased use of emphatic and diagnostic
> interpretations of gestures...and constant
> efforts to assign credit and responsibility
> (p. 106).

Attempts to locate the "intent" of the rule violation
will determine the subsequent action taken to reduce the
harm-doing of the rule violation. If malevolent intent is
attributed to the rule viclator, the probability of violence
is increased.   Many experimental studies have found that the
perception of opponent's intent is a more important variable
in the instigation of aggression than actual physical
attack.   If a given act is seen as aggressive, it
dramatically escalates the probability of counteraggression
(Bandura, 1973; Epstein and Taylor, 1967; Maselli and
Altrochi, 1969).

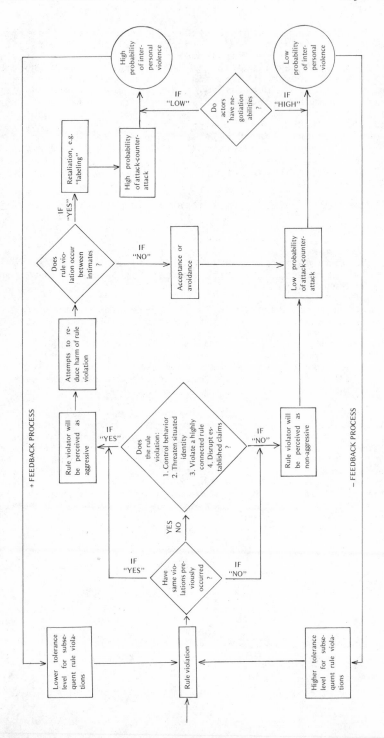

RESPONSE TO RULE VIOLATIONS ATTRIBUTED TO AGGRESSION

The attribution of aggression alone is not sufficient for the initiation of interpersonal violence. Following the imputation, the attributor will evaluate the situation and the possible alternative responses he/she can make. Hepburn (1973) has suggested three possible tactics the attributor can choose to reduce the harm-doing caused by the rule violation (see flowchart).

Avoidance. One tactic that can be used to deal with violations is avoidance. The tactic of avoidance necessitates a physical withdrawal from the location or an emotional disengagement from the encounter. The tactic of avoidance is difficult in intimate relationships where there are external constraints on the participants to remain in the situation (see Foss, Chapter 8).

Acceptance. Another tactic is acceptance of the rule violation. Acceptance of rule violation is also difficult in intimate relationships, where the rules serve to protect the identities of the participants. Accepting the rule violation as appropriate behavior necessarily alters the expectations each has toward the other. Disrupting these stable and orderly interaction patterns makes vulnerable one's identity.

If either acceptance or avoidance is selected as a tactic by which to respond to aggressive rule violations, the likelihood that the encounter will end in violence is greatly diminished.

Retaliation. It is the tactic of retaliation that is most likely to lead to interpersonal violence. When ego adopts the tactic of retaliation he/she risks retaliation by other. Initially, ego will label the rule violation as aggressive, that is, transmit to the violator that he/she attributes intentional harm-doing to him/her. Once the rule violation is labeled, ego can legitimately seek retribution from the rule violator. If the rule violator cannot adequately negotiate the aggressive label, he/she may counterretaliate in an attempt to rid him/herself of the aggressive label. This process accords with Sprey's contention (1971) that successful management of conflict in families requires the ability to negotiate, bargain, and cooperate--to manipulate a range of behavioral skills. If the process of retaliation-counterretaliation continues, the probability of violence is increased.

To summarize the preceding section in propositional form:

Proposition 1. If a rule violation is attributed as aggressive, that is, as

intentional harm-doing, the probability of
interpersonal violence is increased.

If the attribution of aggressiveness is made, an
evaluation of the situation will determine an appropriate
response by which to reduce the harm-doing of the rule
violation. It is posited that:

> Proposition 2. The more intimate the
> relationship, the less likely will acceptance
> or avoidance be used as a tactic to reduce
> the harm-doing of rule violations.

Since acceptance or avoidance is difficult for those
involved in enduring intimate relationships:

> Proposition 3. The more intimate the
> relationship, the more likely will
> retaliation be used as a tactic to reduce the
> harm-doing of rule violations.

If the tactic of retaliation is chosen, chances
increase that violence will ensue; the norm of reciprocity
will legitimize retaliation.

> Proposition 4. If the attribution of aggression
> is communicated to the rule violator, the
> probability of counterretaliation increases.

> Proposition 5. The lower the negotiation
> abilities of the actors involved, the higher
> the probability of counterretaliation.

> Proposition 6. The more the retaliation-
> counterretaliation, the higher the
> probability of violence.

CHARACTERISTICS OF RULES AND RULE VIOLATIONS
THAT ENHANCE AGGRESSIVE ATTRIBUTION

Whether a rule violation is aggressive is typically
inferred from, among other things, characteristics of the
rule violator (e.g., power and status), characteristics of
the situation (presence of alcohol or coercion), and
characteristics of the rule violation itself. This latter
category is of interest here. Certain characteristics of
rules and types of rule violations do seem to lead to the
violator's being seen as aggressive. The characteristics of
rules to be considered in this connection are those that:
(1) control or restrict behavior, (2) threaten situated
identities, (3) are highly connected to other rules, and (4)
disrupt established claims. In the discussion of each of
these characteristics we will attempt to demonstrate how

certain structural features of the husband-wife relationship
may enhance the attribution of aggression for rule
violations.

Control of Behavior

Experimental studies have found that actions that
control the behavior of another, or constrain another's
behavioral alternatives or outcomes, are more likely to be
attributed as aggressive (Brown and Tedeschi, 1974; Cameron
and Janky, 1972; Tedeschi, et al., 1974). When an action
forces a person into a position in which alternative courses
of action are severely limited, the actor probably will
evaluate the action as goal-directed. Are rule violations
that occur between intimates more likely to be perceived as
controlling than rule violations in other social
relationships? It has already been mentioned that a wide
variety of rules between intimates are undefined and
ambiguous. But, in addition, an organizational feature of
the husband-wife relationship may increase the degree to
which a rule violation of one spouse impinges on the
partner.

In many institutional spheres, the violation of rules
is usually examined by some form of civil authority whose
function is to render an objective judgment. For example,
if labor accuses management of violating certain contractual
arrangements about overtime pay and both sides remain
resolute about their "rightness," objective negotiators will
be called in to mediate the dispute. The resolution of the
dispute by recourse to third party arbitration will
temporarily halt each side's feeling "controlled" by the
other. In more intimate social relationships, as marriage,
there is no institutionalized third party arbitration
designed to handle rule violations. For example, if a
husband violates a relational rule by having sexual
relations with another woman, the wife has recourse only to
the husband. In effect, the wife is under the control of
the rule violator. Other alternatives are to have someone
talk to the husband, or to dissolve the marriage, but no
direct authority can mandate an end to the violation.

As Sprey (1971) remarks: "Conjugal love, the bond of
marriage, is the most exclusive of all in our society" (p.
723). The closer the participants in a social relationship,
the more exclusive of strangers it becomes. For our
purposes, and to summarize this section:

> Proposition 7. The more intimate the
> participants in a social relationship, the
> lower the probability of institutionalized
> third party arbitration on rule violations.

<u>Proposition 8</u>. The lower the probability of institutionalized third party arbitration on rule violations, the more one is under control of the rule violator.

<u>Proposition 9</u>. If a rule violation occurs, the more intimate the participants in a social relationship, the more one is under the control of the rule violator.

Threats to Situated Identities

Rule violations that threaten the situated identity of a person have a high probability of being labeled as aggressive. Hepburn (1973) states:

> The perception of a threat to the situated identities is the initial stage in the process which may terminate in interpersonal violence, for it is the perception of a threat that transforms a harmonious, non-identity directed interaction into a hostile identity directed encounter (p.423).

This chapter holds that the attribution of aggression is the initial stage in a process of interpersonal violence. Rule violations perceived as threatening to the situated identities of participants facilitate the attribution of aggression, but are not the sole determinant.

The focus here is not on threat as a verbal or nonverbal message promising unfavorable consequences if demands are not met, but on the perception of threats to situated identities; that is, the perception that one's identity is being jeopardized, or the perception of a negative evaluation of worth. The threat may be intentional or unintentional; what is crucial is that the threat is perceived as harmful to one's sense of who he/she is in a relationship.

As mentioned, intimate relationships involve a mutual concern for the identities of participants. Identities are supported and enhanced through interaction. This support is facilitated because each intimate has an extensive knowledge of the other's collection of social identities, or social biography. In effect, intimates know how to support the identities of each other because each knows about the things that matter to each other. Although this extensive knowledge can be used to support and enhance identities, at the same time, it can be used to damage them.

This process is highlighted in the following passage by William Dean Howells in his novel <u>The Rise of Silas Lapham</u> in a discussion of the nature of marriage:

> Two people by no means reckless of each other's
> rights and feelings, but even tender of them for
> the most part, may tear at each other's
> heartstrings in this sacred bond with impunity;
> though if they were any other two they would not
> speak or look at each other again after the
> outrages they exchange....If the husband and
> wife are blunt, outspoken people like the
> Laphams, they do not weigh their words, if they
> are more refined, they weigh them very
> carefully, and know accurately just how far they
> will vary and in what most sensitive spot they
> may be planted with the most effect (1964:50).

Besides possessing knowledge of other members that can
be used to do harm, intimates are predisposed to impute harm
where no malevolence is necessarily intended. For example,
if in the presence of others, a wife expresses the desire
for certain material goods that are beyond her means, a
husband who is sensitive about his earning potential may
feel threatened by such a statement. While her intent may
have been to share her feelings about things she would like
to have, the comment may be threatening to the husband
because he knows that she knows that he is sensitive about
such things. Because she knows he is sensitive about such
things, he is likely to feel, she would not have said it
unless she meant to comment on his earning capacity. If a
nonintimate had expressed the same desire for material
goods, there would have been no reason for the husband to
perceive such a statement as threatening to his
self-identity.

If a nonintimate asks, "Why don't you ever take your
wife out to dinner?" the question may not be perceived as
threatening even when it _was_ meant malevolently. The
perceiver cannot be certain that the nonintimate knows he is
sensitive about such remarks. Because he knows that his
wife knows he is sensitive to such things, the same remark
by her will be more likely perceived as threatening.

Attribution theory offers some empirical evidence that
this sort of situation may indeed occur. Jones and Davis
(1965) provide experimental research on the knowledge people
use in deciding with certainty an act's intentionality. Two
of their conclusions are of direct concern to intimate
relationships:

> Knowledge and ability are preconditions for the
> assignment of intentions. Each plays a role in
> enabling the perceiver to decide whether an
> effect or consequence of action was accidental
> (1965:221-222).

> The meaning of an action--its intentional
> significance--derives from such consideration of

the alternative action possibilities available
to, but foregone by, the actor (1965:222).

In the above example, to the husband's way of thinking,
his wife could have talked about a variety of things, so why
did she choose to talk about something that she knows him to
be sensitive about? To summarize:

> Proposition 10.   The   more   intimate   the
> participants in a relationship, the more
> extensive   the   knowledge   of   social
> biographies.

> Proposition 11.   The   more extensive   the
> knowledge of social biographies, the higher
> the certainty that other's rule violation was
> intentional.

Highly Connected Rules

The violation of a rule that is highly connected to
other rules increases the probability that the rule
violation will be perceived as aggressive.

When a highly connected rule is violated, it has the
potential to disrupt the entire functioning of the
organization. For example, in the military as in many
bureaucracies, rules are clearly specified and highly
differentiated. The violation of a rule is handled on a
statute basis. The violation is coded, and "suitable
punishment" is predefined. The rules are so fragmented that
it is difficult to violate highly connected rules; though
the rules are connected, each rule is also distinct from
others.

In intimate relationships, relational rules are not
distinct from one another, but vague, undefined, and for the
most part highly connected to one another. As an example, a
rule violation in which a husband refuses to fulfill a task
function by not helping around the house may generate an
argument in which the generalization is made that he is lazy
and doesn't care what happens around the home. He may
retort that his wife does not always please him with what
she does around the house and, besides, he works and she
doesn't. Reference to past events may be brought in, as
well as recourse to dispositional traits to bolster
argumentive points. To summarize:

> Proposition 12.   The   more   intimate   the
> relationship, the more vague and undefined
> the rules.

Proposition 13. The more vague and undefined
the rules, the higher the connectedness of
the rules.

Proposition 14. The more intimate the
relationship, the higher the probability that
rule violations will be violations of highly
connected rules.

Proposition 15. The violation of a highly
connected rule heightens the probability that
the rule violator will be perceived as
aggressive.

Disruption of Claims

Stable interaction patterns, developed over the course
of a relationship, order and make predictable the
expectations of each participant toward the other. Patterns
of "claiming behavior" develop and become stabilized.
Claiming behavior, as the phrase implies, refers to making
claims or demands on another because of your social position
relative to the other. Intimate relationships, as compared
with nonintimate relationships, can be characterized by
relational complacence, wherein patterns of claiming
behavior become taken for granted. Relational complacence
is less likely to occur in groups in which patterns of
claiming behavior are based solely on secondary or exchange
considerations; for example, in employer-employee or
landlord-tenant relations.

Relational rule violations that disrupt established
patterns of claiming behavior have a high probability of
being perceived as aggressive.

The inauguration of asymmetrical claims into an
initially defined egalitarian (symmetrical)
relationship, or of symmetrical claims into an
initially defied authoritarian (asymmetrical)
relationship will disrupt the harmony of the
interaction and threaten the identities of the
participants (Hepburn, 1973:27).

The literature illustrates the effect of introducing
symmetry into initially defined asymmetrical relationships.
Reiss (1968) points out that almost half of the cases of
police brutality involve an open defiance of the officer's
authority. That is, the arrested party sought to disrupt
taken-for-granted claims--in this case, a rejection of the
officer's authority. Westley (1953) reports that when asked
to indicate those circumstances in which they deem violent
techniques appropriate, the police most often cited those
instances in which their claims were defied by uncooperative
persons so that coercion had to be used to maintain their

self-interest. Tedeschi, et al. (1974) argue that one factor that leads persons to label acts as aggressive is the advancement of self-interest. A disruption of established claims is likely to be perceived as the advancement of the other's selfish interests by the party whose interests are being negatively affected.

In intimate relationships, relational complacence may predispose one party to view disruptions of claims as attempts to further self-interest of the other. For example, a previously nonworking wife who decides to get a job could be perceived as attempting to disrupt previously established claims. Her intent may be assertive, not aggressive, but it may be perceived as aggressive by her husband who sees such an action as negatively affecting his self-interest. This process is illustrated in Chapter 10 of this volume in Ralph IaRossa's case study of Joe and Jennifer.

These four characteristics of rule violations are held to facilitate the perception of rule violations as malevolent. If rule violations occur that have one or more of these characteristics, the probability is high that such rule violations will be perceived as intentionally harm-producing.

FEEDBACK PROCESSES

Up to now, we have been primarily concerned with the imputation of intentionality to the actions of others and its role in facilitating violence. Another large consideration in attribution theory concerns locating the "cause" of the action. The perceiver will sometimes attempt to interpret an action by linking it to the environment or the personal disposition of the actor.

A good deal of evidence from attribution theory shows that pressures exist to attribute responsibility to the person, that is, to his/her personality or disposition, the more times aggressive actions occur or are perceived as occurring. Relational rule violations that result in interpersonal violence reinforce the perceiver in viewing the violator as an aggressive person. Experimental evidence from Kelley, et al. (1962) supports this contention:

An effect is attributed to one of its possible causes with which, over time, it covaries.

As the association between rule violations and interpersonal violence becomes stronger, and occurs under different conditions, so does the certainty that the rule violator is an aggressive person.

Other processes also are at work that influence the
perceiver to view the rule violator as an aggressive person
rather than as a victim of his/her environment. For
example, an experiment by Kanouse and Hanson (1971)
demonstrated that people are generally cost-oriented in
forming overall evaluations. When an object or event has
both positive and negative characteristics, people weigh the
negative more than the positive. In the family situation,
where previous rule violations have caused interpersonal
violence, subsequent actions taken by the rule violator,
although containing both positive and negative features, may
be more likely to be seen as aggressive.

More important to our discussion of the imputation of
aggression to the personal disposition of the actor is the
nature of violence itself. Violence is usually a high
intensity, pain-producing act. If in the past attempts to
resolve rule violations have escalated to violence, the
probability is greater of seeing the other as aggressive.
Experimental evidence from both Kelley (1967) and Walster
(1966) points out that the perceiver has an increasing need
to attribute responsibility as the outcomes of actions
become more severe.

In a social-psychological sense, the consequences for
the rule violator can be severe, in that changes in
self-concept may occur as attributions to the personal
characteristics are transmitted. The rule violator may
begin to see him/herself as aggressive or violent and act in
terms of the larger cultural meaning of being an aggressive
or violent person.

This sequence of events may not occur, however, in
social groups like the family. Certain features of intimate
relationships exist that may work against making
attributions to the personal disposition of the person in
favor of attributing "cause" to the environment or
situation. Three notions of attribution theory are relevant
here: Jones and Davis' (1965) concepts of hedonistic
relevance and personalism and Kelley's (1971) concept of
pluralistic ignorance. These authors see these concepts as
important variables in affecting attributor bias because of
the perceiver's felt personal needs. Jones and Davis point
out that one's personal involvement with the actor may
affect one's attribution. The action observed has direct
positive or negative consequences for the perceiver--it is
hedonistically relevant. Also, perceiver bias may occur
because of the relationship of actor to perceiver. When the
perceiver believes that the action he/she observes has been
conditioned by his/her presence, personalism will affect
dispositional attributions.

Because of the high interdependence of the couple,
these two factors are especially relevant to intimate
relationships. Relational rule violations are

hedonistically relevant and personalistic to intimates and
may bias the attribution process. Intimates may be
reluctant to label a spouse as aggressive or violent because
the attribution has implications for both. To label an
intimate as an aggressive or violent person may be too
difficult to reconcile with the image of spouse as a freely
chosen, close emotional partner. The perceiver may tend to
err in the direction of nonrecognition of the spouse's
responsibility and attribute rule violations to the
environment or situation rather than to the partner's
personality. Findings from a study by Yarrow, et al.
(1955), of wives' definitions of husbands' emotional problems
can be thus interpreted. They report a great reluctance on
the part of wives to label their husbands as mentally ill.
Not until all possible interpretations of their husbands'
behavior are examined and found wanting is the attribution
to personal disposition made. In other words, the evidence
has to be overwhelming before the husband is seen as a
mentally ill person in need of professional help.

The other concept relevant to attribution bias among
intimates is what Kelley (1971) calls pluralistic ignorance.
This variable refers to the lack of consensus on an
attribution through either the absence of comparison or the
lack of other observers. The private nature of the family
institution (Laslett, 1973), in which most activities take
place out of view of nonfamily members, heightens the
likelihood of pluralistic ignorance. Attributions made in
the family setting usually take place without feedback from
others. The lack of third party observers and the inability
to observe other sets of intimates during the resolution of
rule violations leads to a lack of certainty as to the
proper attribution. Because of this lack of certainty and
the possibility of error, dispositional attributions may be
made in a conservative direction, blaming the situation
rather than the spouse.

As was mentioned in reference to labeling mental
illness, attribution bias could be an important variable in
accounting for the reluctance of many married persons to
seek help when involved in violent relationships, until the
outcomes become severe for everyone involved.

CONCLUSION

The relationship between husband-wife violence and two
aspects of attribution theory were examined in this chapter.
The first of these aspects, the attribution of intentional
aggression, was seen as an important variable in the
occurrence of interpersonal violence. It was argued that
the violation of relational rules, which are designed to
protect the identities of participants in intimate
relationships, can initiate a process wherein the validity

of the rule is negotiated, and attempts to reduce the harm-doing of the violation are begun. The violation of relational rules may be accidental or deliberate, the significant factor being the meaning of the violation that the other attributes to the violator.

Four kinds of rule violations most likely to be perceived as aggressive are (1) rule violations that control behavior, (2) rule violations seen as threats to situated identities, (3) violations of rules that are highly connected to other rules, and (4) rule violations that disrupt established claims.

We further posited that the family as an intimate group, especially the husband-wife relationship, may have certain organizational features that increase the probability that rule violations of the kind just listed enhance the attribution of aggression. From this perspective, the family is seen as a faulty organization in that (1) no structural arrangements exist for institutionalized third-party arbitration to settle rule violations, (2) knowledge of one another's social biographies is too great, (3) rules are vague, ambiguous, and highly connected, and (4) the family as an organization does not adapt well to change, owing to relational complacence.

The second aspect of attribution theory examined was that concerned with the process of locating the "cause" of the action. Once a perceiver attributes intentionality to another's actions, he/she attempts to interpret the cause of the action. Attributions are made to the environment or situation, or to the personality of the actor. Certain features of intimate relationships were seen as promoting attributional bias, wherein situational and environmental factors are blamed for violent actions rather than the personal disposition of the actor.

NOTES

*A version of this chapter was presented at the Theory Construction Workshop at the annual meeting of the National Council on Family Relations, August 19-20, 1975. The preparation of this chapter was supported by National Institute of Mental Health grant No. 13050. I would like to thank Ms. Joyce E. Foss and Ms. Saundra L. Atwell for many helpful suggestions throughout the formulation of this chapter.

1. Aggression is here defined as a physical or psychological act or acts, occurring in an interpersonal situation, that are judged to be intentionally

harm-producing. The distinction between aggression and violence is so problematic that it would take an entire chapter to deal with the matter (see Gelles and Straus, 1978). This chapter focuses on how attribution processes facilitate violence by producing a cycle of escalating aggression.

2. Identity is seen here as a social phenomenon. Through our position-sets, in the social structure in relation to other position-sets, it is established where and what we are. Most basically, identity is the answer to the question, "Who am I?"

3. Situated identity refers to the location of one's social self in relation to a specific social position. For example, a husband in relation to his wife, or a student in relation to his/her teacher.

Part IV The Interplay of Culture and Social Organization

The chapters in the preceding section
emphasize that certain aspects of family
organization increase the probability of
conflict. But conflict is not the same as
violence; there are many nonviolent ways of
settling conflict. However, in a group
characterized by a high degree of conflict,
where norms legitimize the use of physical force
(as shown in Part II), the stage is set for a
high level of violence. This combination of
social organizational and cultural factors forms
the focus of all three chapters in Part IV.

The three chapters have something else in
common. All illustrate what Allen and Straus in
Chapter 12 call the "ultimate resource theory of
violence." This theory states that violence will
be used as a resource when other resources are
lacking. Thus a family member with little
power, money, or status is more likely to resort
to violence as a means of winning a conflict.

To understand why some families resolve
conflict violently and others do not involves a
number of closely related questions. For
example, why do many men feel they should
automatically be the "head of the household,"
while others feel equalitarian relationships are
the acceptable norm? Why is the probability of
the occurrence of violence higher in families
where the wife's resources exceed those of the
husband? How does employment outside the home
affect the balance of power in marriage?

The chapters in this section use vastly
different methods, but each comes to grips with
the type of questions just listed. First, a
case study is presented that enables us to grasp
the dynamics of marital conflict and violence by
sharing the experiences of a young couple. This
history is followed by a chapter that traces the
logical implications for marital violence of the
changes in employment of married women and
changes in the way masculinity is defined.
Finally, the third chapter in the section uses
statistical analysis of a large sample of
couples to test the "utlimate resource theory"
of marital violence.

Chapter 10

"And We Haven't Had Any Problems Since": Conjugal Violence and the Politics of Marriage

Ralph LaRossa

* *

Joe and Jennifer, the couple whose story we follow in this chapter, is not the study of a "disturbed" couple. They, like other couples in varying degrees, have certain conflicts of interest--some of which may end in violence. Their story gives us an inside view of the interplay of cultural and social organizational factors in producing marital violence. As pointed out in earlier chapters, the fact that cultural norms permit violence among family members does not automatically mean that violence will be used to resolve conflict situations. We must also understand the social organization of the marriage. This is vividly illustrated when Joe relates the time he slapped Jennifer "three or four times." This occurred during a period in their marriage when Joe perceived Jennifer as attempting to dominate their relationship. Joe responded to this attempted coup with violence because he felt he "had to do something to stop the bad progression of events." In short, violence was used when other factors that in his mind would validate his claim to dominant power were lacking.

* *

In an attempt to help fill the need for ethnographies of American marriages, I recently conducted a qualitative study of sixteen married couples expecting their first child (LaRossa, 1977).*1 My conversations with these couples led me to conclude that, contrary to popular opinion, confrontation and struggle as well as consensus and equilibrium are at the root of the marital union. The idea that marriage is a conflict system is hardly novel (see

Sprey, 1969, for example). What evidently has been lacking however is empirical support for this contention.*2

The purpose of this chapter is to present an illustration of the conflict theme. The case study that follows tells the story of Joe and Jennifer (pseudonyms), a couple whose power struggle is manifested in a variety of ways. Their story is particularly significant because of the violent side to their relationship. Through their experience, the cold war metaphor, implicit in the conflict approach, truly comes to life.

JOE AND JENNIFER

The first pregnancy meant essentially two things to Joe and Jennifer. It meant that after having waited nearly four years they were finally starting a family, something they had always wanted to do. It also signaled a change in their work structure. For the first time since they were married Jennifer would not be working. More important, for the first time since they were married Joe would be the sole wage earner. The significance of this latter point is that Joe intended to use his new position to make a claim for dominance in the marriage.

Joe was a metaphorical speaker. Often, while discussing an issue, he would (to "clarify" a point) bring in anecdotes from his personal experiences or relate the issue to the international state of affairs. There were times during my interviews with this couple, I must confess, when I wished he would have been more specific in his answers. I learned however that I had to accept, as others had, that Joe was just "deep."

> Jennifer: Joe is a very deep thinker, and he
> always has something on his mind. He can
> drive you right up a wall!

Though Joe did most of the talking, Jennifer was not at a loss for words. Sometimes she found it difficult to get a word in edgewise or remember what question I had asked after Joe had picked it up and run with it for a while, but then so did I. When Jennifer did speak, she said what was on her mind--as did Joe; but, as she once said, what it took Joe to say in a paragraph, she said in a sentence. On a number of occasions during the interviews while Joe was building an argument (and this was particularly true if Joe's argument was an attempt to justify why he should be in charge) a few well placed words by Jennifer and Joe's edifice would come tumbling down.

Joe and Jennifer had known each other since high school. Their first reaction to each other was, as Jennifer put it, "mutual disgust." Both attribute this to the fact that they are each honest types--if they don't like you, they tell you--and, in the beginning, they told each other more of what they didn't like than of what they liked. In time, their hatred turned to love. What attracted them to each other was their similarities--their openness, their aggressiveness, and, interestingly, what they saw as the inability of either to dominate the other. It was a relationship built explicitly on conflict and honesty. (Joe once described Jennifer as his "confessor," and he hers.)

The couple could not recall any specific point at which they decided to get married. "Someplace along the line," it was just assumed. Though they may not have gone through the marriage proposal ritual, the transition to the married state was one they took very seriously. Joe and Jennifer were a religious couple. Joe, in particular, prided himself on his interpretations of the Bible. They did not believe in divorce. They felt it reflected weakness--a couple's inability to face life's problems.

When they got married, they lived solely on Jennifer's income. Having graduated from high school with a business diploma, she worked as a bookkeeper. Joe was just beginning his third year of college, studying to be an accountant. Actually, for the first three and a half years of their marriage, Jennifer would be the primary wage earner. This was because after Joe was awarded his bachelor's degree, he went on to attend a postgraduate business school which took him a year and a half to complete.

Both believed that the way they were each raised explained their personalities and why they complemented each other. Jennifer described her pre-marriage family life as one in which she was the primary decision-maker.

> Jennifer: I was always very independent before
> I got married. As a matter of fact, my
> parents were never my rule. I was the rule
> of my parents.

Joe, on the other hand, was brought up in a patriarchal home--all decisions were made by his father.

> Joe: ...And at my house it was just the
> opposite. My father was a very strong father
> image, traditional. "Come to him, your
> father will decide for you."...He wouldn't
> give me any responsibility.

Jennifer's independence, they felt, was a function of her having been forced to be independent all along. Joe's was a manifestation of his rebellion against his father's

autocratic style ("I had to sort of assert myself").
According to Joe, Jennifer came to the marriage wanting to
"get rid of" some of her power, and he came "wanting more,"
so their relationship "worked out all right." Neither would
try to dominate the other.

Although Joe claimed that Jennifer wanted less power
and that she would not try to dominate him, this evidently
was not the case. Sometime during the first two years of
their marriage, Joe and Jennifer got into an argument that
ended in violence--Joe struck Jennifer. The conflict was a
power struggle; Joe supposedly hit Jennifer because
Jennifer was trying to dominate. He responded with force
because he felt he "had to do something physical to stop the
bad progression of events." The sequence opens with my
asking Jennifer whether she thought she ran things now--that
is, does she believe she is "the rule" of Joe as she was
"the rule" of her parents and sisters.

> Interviewer: Do you think you run things now?
>
> Jennifer: No, I tried hard, though!
>
> Joe: She tries. One day we had a conflict and
> she more or less tried to run me and I told
> her no, and she got hysterical and said, "I
> could kill you!" And I got rather angry and
> slapped her in the face three or four times
> and I said "Don't you ever say that to me
> again." And we haven't had any problems
> since. So she's sort of learned that she
> isn't going to dominate.
>
> Jennifer: Yes, and I kind of like the idea,
> too.
>
> Joe: She threw a temper tantrum when she
> realized that she couldn't dominate me, and
> when she started getting hysterical,...that's
> the last time, kid! Yeah that's the worst
> argument we ever had! That was a drawn out
> bang out fight. It lasted about four hours.
> It sort of built and built...
>
> Interviewer: Were you surprised when Joe hit
> you?
>
> Joe: Oh, boy, was she.
>
> Jennifer: Yeah.
>
> Joe: She started crying not because I hurt her
> but because she was shocked--"How dare you!"
>
> Interviewer: Why did you hit her?

Jennifer: That was a long time ago.

Joe: That was a real long time ago. It's just
like if you want to do something like tear
down a house, what do you use? Do you use an
atom bomb, or do you use a crane and hammers
and stuff like that? It's just like physical
force. You don't use it until you're forced
to use it. At that point, I felt I had to do
something   physical   to   stop   the   bad
progression of events. I took my chances
with that and it worked. In those
circumstances, my judgment was correct and it
worked.

Jennifer: Joe doesn't usually use force. That
was the first and the last time he'll ever do
that. It was my fault. I was trying to
dominate him, that's for sure. But I was
always that type of person, that's why. I
always had to be that type of person, because
I always had to make my own decisions. I
never had anybody else make my decisions.

Joe: I'm a very dominating person, too, so
there was a conflict there.

Jennifer: I think that's one of the reasons we
got along so well, because he was the first
person I went out with that I couldn't
dominate. So he was a challenge.

Joe: That was a severe conflict. I don't know
if we hadn't solved that problem, if we would
still be married, because of the tension.
I'm not the kind of person that's going to be
dominated.

Jennifer: And I'm not either.

Joe: So we've had to agree, through a process
of compromise, and talking this out. We're
living on reconciliation and compromise and
understanding.

Though lengthy, the sequence is important. It is
important not only for what is said, but for how as well.
For example, the tenor of Joe's comments--he speaks as if
Jennifer were guilty of disrespect or even insubordination
("Don't you ever say that to me again!"..."That's the last
time, kid!"). Even more, there is undoubtedly a certain
amount of pride expressed--he _knew_ he had won that argument.
Jennifer, on the other hand, is quick to point out "that was
the first _and_ _the_ _last_ time he'll ever do that [hit her]."
She wanted to make it perfectly clear to me, but more

importantly to Joe, that she too had no intention of being dominated--and, perhaps, that she considered Joe's gloating an attempt to do just that! She goes on to admit that she married Joe because "he was a challenge." Does she mean by this that she considers Joe her opponent? The conflict nature of their marriage is explicitly acknowledged when Joe concludes by saying that their relationship works on "reconciliation and compromise" (words which connote "conflict" as well as "understanding."

As noted, Joe was a student for the first three and a half years of their marriage. When he graduated, he accepted an offer to work as an accountant with a local firm. One month after Joe took the job, the couple began trying to conceive a child. Four months later they found out that Jennifer was pregnant. They were evidently just biding their time, waiting for Joe to finish school--the point at which they felt it would be time to start a family. They always intended to have children. As Jennifer put it, they never "really seriously" considered not having children.

> Joe: I think having children is a fulfillment... People that are married and don't have children tend to get more selfish as they get older. And I think there's a lot of truth in that.

> Jennifer: If you see people without children, they tend to be very selfish, self-centered people.

> Joe: I think people who have children tend to be more outgoing, and have a healthier attitude toward life.

They also believed the child would bring them closer to each other.

> Joe: I think it's going to pull us together more... Each and every little item that you do together or can discuss together or have in common brings you closer together.

In addition to these reasons, the couple offered yet another reason why they opted to have a child. They wanted to start a family before Jennifer got "too ambitious" in her job. The fact is that while Joe may have just been starting his career, Jennifer had become quite established in hers. She had become the supervisor of the bookkeeping department in the company she had been working for since they were married.

> Jennifer: I figured I better have one before I got too ambitious in my job. I was getting a

lot of promotions and I decided if I got too
ambitious I may not want children. I might
get too involved in material things.

And in another interview--

Jennifer: There's a point in your life when you
should have a family... If you wait too
long, you start to believe that money is more
important than family life. I've seen that
happen to some other people.

Joe and Jennifer's deemphasis of "material things" and
their positive regard for "family life" was, to a large
degree, an outgrowth of their religious beliefs. At the
core of these beliefs is the notion that working is for
personal fulfillment and not for the monetary rewards it may
bring. Jennifer spoke of being a full-time mother, so I
asked her whether she believed she would ever return to
work. She assured me she would, that she would like to work
as a consultant eventually, if only part-time. She felt it
was important for her to pursue her career, that "in this
day and age, you need more than just the family." It was
apparent that Jennifer's concept of self was related to her
career as well as to her family. So was Joe's. While
Jennifer's ambitions were being stifled, Joe's ambitions
were being raised. Jennifer once said that when her
"quiet," "subdued" family first met Joe, they were "shocked"
by his frankness. The impression the couple give however
when they speak of the effect which moving from student to
worker had on Joe is that he had lost some of his
assertiveness in the interim. Through his work he was
evidently regaining his independence and self-confidence.

Jennifer: I think Joe is getting more
independent... He's been working well with
all the business people he's been dealing
with lately. He's getting more
self-confident...

Interviewer: Do you feel that Joe lacked
self-confidence?

Jennifer: I think that when you first get out
of school you do. You're not used to being
with business people. You're used to being
with students.

Interviewer: What do you think about your self-
confidence, Joe?

Joe: I think I'm gaining more self-confidence.
With more experience you know what to do.

Another self-confidence builder which Joe was involved with

was studying for the Certified Public Accountant (CPA) exams. He didn't want to be a CPA. He just wanted to pass the exam and, as he said, "stick my tongue out." (At whom? He didn't say.) Jennifer also wanted him to take the exam so that he would be more flexible. If he didn't like one job, he would be able to move to another with more ease.

The fact that both Joe and Jennifer's individual concepts of self were so related to their respective careers is particularly interesting. When the subject of arguing came up (I asked all the couples what they usually argued about), Joe and Jennifer said that the thing they argued about the most was accounting and bookkeeping. When I asked them why they argued so much about accounting and bookkeeping, it became apparent that they consider themselves, more or less, in the same business--the business of handling money--and that in this business they both have their own ideas. Actually, they seem to approach the business from two different points of view. Joe, as an accountant, represents the abstract or theoretical viewpoint. Jennifer, as a bookkeeper, represents the concrete (down to earth) view.

> Interviewer: Why do you think you end up arguing about it?
>
> Jennifer: I think that's something we both have our own ideas on.
>
> Joe: Sometimes I'm inconsistent and she points it out. At other times her knowledge about the subject is not as high as mine, so I have to sort of educate her.
>
> Jennifer: I'm more accurate and he's more knowledgeable. Put it that way.

And later on,

> Jennifer: He's an accountant, and I'm a bookkeeper.
>
> Joe: Yeah, she's a bookkeeper. Bookkeepers can find errors, and accountants can make up systems and can decide how the systems can run or why, and the bookkeepers can find errors.
>
> Jennifer: Bookkeepers can correct accountants' mistakes.

The classic conflict--education versus experience-- seems to be at the root of their discussion. Despite what may appear to most of us as an intellectual exercise, the fact that Joe and Jennifer's individual concepts of self are

so related to the money handling business makes their
confrontations more than a diversion. They were, I believe,
manifestations of the same conflict that had been going on
between them since they met in high school--who dominates
whom?

Given that the onset of pregnancy signaled a change in
the work structure of the couple's marriage, one might also
suspect that their perennial conflict would develop into
some interesting power plays and parries. This is, in fact,
essentially what happened. Joe may have rebelled against
his father's attempt to exert control as the husband-father.
There were, however, indications that Joe too would have
liked to command Jennifer's respect and subordination
because he too was now the man of the house.

> Joe: Well, I'm a pure male chauvinist pig, and
> I'll admit it.

> Jennifer: Yeah.

Joe's chauvinism, or more precisely his belief that he
should dominate Jennifer because that's the way it should
be, was often not as explicit as the above admission, but
there was no mistaking its existence in some of Joe's other
comments. For example:

> Joe: I don't really discuss the pregnancy that
> much with others. I let Jennifer do all the
> discussing... My background with the people
> in this area; the men just don't discuss
> pregnancy...we let the women take care of
> that.*3

> *

> Joe: It seems like there's a breakdown in
> roles, if you know what I'm getting at. It
> seems like all the women want to be coal
> miners all of a sudden. It seems to be the
> thing to do. My theory is: that the women
> would be better off to stay home and take
> care of the kids and take care of the social
> clubs and that sort of stuff. And the men go
> out and earn the money... I think the basic
> problem with juvenile delinquency and the
> whole mess that this country is in is that
> the man goes out and works, and the woman
> goes out and works, and the children are left
> home...

Unfortunately for Joe, Jennifer wouldn't buy his
ideological (the culture says that's the way it's supposed
to be) theory on who dominates whom. To be a master, one
must have a slave. But the byproduct of

parenthood--Jennifer leaving her job, he becoming the breadwinner--offered Joe another avenue to justify a claim to power. The justification he switched to is sometimes called the resource theory of power. This theory argues that the allocation of tasks and power is based (or should be based, if you're using it as a maxim which Joe was) on the comparative resources of the members of a society and by the life circumstances within which they live. In more simple terms, what this means for the micro society, marriage, is that the division of work and, most importantly, power is determined not by ideology but by who brings in more resources. A resource is defined as anything that one partner may make available to the other, helping the latter satisfy his or her needs or attain his or her goals (Blood and Wolfe, 1960:12). Money and expertise, for example, might qualify as resources.

Within the resource theory system, Joe's claim to power would be structurally based on the assertion that he was bringing in what some couples consider the most important resource--money. Perhaps Jennifer tried to use this justification to dominate Joe during the first three and a half years of their marriage. She was then the breadwinner. And perhaps Joe, though he (literally) fought her attempts during the early years of their marriage to make such a claim, eventually was convinced of her definition of the situation. Would this explain his loss of self-confidence that getting a job (resources?) helped him to regain? Whether or not Joe was making a claim based on rules which had existed all along, it was obvious he anticipated using what he saw as his comparatively greater resources to support his domination. With the transition to parenthood he would become the breadwinner, he would have the responsibilities, and he would be in charge...or so he hoped.

> Joe: I'm sort of proud and happy now that my wife's pregnant and we're going to have a child, and it was the motivating force in terms of me thinking about being the breadwinner, assuming a specific role. She's going to be staying home. Before, I was just another person going out and working and now I'm going to be the breadwinner...

> Interviewer: Do you like that?

> Joe: I think it's nice to feel that you're taking charge... When you have responsibilities, you end up being in charge.

Once again, to Joe's frustration, Jennifer wouldn't buy his theory on who dominates whom. She made it clear a number of times during the interviews that she had no intention of endorsing Joe's claim. The sequence which follows illustrates Joe's moves and Jennifer's countermoves in their negotiation of power.

> Interviewer: In the organization of your marriage, are you the boss?

> Joe: In the circumstances here, in the way we're dividing the authority, now she's going to be the housewife and I'm going to be the principal breadwinner. That moves me up a notch in terms of being the breadwinner and having the say in financial matters. She's going to be in control of the house exclusively. She's going to have more say in what goes on with it, even more so with the furnishings of the house.

> Jennifer: I don't think he's the boss, because I never thought of myself as being the boss either.

> Interviewer: What do you think of Joe's notion that if he's making the money, he's a notch up on you?

> Jennifer: Oh, that's his idea.

> Joe: Well, I think when...anybody does something to assume responsibility in a specific area, there is sort of a raising of him there in authority in that area. That's all I'm trying to get at. Because I will be the sole breadwinner, my authority will go up slightly.

> Interviewer: So your authority is going up here and Jennifer's is going down here. [I motioned with my hands to indicate two different levels.]

> Jennifer: I'd still work on that one... It's still going to work that mine will go up there. [Translation: I will still have as much authority as he has.] He thinks that way [but I know better].

> Interviewer: Do you believe he's the boss because he's the breadwinner?

> Jennifer: He can believe it if he wants.

> Interviewer: What do you think he believes?

> Jennifer: I think he's more of a householder. That's a better word.

Joe: Yeah.   I   get   stepped   upon!
[Laughter]...for   example, if there should be
a prowler in the house and they had a gun, I
would probably assume responsibility in that
circumstance because I'm in charge of the
weapons, and I'm the more physical, violent
personality! [Laughter] So I would take more
responsibility in that circumstance because I
am more knowledgeable.   Now if she was
gung-ho on guns, I'd say, "Here, you go
downstairs..." [Laughter] That sort of thing.
In times of emergency I take over... We each
assume our own responsibilities in our own
area.

Interviewer: But you're going to be head of the
household.

Joe: Yeah. [Laughter] I like the way you said
that!

Interviewer: What does it mean to be head of
the household?

Jennifer: It means nothing. [Laughter]

Joe: This is what it means. It means nothing,
but when a job is botched up, the buck stops
here. That's what it means!   [Laughter]...
What   I'm   saying   is   if I'm the sole
breadwinner, I think over a period of time
I'll be feeling more authority in specific
areas due to the circumstance that   I'm
familiar with.   If she should get a job, my
responsibility as sole breadwinner would have
to go down.   And hers will start to rise.
She's the one who's going to be in contact
with the kid more time than I am, so I'm
going to have to lean over and say.   "OK,
she's the boss when it comes to taking care
of and making decisions about this little
kid." See what I'm getting at? Because this
turns the area of responsibility, because
she's more in touch with it, and so on and so
forth. So what happens is that there are
many areas of responsibility.   So at any
given point in time, you assume "boss of the
car," "boss of the weapons," "boss for home
defense," "boss for being breadwinner," "boss
for heavy manual labor," "boss for repairs
and replacements," "boss over the tools."
Her--"boss for childbearing, childcaring,
food, shopping, household decisions"...I was
just trying to explain that because I am
earning the money solely that I probably will

> end up having more decision making power in
> that area.
>
> Jennifer: Yeah, but I know how to handle it
> more.

There are a number of things worth noting in the above
sequence. First of all, Joe's claim is bound to run into
trouble from the start. He is attempting to argue that
since he is the breadwinner, he is to have "the say" in
financial matters. Given their sensitivity to money
handling, Jennifer's final reply, "Yeah, but I know how to
handle it [money] more [because I'm a bookkeeper and you're
an abstract accountant]," is predictable. Secondly,
although Joe elaborates on his claim by arguing that
responsibility implies authority, and that Jennifer will,
because of her responsibilities, be "boss" of some areas
too, the fact is some areas have more weight than others.
The area in this household which carries the most weight is
the financial area. Joe knows this, but then so does
Jennifer. She refuses to give Joe's claim validity by
denying it access to their world of consensual rules ("Oh,
that's his idea..." "He can believe it if he wants..." "It
means nothing").

Toward the end of the pregnancy, it appeared that Joe
had not given up on an ideological claim to power, that he
in fact would resort to both ideology and resources to
support his power play. By the fourth interview, Jennifer
had quit work and was trying to adapt to being a housewife.
It was difficult for her. She took a great deal of pride in
the work she had done, the books she had set up, the
department she supposedly had straightened out. When she
left, everything in the department started to "fall apart."
The person who took Jennifer's place didn't want to learn
what to do, so they claimed, and as a consequence Jennifer
had been called a number of times to give assistance over
the phone. The whole affair provoked a conflict between Joe
and Jennifer. In spite of Jennifer's attachment to her
previous job, Joe wanted her to "let go." He was actually
quite vehement about it. His threat of what he would do "if
they [Jennifer's former co-workers] call up" is interesting.
He says he is going to "act like a father" when he tells
them to stop calling. Is it his father he is going to act
like, his father the patriarch who made all the decisions
for Joe? And for whom is he acting--Jennifer's former
co-workers or Jennifer, herself?

> Joe: ...If they call up here, I'm going to get
> on the phone and act like a father. And I'm
> going to tell them, "Hey, you'd better hold
> up now, and if you call once more, I'm going
> to punch you in the mouth." And I'm going to
> hang up on them. And I know they are going
> to bother her. I don't want that to happen.

Joe once said that he felt the pregnancy made him more of a man and Jennifer more of a woman. Perhaps what he meant by this is that finally he can draw that line as his father drew the line. Whether Jennifer will be able to continue to resist remains to be seen.

CONJUGAL VIOLENCE AND THE POLITICS OF MARRIAGE

Joe and Jennifer's relationship appears to be built on interpersonal conflict--"an incompatible difference of objective . . . a desire on the part of both contestants to attain what is available only to one, or only in part" (Dahrendorf, 1959:135). The conflict between them may be viewed in essentially one of two ways--as a sign of a "disturbed" or "sick" relationship, or as a normal consequence of the marital bond. The first conception, the consensus approach, assumes that the husband-wife union is a relationship based on agreement and homeostasis. The second conception, the conflict approach, assumes that dissensus and struggles for power are inherent qualities of a marriage. The first conception is the popular one. However, the validity of this conception has been questioned in many of the chapters of this book and by sociologists such as Sprey. Sprey (1969), for example, argues that the consensus approach is based on two fallacies: (1) the belief that participation in the family is a voluntary matter, and (2) the notion that the family is a buffer between the individual and society.

To dispute these claims, Sprey notes first that membership in one's natal family is obviously not by choice, and that there is no real normative alternative to the married state as a life career in our society, and secondly that conceiving the family as a world into which one may withdraw from the conflicts of everyday life erroneously assumes that individuals are somehow apart from rather than involved in society. A conflict approach is of course not new to social science (cf., Hobbes, Marx, Simmel). For some reason, however, it has traditionally been reserved for explaining macro level relations (for example the class struggle) and nonfamilial micro encounters (the presentation of self in everyday life). The approach is just beginning to gain significant support among family researchers.

Presented here as an isolated case, Joe and Jennifer's story may come across as a document of a "disturbed" relationship. Considered in conjunction with the other couples in the larger study from which this case study was taken, however, Joe and Jennifers's marital experience does not seem that unusual. The fact is all the sample couples, in one way or another and in varying degrees, were involved in an ongoing interpersonal confrontation. What about Joe's violence toward Jennifer during the first two years of their

marriage? Is this "usual?" It is true that of the sixteen
couples in my sample only two disclosed a violent encounter
(the other couple also said the wife was the victim;
alcohol seemed to be a precipitator). Not to be overlooked
however is the fact that recent inquiries into the incidence
of family violence suggest that conjugal violence may indeed
be a usual occurrence (see Chapters 1 and 2). The research
indicates that Joe and Jennifer's marriage may be more
typical than we realize, or would like to believe.

     Recent attempts to explain family violence have, in
fact, resulted in the development of theories which
complement the conflict approach. The conceptualizations
proposed by Allen and Straus (Chapter 12) and by Brown
(Chapter 11) are cases in point. Each of these theories
sees husband-wife violence as a consequence of an interplay
between cultural and social structural variables rather than
psychopathological factors. Implicit in each is the
assertion that social conflict is built into the
organization of the conjugal system and of the larger
society with which that system transacts.

     Drawing from the work of Goode (1971), Rodman (1972),
and Rogers (1974), Allen and Straus' chapter proposes the
"Ultimate Resource" theory of conjugal violence.
Essentially the theory suggests that in an
individualistically oriented urban-industrial society (for
example the United States) where male superiority norms are
weak and somewhat ambiguous and where the presumption of
male superiority must be validated by superiority in
"resources" (such as material goods and valued personal
traits), violence will be invoked by an individual who lacks
other resources to serve as a basis for power. In other
words, violence may be understood as the "ultimate resource"
for sustaining a power claim. Allen and Straus' theory
offers a cogent explanation of why Joe resorted to violence
to stop what he saw as "the bad progression of events." At
the time of the encounter, Joe lacked the resources to
ground his patriarchal ideology ("I'm a pure male chauvinist
pig, and I'll admit it"). Economically supported by
Jennifer, he could not rely on any "extrinsic" resources
(economic and prestige conferring characteristics) as a
basis for power. Furthermore, Jennifer implies that Joe's
"intrinsic" resources (valued personal traits) were also low
during this time when she remarks later on that Joe seemed
to be "getting more independent...more self-confident" as a
result of his (now) being with "business people" rather than
"students."*4 Given this imbalance--husband dominant
ideology versus wife dominant resource structure (an
imbalance that Allen and Straus see as characteristic of the
working class)--one would expect (assuming the validity of
the "Ultimate Resource" theory) that Joe would resort to a
slap in the face "three or four times" to show Jennifer that
despite his lack of "extrinsic" and "intrinsic" resources,
he is "not the kind of person that's [sic] going to be

dominated."

Joe's threat of violence during the final weeks of the pregnancy may perhaps also be interpreted within the Allen and Straus framework. Was Joe threatening Jennifer's co-workers ("If you call once more, I'm going to punch you in the mouth") or was he in fact indirectly threatening Jennifer? As long as Jennifer held on to her job, Joe could not base a claim for power on his greater economic position. The education versus experience debate makes it clear that Jennifer did not see her occupational status as below Joe's. Was he communicating to Jennifer that if her career was going to continue to interfere he would have no choice but to fall back on the "ultimate resource" to show her he intended to be "boss?"

Joe and Jennifer also illustrate the processes described in Brown's chapter on "Wife Employment, Marital Equality, and Husband-Wife Violence" (Chapter 11). Brown notes the increase in the number of working wives in America and the corresponding decrease in husband power that this change implies ("Since money is a resource in marriage, we may assume that as more wives contributed to the family income the power of the husband was affected inversely"). Brown develops a theory that "traces out the known and theoretical consequences of wife employment and seeks to answer the question of whether one of the consequences of wife employment is an increased level of husband-wife conflict and violence."

The argument is made that one consequence of the increased economic independence of the wife is a change in her authority expectations from husband dominant to equalitarian. Since the male has traditionally been ascribed superior status in our society, this attitude shift leads to a conflict between the wife's equalitarian authority expectations and the husband's male superiority norms. The critical question from Brown's point of view is "Does the husband accept the equalitarian authority structure?" If the answer to this question is no, the conflict will be seen as illegitimate and the husband will revert to traditional dominating techniques increasing the likelihood of violent conflict. If the answer to the question is yes, the intimacy in the couple's relationship will increase (owing to shared aspects of life) and this increase will in turn increase the conflict in the marriage. ("Increasing intimacy brings with it an increasing awareness of, and confrontation with, the uniqueness of the other." Sprey, 1971:724.) However, the conflict brought on by the increased intimacy will be seen as legitimate--that is, constructive and highly desirable--decreasing the likelihood of violent conflict. Whether Jennifer's economic independence prompted a change in her authority expectations is not clear. She may have held equalitarian or wife dominant expectations before she became a bookkeeper. Be that as it may, there is no doubt that Jennifer's ideas on who should be in charge conflicted with Joe's traditional thoughts on the subject. Confronted with the conflict between Jennifer's authority expectations, and his own male superiority norms, how does Joe react? He continually refuses to accept the authority structure which Jennifer proposes. It could be said (assuming the validity of Brown's theory) that Joe's slap was one manifestation of his resorting to traditional dominating techniques when his superiority was threatened.

Particularly significant is the meaning which Joe and Jennifer impute to the violent incident. Both see the encounter as an act that was appropriate, given the situation (Joe: "I had to do something physical..." Jennifer: "It was my fault.") Their responses provide an example of what Gelles (1974:59) calls "normal violence"--violence that is accepted, approved, and even mandated in family interaction. The existence of this type of violence is yet another demonstration of how social conflict can be built into the organization of a marriage.

It is noteworthy that marital violence is being conceptualized by these researchers as an act that has both ideological and social structural antecedents. Their dual focus is in accord with my conclusions on the conflict approach. Specifically, the conflict approach suggested by the interviews does not imply simply an exchange framework. Rather, the conflict process emerges as a system*5 in which the marital symbol structure (conventional sign structure) as well as the marital exchange structure (resource structure) influence, and are influenced by, the marital power structure (the ability of the husband to affect marital life versus the ability of the wife to affect marital life). In other words, marital politics (the distribution and exercise of power) is not based simply on ideology (for example, the husband is in charge because that's "the way it's supposed to be") or on exchange (the husband is in charge because he is bringing to the marriage rewards--money, status--that satisfy his wife), but on a synthesis of the two.*6

NOTES

*I am indebted to Maureen LaRossa and Howard M.
Shapiro for their helpful comments on an earlier draft of
this chapter. This excerpt is reprinted from Conflict and
Power in Marriage: Expecting the First Child by Ralph
LaRossa, Sage Library of Social Research, Vol. 50, (c)
1977, pp. 69-82 by permission of the Publisher, Sage
Publications, Inc. (Beverly Hills/London).

1. The research is essentially two studies in one.
Manifestly, it is a study of how married couples respond to
the first pregnancy--to the transition to parenthood. More
important, and at a higher level of abstraction, it is a
study of the structure and phenomenology of the husband-wife
relationship. Sixteen married couples were interviewed
during the twelfth, twentieth, twenty-eighth, thirty-sixth
weeks of their respective first pregnancies. The interviews
were conjoint (husband and wife together) and unstructured
(nonstandardized). They were conducted in the couples'
homes, were taped and later transcribed. Analysis of the
interview transcipts was qualitative (the conceptual
components of explanation were developed, for the most part,
from the data).

2. Sprey (1969) cites research that he feels
"chronicles" or "illustrates" the conflict framework (Bach
and Wyden, 1968; Brim et al., 1961; Hawkins, 1968; Lewis,
1967; Scanzoni, 1968). To these one could add Larson
(1974) and Rausch et al. (1974). Each of these
investigators does offer some finding(s) that may be
interpreted as support for the conflict approach. None of
these studies, however, confronts the major assumptions of
the conflict approach. In other words, none addresses the
question of how conflict is intrinsic to family life, or how
families manage rather than resolve conflicts. None of
these studies focuses on the political dimension, the
nucleus, in my opinion, of the family as a conflict system.
Of the studies cited, Bach and Wyden (1968) perhaps comes
the closest to addressing these issues. Their research is,
however, based on clinical impressions.

3. Joe's reference to "the people in this area" is
interesting. Born and raised in rural New England, Joe
seems to be claiming that there exists a geographically
based subculture and that he is part of it.

4. The identification of "extrinsic" and "intrinsic"
resources is from Blau (1964:20-22).

5. The definition of a system subscribed to is
Buckley's (1968:493). "We define a system in general as a
complex of elements or components directly or indirectly
related in a causal network, such that at least some of the
components are related to some others in a more or less

stable way at any one time. The interrelations may be mutual or unidirectional, linear, non-linear or intermittent, and varying in degrees of causal efficacy or priority. The particular kinds of more or less stable interrelationships or components that become established at any time constitute the particular structure of the system at that time."

6. Sprey (1972:237) makes the point that a conflict approach "implies a framework of exchange." He does not explain what he means by this. If however he is saying that cognitive sociology (symbolic interaction, phenomenology) has no place within a conflict approach, then I must disagree. In my opinion (and I believe family violence researchers would concur with me on this), a more appropriate way of stating the case is that a conflict approach implies politics (the distribution and exercise of power), and politics entails not only the ability to affect reinforcement contingencies (exchange) but also the ability to affect the definition of the situation (symbols). For a discussion of this issue as it applies to the study of marital power, see Safilios-Rothschild (1971).

Chapter 11

Wife-Employment, Marital Equality, and Husband-Wife Violence

Bruce W. Brown

* *

A theme in the previous chapter that pervaded the dialogue between Joe and Jennifer was the issue of wife employment. In this chapter, Brown suggests that one consequence of wives working is an increased level of husband-wife conflict and violence. The increased economic independence of the married woman changes her authority expectations from husband dominant to equalitarian, and leads to a conflict between the wife's new authority expectations and the husband's male superiority norms.

A crucial contingency in Brown's formulation is whether the husband accepts the equalitarian authority structure. If not, attempts to disrupt his power claims may be met with violent resistance, especially if he is lacking in other resources. In the case of Joe and Jennifer, Jennifer's attempt to alter the authority structure of their marriage caused Joe to use violence.

A further contribution of Brown's chapter is his investigation of the factors that influence the husband's acceptance or rejection of equalitarian authority patterns. As the reader will note, many of the factors he lists are bound up in male sex role expectations that leave men unprepared for developing relationships that call for shared power and equal task allocation with women.

* *

Research on family power has emphasized the beneficial effects of the equalitarian marriage style. It has been heralded in the popular culture as a cure-all for the ailments of contemporary marriages. However, others such as Straus in Chapter 6, Kolb and Straus (1974), and Whitehurst (1974) who have studied the emerging equalitarian marriage style concluded that, whatever the ultimate benefits, during the transition period, the move toward equality between the sexes may cause many problems.

> Such a change toward true sexual equality in the family, like any other drastic change in the social structure, poses problems, at least during the transition period. Individuals socialized to operate in one system of family organization may have difficulty operating under new standards (Kolb and Straus, 1974:756).

The focus of this chapter is an explanation of one of the factors that led Whitehurst (1974:76) to suggest "...that the conflict between the emerging equalitarian social structure and the continuing male-superiority norms will tend to increase rather than decrease conflict and violence between husbands and wives." This chapter traces out the known and theoretical consequences of wife-employment and considers the question of whether one of the consequences of wife-employment is an increased level of husband-wife conflict and violence.

LEGITIMATION OF MARITAL POWER

Blood and Wolfe (1960:11) think that no change in the American family is more significant than the shift from one-sided male authority to the sharing of power and/or authority by the husband and wife. Power and authority are involved in practically every aspect of marriage.*1 As Kolb and Straus (1974:757) state:

> ...the degree of control exercised by family members over one another is an element of family structure affected by and in turn affecting many other aspects of family integration and interaction.

Blood and Wolfe's (1960:12) analysis contrasts two sources of power in the marital relationship: "culture and competence." Briefly, their cultural explanation of power states that power lies in the hands of the partner who the culture dictates should have that power. In this case, Blood and Wolfe apparently are speaking of authority, the right to exercise power. In our own culture, the popular view has been that "the man should be the head of the house."

The competence explanation of power states that the
power lies in the hands of the partner who contributes the
greater "resources" to the marriage. A resource is defined
as anything that one partner makes available to the other,
helping the latter satisfy his needs or attain his goals
(Blood and Wolfe, 1960:12; Safilios-Rothschild, 1976:356).
As Blood and Wolfe (1960:14) point out, the question is not
an "either-or" one; both cultural norms and resources must
be taken into account. They do, however, qualify this
notion by stating that the competence explanation appears to
account better for family-to-family differences in marital
power.

EMPLOYMENT AND POWER

Many researchers think that no other factor has
affected the balance of power in American marriages more
than the increase in the number of working wives. Aldous
(1974:232), for example, says that:

> ...with 65.7 percent of married women presently
> engaged in gainful employment, including 20.6
> percent of women with children under six years
> of age, people no longer are willing to accept
> the norms legitimating and prescribing a
> segregated conjugal role organization.

According to the resource theory of power the increased
resources of working wives have important implications for
marital power and for ideology concerning marital authority.
Since money is a resource in marriage, as the wife's
resources increase, her power presumably also increases and
she is in a better bargaining position to suggest or demand
a more equalitarian authority structure.

As the case of Joe and Jennifer illustrates, this
transition to a more equal sharing of authority appears to
be particularly difficult for husbands. No doubt, many
contemporary husbands and wives view the wife's employment
as a necessary income supplement. This, however, does not
guarantee that husbands will find some of the "unintended
consequences" of wife-employment easy to adjust to. Burke
and Weir (1976:284), for example, found that husbands of
working wives were less satisfied with their marriages than
husbands of nonworking wives. Furthermore, even profeminist
men seem to prefer "family women" to "career women" (Stapp
and Pines, 1976). The reason for husbands' difficulty with
an equal sharing of authority is essentially a conflict
between the two bases of power just discussed--cultural
norms and individual resources. In terms of individual
resources, employed wives should share in the authority
structure of the marriage. However, the popular culture and
the legal system (Weitzman, 1975) tell husbands just the

opposite. Kolb and Straus (1974:761) cite a recent Harris
Poll to support their statement that "both in law and in
popular opinion, the husband is still expected to be the
family 'head' or leader."

WIFE-EMPLOYMENT AND THE CHALLENGE TO ASCRIBED MALE AUTHORITY

The remainder of this chapter is concerned with an
explanation of the hypothesized relationship between
wife-employment and husband-wife violence. "Violence," as
used in this chapter, refers to physical violence between
husbands and wives.

The reader should not assume that wife-employment is
the only possible explanation for violence. Other strains
related to wife-employment, such as those concerning child
care and housekeeping, may also play a part in husband-wife
violence. The importance of this theory is that it does
identify one crucial aspect of the overall explanation of
husband-wife violence.

We begin with the proposition that employment of the
wife provides her with increased resources. These resources
in turn lead to increased power. In the majority of
studies, power has been construed as decision-making and the
two concepts have come to be used interchangeably
(Safilios-Rothschild, 1970). A number of these studies
found that working wives exert more influence in
decision-making.*2 With this shift toward more equal power
between husband and wife, the wife comes to expect a change
to equalitarian authority (Blood and Hamblin, 1958). To the
extent that this change occurs, wife-employment may lead to
an undermining of ascribed male authority patterns. As
Scanzoni (1970:148) states, "The wife is more motivated to
'go along' with him, to 'give in' to him, to let 'him have
his way' to the extent that he provides maximum economic
rewards." If the husband is no longer providing maximum
economic rewards, because the wife is now involved in this
function, she is not as inclined "to go along with him."
Homans (1961:287) put this idea more generally in the
proposition that "the most important single factor in making
a man a leader is...the ability to provide rare and valued
rewards for his followers." If a husband no longer provides
rare and valued rewards for his "follower," because she
herself now provides them, the husband no longer is in a
position to be the unquestioned leader. The result is an
attempt to shift from a dominant-submissive to an
equalitarian authority structure within the marriage.

The attempted shift to an equalitarian authority
structure leads to conflict between the wife's equalitarian
authority expectations and the husband's male superiority

norms. Empirical data show the existence of such conflicts.
Specifically, Gianopulos and Mitchell (1957), Nye (1958 and
1963), and Glazer-Malbin (1975:Table 7) found that marital
conflict is more frequent among couples in which the wife is
employed. As stated earlier, Whitehurst thinks that the
conflict between the emerging equalitarian authority
structure and male superiority norms will increase
husband-wife violence. The remainder of this chapter deals
with the conditions under which Whitehurst's assertion may
be correct.

FACTORS INFLUENCING HUSBAND ACCEPTANCE OF
THE EQUALITARIAN AUTHORITY STRUCTURE

The husband's acceptance or rejection of the
equalitarian authority structure is contingent upon a number
of variables. The present theory deals with four of these
variables:

1. degree of compulsive masculinity
2. degree of anticipatory socialization
3. degree of role clarity
4. degree to which the transition facilitates goal
   attainment.

Compulsive Masculinity. Parsons (1947) sees
"compulsive masculinity" as the result of the effort on the
part of men to assert their masculinity and repudiate a
natural identification with their mothers. Elements of the
compulsive masculinity syndrome have been analyzed by a
number of other sociologists. For example, Balswick and
Peek (1971) think that American men are socialized to be
tough and to avoid showing emotions. Evidence for the ideal
of toughness in men is supplied in a Canadian survey
conducted by Goldfarb (1970, as cited in Whitehurst,
1974:80), in which 61 percent of the respondents felt men
should be tough and not back away from a fight. Ross
(1972), in a toy-selection study, confirmed the enormous
pressures by family and society for boys to behave in the
accepted masculine way. When boys were given a toy
appropriate for the opposite sex, they showed anxiety,
indicating that an inappropriate toy would mean
embarrassment and possibly punishment.

One aspect of the "accepted masculine way" is for
husbands to be dominant over their wives. For many
husbands, an equal sharing of authority within the marriage
may be viewed as a "lack of masculinity" on their part. We
are moving toward an age of equality between the sexes, and
our difficulty in making this transition depends in part on
the degree of compulsive masculinity exhibited by husbands
in our society.

Anticipatory Socialization. Anticipatory socialization
is defined as the adoption of the norms and values of a role
before being in a social situation where it is appropriate
(Merton, 1957:265 and Burr, 1973:125). Husbands in American
society have not received much anticipatory socialization
for an equal sharing of marital authority. In fact, just
the opposite seems to be true of American boys, who hold
sexist attitudes by the tender age of two (Kuhn, 1976).
However, to the extent that a new and more equalitarian
marital ideology permeates the culture through the mass
media, the feminist movement, and family and sex education
in the schools, men will find it easier to accept this new
marital authority structure when faced with the issue in
their own marriage.

Role Clarity. Cottrell (1942:618) defines role clarity
as "the degree to which there is a set of explicit
definitions of the reciprocal behavior expected." As
mentioned previously, the transition to equalitarian marital
authority structures is a difficult one, especially for
husbands. Komarovsky (1973) found that although males agree
verbally with equality between the sexes, they are still
attached emotionally to traditional attitudes and patterns
of behavior. Since the amount of role clarity influences
the ease of transition into roles (Burr, 1973:127), one of
the reasons husbands are experiencing difficulty may be the
lack of clarity concerning their roles as marital partners
in an equalitarian authority structure.

A role-model of an equalitarian husband is hardly to be
found in our culture and, therefore, no explicit set of
definitions exists for the husband to follow. Marital role
prescriptions, although moving in the direction of increased
equalitarianism since 1900, still tend to relegate husbands
to the provider role and wives to the homemaker and
child-rearer roles (Brown, 1978). The mass media, in
particular, advertising during sports events, emphasize the
"real man" image (Brown, 1973). The "real man" is
physically tough, is dominant over women, and has the
freedom to do what he pleases when he pleases. These
characteristics are in direct opposition to characteristics
needed for a viable relationship with wives who subscribe to
an equalitarian marital authority structure.

Facilitation of Goal Attainment. As Burr (1973:134)
points out, the amount that a role facilitates attaining a
goal influences the ease of transition into a role. In
other words, if the result of a role transition is
desirable, it makes the transition easier. Many American
husbands believe that by sharing authority equally with
their wives, they have nothing to gain and much to lose.

Subliminally, this message is brought across in the
media. Husbands who are not dominant tend to be portrayed
on television as somewhat ridiculous, incompetent, and

confused (LeMasters, 1971). The comics not only reflect, but also shape husbands' attitudes toward sharing marital authority.

> Dagwood Bumstead represents an important archetype in the American psyche--the irrelevant male. Dagwood is browbeaten by a domineering and assertive wife, is abused by his boss, and is generally a failure in everything he tries (Berger, 1974:105).

Failure and nonattainment, then, are believed to be the outcome for husbands who let their wives share equally in marital authority. Until men come to perceive some of the advantages to themselves of an equalitarian relationship they will resist change in that direction.

Rejection of the Equalitarian Authority Structure. These four variables--degree of compulsive masculinity, degree of anticipatory socialization, degree of role clarity, and degree to which the transition facilitates goal attainment--all play a part in the husband's decision to accept or reject the equalitarian marital authority structure.

Husbands who do not accept the idea of equality in authority view the conflict between the wife's equalitarian authority expectations and their own male superiority norms as illegitimate. Because this conflict is seen as illegitimate we find husbands reverting to traditional dominating techniques to resolve the conflict. Rueger (1973:76) thinks that:

> Men are trying to cope with the changes through the traditional attitudes. When the old dominating techniques no longer prove effective, men become insecure and anxious because of the ominous specter of 'failure.'

What are these "old dominating techniques?" Greater monetary resources is one, but the ever-increasing proportion of employed wives makes this resource less and less available. A higher level of education is another, but with the increasing enrollment of women in college, that also is increasingly less true. In fact, increases in educational attainment may be one of the causal factors of the emergence of prescriptions for joint marital decision-making (Brown, 1977). If nothing else, at least men used to have the normative prescriptions concerning marital authority on their side, but that also has been slowly but surely changing (Brown, 1978). However, one advantage that husbands still have over their wives is their greater physical strength. As Whitehurst (1974:78) notes:

When all other resources of masculine identity
fail, men can always rely on being 'tough' as a
sign of manhood. Handling wives in aggressive
ways is in some respects an extension of the
normal ways men learn to handle a variety of
problems....

Similarly, Komarovsky's (1962:227) study of blue collar
families led her to conclude that the threat of violence is
another ground of masculine power. Finally, Wolfgang (1969)
points out that "violence is a means of seeking power and
may be defined as an act of despair committed when the door
is closed to alternative resolutions." No doubt, many
contemporary husbands feel that the doors not only have been
shut, but actually slammed in their faces.

VIOLENCE IN THE EQUALITARIAN AUTHORITY STRUCTURE

Up to this point, the chapter has been concerned with
the conflict over the transition to equalitarian marital
authority structures. However, this is not to suggest that
the husband's rejection of an equalitarian authority
structure is the only source of conflict and violence.
Husbands who accept equality in authority find that this
leads to increased intimacy and companionship in their
marital relationship owing to the increase in shared aspects
of life. Blood and Wolfe (1960:160) found that the more
decisions were shared by the husband and wife, the more
satisfaction was expressed with marital companionship.

This increased intimacy would appear to be a plus for
equalitarian marriages, but Coser (1969) and Sprey (1971)
caution that the more intimate social relations are, the
more likely thay are to give rise to conflict. Green (1941)
found that in ethnic groups in which there are lower
expectations of emotional attachments between husband and
wife, marriages tend to be more stable. Goode (1962)
concludes that marital strain is likely to be reduced when
the partners lower their expectations of emotional
performance and comply with minimal role obligations.
Therefore (and somewhat paradoxically) marital conflict can
be expected to increase as the marital partners share more
aspects of life.

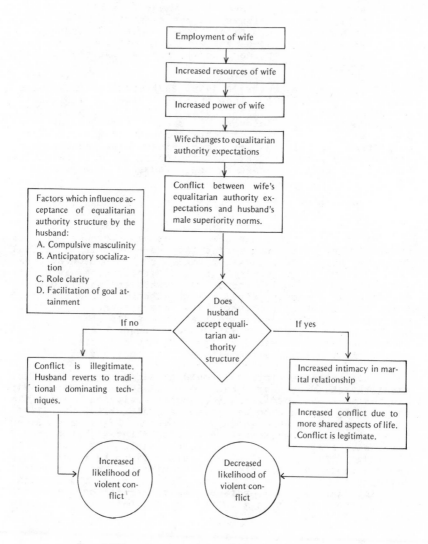

Figure 1. Wife employment, marital equality, and husband-wife violence

Another aspect of this paradox is that if an equalitarian authority structure is accepted by both spouses, conflict will be viewed as legitimate, because both partners have equal rights to have their views prevail. Bach and Wyden (1968:98) suggest that "verbal conflict between intimates is not only acceptable, especially between husbands and wives; it is constructive and highly desirable." Since the conflict is viewed as legitimate, the likelihood of husband-wife violence as a means of conflict resolution is decreased. In short (and again somewhat paradoxically), the higher level of conflict is likely to be associated with less physical violence.*3 However, at the same time, the increased conflict may lead to a decreased stability of the marriage. After experiencing what might be termed "intimate conflict," the couple may come to the conclusion that divorce is their best option. Regardless of the arguments "for and against" divorce, it seems obvious that divorce is a more desirable solution to marital conflict than husband-wife violence.

PROPOSITIONAL AND DIAGRAMMATIC SUMMARY

Rather than attempt to summarize the contents of this chapter in running text, a more useful device is to set forth the main elements of the theory in a series of propositions. As a final summarizing device, Figure 1 presents the causal connections specified in the theory in the form of a flow chart.

Propositions: Employment of the wife leads to increased resources of the wife.

Increased resources of the wife lead to increased power of the wife.

Increased power of the wife leads the wife to change to equalitarian authority expectations.

The wife's equalitarian authority expectations conflict with the husband's male superiority norms.

The husband's decision whether or not to accept the equalitarian authority structure is influenced by:

1. compulsive masculinity
2. anticipatory socialization
3. role clarity
4. facilitation of goal attainment.

 If the husband does not accept the

equalitarian authority structure, then he
reverts to traditional dominating techniques.

Reverting   to   traditional   dominating
techniques   by   the   husband   leads to an
increased   likelihood   of   husband-wife
violence.

Acceptance of the equalitarian authority
structure by the husband leads to increased
intimacy between the husband and wife.

Increased intimacy between the husband and
wife leads to increased legitimate conflict
between the husband and wife.

Legitimate conflict leads to a decreased
likelihood of husband-wife violence as a
means of conflict resolution.

NOTES

*Revision of a paper presented at the annual meeting of
the National Council on Family Relations, Salt Lake City,
Utah, August 20-23, 1975. The preparation of this paper was
supported by National Institute of Mental Health grant No.
13050. The comments and criticisms of Lee Crandell and Dean
Knudson aided in the revision of the paper.

1. As used in this chapter, "power" refers to the
potential ability to control another's behavior, and
"authority" refers to legitimized power (Blood and Wolfe,
1960:11).

2. Bahr, Bowerman and Gecas, 1974:366; Blood,
1963:294; Blood, 1965:195; Blood and Wolfe, 1960:40;
Heer, 1958:347; McKinley, 1964:149; Scanzoni, 1970:160;
Wolfe, 1959:109. The studies just cited are all
investigations of American families. Although similar
results have been found in some cross-cultural studies
(Abbott, 1976:172; Blood, 1967:159; Buric and Zecevic,
1967:328; Lupri, 1969:144; Michel, 1970:159; Oppong,
1970:678; Richmond, 1976:262; Safilios-Rothschild,
1967:346; Weller, 1968:439), contradictory results were
found by Centers, Raven, and Rodrigues, 1971:276; Hoffman,
1960:224; Kandel and Lesser, 1972:134; Middleton and
Putney, 1960:608; and Straus, 1977.

3. The validity of this assertion depends on
distinguishing between conflict (in the sense of "conflict
of interest" as described in Chapter 8) and aggression (in
the sense of a malevolent act). If Bach and Wyden's

assertion is read as suggesting that verbal aggression helps
avoid physical aggression, the evidence is overwhelmingly
the opposite (Straus, 1974a).

Chapter 12

Resources, Power, and Husband-Wife Violence

Craig M. Allen and Murray A. Straus

* *

Both LaRossa's case study and Brown's theoretical analysis suggest that "resources" like the income provided by a wife's employment outside the home increases her power, and increases also the likelihood that the husband will use violence to "stop the bad progression of events," as Joe puts it in Chapter 10. But neither a case study nor a logical deduction are sufficient evidence for a scientific conclusion. Such a conclusion depends on additional data, and that is what Allen and Straus's study of approximately 400 couples provides.

In addition to the statistical findings, this chapter takes the theoretical analysis of LaRossa and Brown one step further. It puts forward the "ultimate resource theory" to explain the relationship between power and violence by taking into consideration cultural norms regarding family power. The theory holds that in individualistic, achievement-oriented societies, norms supporting male superiority are weak or ambiguous. For a husband to be more than a census tally in the statistics on "household heads," he has to validate his position by superior "resources" such as money, occupational status, or valued personal traits. If the husband lacks such resources, and feels entitled to a position of dominance, violence may be used as the "ultimate resource" to back up feelings of power entitlement. Data from approximately 400 couples support these ideas, but only for working class couples.

* *

A number of sociological theories of family violence, such as those by Gil (1975), Goode (1971), and Straus (Chapter 6), hold that the use of physical force is the ultimate sanction that underlies the maintenance of the present male-dominant pattern of family organization. Although the analyses of these authors may seem plausible, they rest on piecing together scattered, often impressionistic evidence. We need specific tests of the idea that the threat of physical violence underlies the existing family structure. These data, although limited in several ways, are a step in that direction.

THEORIES OF RESOURCES AND POWER

Following the work of French and Raven (1959), Blood and Wolfe introduced the "resource theory" of family power. They defined a resource as "...anything that one partner may make available to the other, helping the latter satisfy his needs or attain his goals" (1960:12). The Blood and Wolfe study found that the spouse with the greater number of resources tends to have more power over his or her partner.*1 However, Rodman's (1967) analysis of data from several countries found the theory to be supported in the United States and France, but not confirmed by data from Greece and Yugoslavia. In the latter two countries, the correlations of father's education and occupation with power were in the opposite direction from that predicted by the resource theory. Rodman concluded that, to explain the distribution of marital power, the cultural context from which norms defining appropriate resources are determined must be taken into account (see also Fox, 1973). In a subsequent comprehensive review of findings related to the resource theory, Rodman (1972) developed a theory of "resources in a cultural context" in which he suggests that the dynamics of exchange in the marital dyad can be understood only in the context of the culture of which the dyad is a part:

> The balance of marital power is influenced by the interaction of (1) the comparative resources of husband and wife and (2) the cultural or subcultural expectations about the distribution of marital power (1972:60).

THE ULTIMATE RESOURCE THEORY

Goode (1971), Rodman (1972), and Rogers (1974) suggest that violence is a resource invoked when individuals lack other legitimate resources to serve as bases for their power.*2 According to Goode (1971), a spouse who lacks the prestige, money, or skill necessary to induce the other

spouse to perform some behavior might resort to violence as
a final resource, even though the exercise of violence is an
illegitimate or negatively sanctioned mode of exercising
power. Rodman (1972) asserts, however, that this pattern
will be found only in a society in which (1) the norms which
legitimatize the exercise of power are weak and somewhat
ambiguous, (2) the actual exercise of legitimate power must
be validated by the resources in the form of personal
qualities and material possession. The United States
typifies this kind of society, because (1) equalitarian
norms are replacing patriarchal norms in the marital dyad,
(2) as a consequence, there is normative ambiguity about the
distribution of marital power; and (3) additional power can
be obtained by increasing one's resources relative to those
of his spouse.

These considerations constitute what can be called the
"ultimate resource" theory of violence, suggesting that
violence will be invoked by a person who lacks other
resources to serve as a basis for power. This theory
implies a correlation between power and violence only under
certain circumstances, since power can be maintained by the
use of resources other than violence. In short, the
relationship between power and marital violence is
contingent on what resources other than violence are
available. These considerations are the basis for the main
hypotheses to be tested.

> 1. When resources of a spouse are low, the
> greater that spouse's power, the greater his or
> her use of violence.
>
> 2. When resources are high, there is no
> relationship between power and violence.*3

Class Differences. Although equalitarian norms are
replacing patriarchal norms of authority in our society, the
working class lags behind the middle class in this normative
transition (Hoffman, 1960; Komarovsky, 1962; McKinley,
1964; Lopata, 1971:108; Scanzoni, 1975; Young and
Willmott, 1973). As a consequence, husbands in the working
class adhere more to traditional or patriarchal norms of
authority than do husbands in the middle class. However,
their actual power tends to be lower than that exercised by
middle class husbands. This contradiction arises out of one
of the cruel tricks of the social structure: Working class
husbands, whose ideology emphasizes male power, tend to
possess fewer resources that can serve as a basis for power
than do middle class husbands. The interacting effect of
fewer resources with stronger adherence to patriarchal norms
leads us to expect that the lower the occupational status of
the husband the greater the correlation between resources,
power, and violence. Lacking monetary, prestige, and
educational resources on which to base power, low status men
are more likely to compensate by using actual or threatened

physical force as a basis for power.

SAMPLE AND METHOD

Sample. The data to be reported are from a study of the families of students in introductory sociology and anthropology classes at the University of New Hampshire in the fall of 1972. The data were obtained by questionnaires completed on a voluntary basis during a class period. Of the 583 questionnaires distributed, 555 or 92 percent were completed. Since the analyses to be presented depended on both the student's and both parent's living at home during the student's senior year in high school, further cases were lost because a parent or the child was not living at home that year. In addition, there was the inevitable loss of some cases because certain questions were not answered. The resulting final sample size ranges from 324 to 437, depending on the variables included in a given table. Of these cases, 26 percent are families in which the husband is a manual worker.

Measure of Violence. Data on husband-wife violence was secured from one of the couple's children because of (1) the difficulty of directly observing the occurrence of violent behavior between spouses, particularly the more extreme forms; (2) the ethical problems entailed in devising an experimental situation in which violent behavior between husbands and wives could be precipitated; and (3) the fear that the strong negative sanctions in our society against the practice and even the admission of violence would lead to refusals and/or underreporting by husbands and wives.

The validity of interview data on family patterns is always open to question once one goes beyond such subjects as the ages and sex of children, and some researchers feel that this procedure is even more questionable when a child is the source of the data. However, Calonico and Thomas (1973) found that children can predict their parents' behavior under certain circumstances slightly more accurately than their parents can of one another. They attributed this finding to the familiarity of the children with their parents' past behavior. Bahr, Bowerman, and Gecas (1974) found that adolescents across various age categories were quite consistent in reporting their parents' behavior. They suggest that it would be extremely difficult for parents to hide their behavior from adolescent children over a long period of time. A more comprehensive examination of this issue, together with data on the validity of the violence measure used in this paper, is given in Bulcroft and Straus (1975). That analysis shows a high degree of agreement between student reports of husband-wife violence and data provided independently by the spouses themselves.

The specific technique used to measure physical
violence is the Violence scale of the family Conflict
Tactics Scales (CTS) instrument (Straus, 1974a:15; 1979).
In this technique, the respondent is first asked to identify
the major sources of disagreement and conflict during the
referent year. Following this, a series of questions are
asked concerning partner's responses to conflicts during
that year. These questions are arranged in gradually
increasing order of coerciveness of responses, beginning
with discussing things calmly, and ending with hitting the
other person with something hard.

The Violence index consists of the final five items. A
complete list of the CTS questions is given in Straus
(1974a; 1979), together with data on the internal
consistency reliability of each index. Validity data are
given in Bulcroft and Straus (1975).*4

Power Measure. The conceptualization and measurement
of conjugal power has posed many difficulties, as evidenced
by several critical studies (Cromwell and Olson, 1975;
Heer, 1963; Olson, 1969; Olson and Rabunsky, 1972;
Safilios-Rothschild, 1970; and Turk and Bell, 1972). Our
definition is explained in Straus, 1977 and Straus and
Tallman, 1971. The specific measure used in this chapter is
the Decision Power Index of Blood and Wolfe (1960).*5

Although it has been widely criticized (in part because
it is the most widely used measure), Blood and Wolfe's
measure seemed best suited to this research for the
following reasons: (1) It uses a convenient list of
indicators in which power is theoretically most likely
evident--who has the final say in important and typical
family decisions. (2) Its wide use in the past decade and a
half permits comparison with many previous studies. (3) The
many correlates of power as measured by this method provide
what is, in effect, "construct validation" evidence, and a
recent paper by Straus (1977) provides evidence of
concurrent validity. (4) Research on power in families has
increasingly demonstrated the multidimensional nature of the
concept.

The theory being tested requires a measure restricted
to what Cromwell and Olson (1975) call the "power outcomes"
dimension. This, of course, deliberately omits other
crucial dimensions such as the processes by which decisions
are reached. Although for convenience in exposition we
follow the convention of using the word power for the
particular aspect measured, the reader must bear in mind
that this use refers only to who makes certain somewhat
arbitrarily selected decisions. In particular, the measure
explicitly excludes what French and Raven (1959) call the
"basis" of power, such as "reward power" (the ability to
provide rewards because of control of money or other valued
goods or services), "expert power" based on perception of

superior knowledge, etc. A "power outcome" type measure was
necessary because the theory being tested concerns the
relationships between certain of French and Raven's "bases"
of power (which we prefer to identify as "resources") and
power outcomes, in the sense of who makes critical
decisions.

Since the Blood and Wolfe technique examines answers
that indicate "who has the final say" in respect to the six
decisions, and since the measure is scored so that high
scores show that the balance of power is on the side of the
husband and low scores show that the wife has relatively
more decision power, we will sometimes use the term "Final
Say Power Index" or "Relative Power Index" to identify this
instrument.

Resource Measure. For each spouse, an Absolute
Resource Index and a Relative Resource Index were
constructed. The Absolute Resource Index consists of the
sum of four items referring to economic and prestige
conferring characteristics (education, occupation, income,
satisfaction with income) and four items referring to valued
personal traits (high self-esteem, achievement orientation
and sociability, and low anxiety). The former can be
thought of as corresponding to what Blau (1964:20-22) would
call "extrinsic" resources, and the latter as what he
identifies as "intrinsic" resources. A parallel Relative
Resource Index was also computed for each spouse, by first
calculating the extent to which a particular spouse had a
higher score on each resource and then summing the positive
scores.*6

POWER AND VIOLENCE

The most elementary empirical data on the issue of this
paper is the correlation between the balance of power in the
family (as measured by our version of the Blood and Wolfe
"Decision Power Index") and the frequency of physical
violence between spouses. However, as was explained in the
introduction, and as we note again below, such correlations
are not an adequate test of ultimate resource theory because
they do not take into account the resources that give
legitimacy to each actor's power position. Nevertheless,
these simple correlations are an appropriate point at which
to begin the data analysis, if for no other reason than to
demonstrate their inadequacy.

The upper arrow of Figure 1 gives the correlations between the relative power index and the use of violence by the total sample, by the working class part of the sample, and by the middle class part of the sample. The correlations between the Relative Power Index and the wife's violence are shown in the lower arrow. In general, Figure 1 shows only low and variable correlations between power and violence. However, to the extent that conclusions can be drawn, Figure 1 suggests that in the middle class, there is no relationship between relative power and the husband's violence, but as the husband's power increases, the wife's violence decreases (-.16). The pattern is reversed for the working class, where there is a slight tendency for the husband's violence to increase as his power increases, but no relationship is shown between his power and her violence. The pattern for the total sample is the same as the pattern for the middle class, largely because the preponderance of cases are middle class (75 to 80 percent, depending on the variables in a given set of tabulations).*7

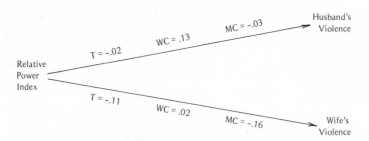

Figure 1. Correlation (r) of relative power index with violence by husbands and wives, for total sample, working class, and middle class

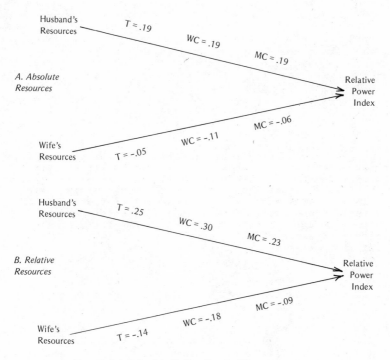

Figure 2. Correlation (r) of husband's and wife's resources with relative
power of husband and wife

RESOURCES AND POWER

Absolute Resources. Part A of Figure 2 shows that for
all samples, as the husband's resources increase, there is a
tendency for his power to increase (r = 0.19). Hardly any
relation is seen between the wife's resources and the
balance of power in the family. But to the extent that a
relationship exists, the negative correlations suggest the
other side of the coin shown by the findings for the
husband; that is, the more the wife's resources the less
the husband's power.

Relative Resources. Correlations between relative
resources and the husband's balance of power are given in
Part B of Figure 2. These correlations reveal the same
pattern as was found for absolute resources except that the
correlations are larger (an average of 73 percent greater).
Therefore these data show that both absolute and relative
resources affect the balance of power in the families
studied. However, even within the context of the low
correlations that one expects in analyses of a single causal
factor, only the husband's relative resources seem to have a
substantial relationship to who has the final say.
Furthermore, for both husbands and wives, the correlation
between resources and power is stronger within the working
class than within the middle class part of the sample.
Despite these qualifications, the correlations in each
sample, for both husbands and wives, and for both types of
resources, are in the same direction as that predicted by
the resource theory.*8

THEORIES OF RESOURCES AND VIOLENCE

Up to this point we have shown only a weak and erratic
relationship between violence and the balance of power in
family decisions. We suggested that the simple correlation
between power and violence fails to take into account the
dimension of legitimacy in exercising power. In a modern
industrial society, as in most other societies, power is
usually ascribed to the husband. But the husband must also
possess the personal and material resources that are valued
in such a society. In short, it was argued that despite the
normative assumption that the husband will be the family
leader, this status must be validated by means of
appropriate resources. Therefore, power and violence will
be related only if the exercise of power is illegitimate.

As a first step in testing this more specific theory of
the relation between power and violence, recall that the
preceding section showed resources to be correlated with
power; that is, on the average, husbands exercising
superior power have validated this position by superior

resources.*9 In this section, we take the next step in assessing the complex set of relationships between power and violence by examining the correlations between resources and violence, as shown in Figure 3.

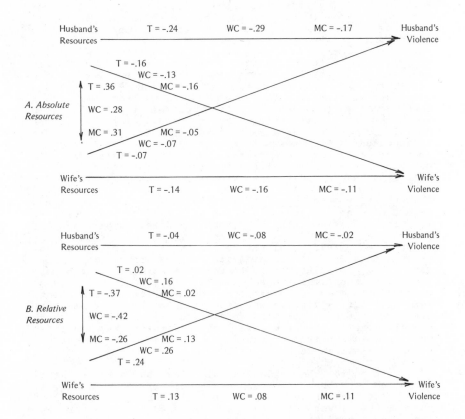

Figure 3. Correlation (r) of husband's and wife's resources with violence by each spouse

Absolute Resources. The correlations in the top line of Figure 3, part A, show that the greater the husband's absolute resources, the less his use of physical violence. For wives, the correlations shown in the lower arrow of part A are small but in the same direction as those for husbands: the greater her absolute resources, the less her violence. For both spouses, but especially for the husbands, the correlations are stronger for the working class than for the middle class.

Turning to the correlations between husband's resources and the wife's violence, the upper diagonal arrow of part A indicates the same trend: as the husband's absolute resources increase, the wife's violence decreases. This same tendency is evident from the correlations of wife's resources with the husband's violence, except that the correlations, although all negative, are also all near zero in magnitude. It appears from these data that the husband's absolute resources are more related to the wife's and his own violence, than the wife's absolute resources are related to her husband's and her own violence.

Relative Resources. At first glance it seems as though part B of Figure 3 shows only low and erratic relationships. To a certain extent, this is correct. However, part of what seems at first to be erratic variations turn out to be theoretically meaningful reversals in the "sign" of the correlations. Let's begin with the top arrow. This shows essentially no relationship between the extent to which the husband's resources exceed those of his wife and his use of physical violence. However, the bottom arrow shows a slight tendency for wives whose resources exceed those of their husbands to use physical violence. Although these correlations are low, we suggest that they indicate reactions to a situation that goes against the leadership norms in American society.

Turning to the relation of each spouse's relative resources to the violence of the other, for husbands, we find again that there is little relationship. However, for wives, the lower diagonal arrow shows that the more her resources exceed those of her husband, the greater his violence. Our interpretation of this finding is that the counternormative situation of a wife having greater resources than her husband is associated with greater violence on the part of both spouses, but especially by the husband whose ascribed position is being threatened. In other words, the finding reflects efforts by wives to assert power on the basis of having superior resources, in the mistaken belief that such superiority in resources makes equal or superior power legitimate. This is a reasonable expectation in view of the requirement that husbands validate their ascribed superior position by appropriate superiority in resources. But as countless women have discovered, society stacks the cards against them by

creating a dual set of requirements that are impossible to
satisfy: to exercise legitimately superior power in the
family, one must both have superior resources and be a man.
Obviously only husbands can meet both requirements!

RESOURCES AND THE LEGITIMACY OF POWER

Although the findings in the preceding three sections
are interesting in their own right, they were presented
primarily to lay the groundwork for a more specific test of
the two main hypotheses derived from the ultimate resource
theory. Specifically, in an individual-achievement oriented
society such as the United States, the pattern of
normatively prescribed male family leadership that
characterizes so many societies is supplemented by the
further requirement that the husband demonstrate his
eligibility to occupy a leadership position in possessing
valued personal characteristics and providing economic
goods. If he does not, then the legitimacy of his power is
undermined. Under these circumstances, we suggest, male
power will be associated with violence.

Table 1. Correlation of Power with Violence, Controlling for Resources for Each Spouse

		Correlation (r) of Power with:			
		Husband's violence when specified		Wife's violence when specified	
Resource Category and Sample	Social Class	Resources are:		Resources are:	
		High	Low	High	Low
A. Husband's Resources					
Absolute	Middle	.01	.04	-.12	-.17
Relative	Middle	.01	-.11	-.14	-.26
Absolute	Working	-.04	.49	-.13	.31
Relative	Working	.07	.17	-.04	.05
B. Wife's Resources					
Absolute	Middle	-.04	-.04	-.14	-.20
Relative	Middle	.03	-.13	-.13	-.20
Absolute	Working	.10	.18	.10	-.05
Relative	Working	.13	.20	.10	-.07

Note: The approximate N's for the subgroups are Middle Class: low husband resources = 120, high husband
resources = 160, low wife resources = 115, high wife resources = 170. Working class: low husband resources
= 30, high husband resources = 50, low wife resources = 30, high wife resources = 50.

The findings can be summarized under two headings: a
high   resource   group   and   a   low   resource group.*10
Correlations between power and violence were then computed
within   each   of   the   resource   groups.   This process was
repeated for each of the four resource indexes.

Husband's Violence.   Table 1 gives the correlations
between   our   measures   of   power and violence separately for
those high and low in each of the resource indexes.
Starting with the four correlations shown in the upper left
under "husband's violence," within the middle class part of
this sample, essentially no relation is seen between the
balance of power in the family and the husband's violence.
However, within the working class (next four correlations in
the left panel), the correlations of -0.04 for the high
resource husband and 0.49 for the low resource husband
provide strong support for the hypothesis that male power is
not associated with violence if the husband has resources to
validate his position, but is associated with violence when
the husband lacks such resources.

What effects do the wife's resources have on the
relation between power and the husband's violence? We have
not specified a hypothesis for this issue, so   the
correlations shown in part B of the left panel of the table
are purely exploratory. The block of four correlations for
the   middle class, like the equivalent block for the
husband's, shows that for this social class group, the level
of the wife's resources does not alter the finding of no
relation between power and violence on the part of husband.
But within the working class part of this sample, there is a
small but consistent tendency for male power to be
associated with male violence.

Overall, to summarize the data on husband's violence
shown in the left columns of Table 1, it seems as though in
the middle class, violence is not associated with male
power.   This is also true for those working class men who
are high in resources. But for working class men who are
low in resources maintaining a superior power position is
associated with the use of physical force.   Taking into
account the resources of the wife does not alter these
conclusions for the middle class.   But for the working
class, in each of the wife resource groups, a small but
consistent tendency exists for male power to be associated
with male violence.

Wife's Violence. The right panel of Table 1 shows the
correlations between the dyadic balance of power and the
frequency with which wives use physical violence.   These
correlations were also computed for exploratory purposes,
since we did not formulate any specific hypotheses regarding
the way low versus high resources might affect the relation
of power to violence on the part of wives.

Within the middle class (top four correlations in the right panel) the negative correlations show that the more the balance of power is in favor of the husband, the less the wife's violence. This tendency is present both when the husband's resources are high and when they are low, but the correlation is stronger in the latter case. Within the working class part of the sample, controlling for the husband's resources (second block of four correlations in the right panel of Table 1) produces a much more complicated set of correlations: When the husband's resources are high, there is a slight tendency for high husband power to be associated with low wife violence (as in the findings for the middle class). But when the husband's absolute resources are low, then the greater his power, the more her violence ($r = 0.31$). Both these findings, and especially the difference between the correlations for low and high resource husbands, are consistent with the theory that specifies that violence will occur when husbands who lack the resources to legitimize their ascribed power try to exercise that power. On the other hand, we have not as yet formulated any satisfactory explanation for the finding that when the control for resources is on the basis of the relative resources of husband and wife, the correlations are near zero, even though they show the same shift from negative for the high resource group to positive for the low resource group.

The two right columns in Part B of Table 1 show the correlations between the husband's power and the wife's violence when controls are introduced for the wife's level of resources. The middle class block of four correlations shows a pattern similar to that found when the control was on the basis of the husband's resources; namely, for all resource groups, the more the husband's power, the less violence on the part of the wife. But when we look at the last four correlations in the lower right corner of Table 1, still a different pattern is revealed. First, the correlations are all very low. However, the pattern of these correlations fits our theory exactly: When the wives are high in resources, high power on the part of the husband is associated with a tendency towards violence on the part of the wife--perhaps as a means of resisting male dominance on the part of women whose resources lead them to desire a greater share of the power. Conversely, when resources are low, high power on the part of the husband is associated with less violence on the part of his wife (although the negative correlations between male power and the wife's violence are low). We can speculate that this correlation represents an acceptance of the traditional family power hierarchy on the part of women who lack the resources to claim greater equality.

Overall, the data on violence initiated by wives are like those for male violence. In both instances, the data are consistent with the resource theory only within the

working class part of the sample. Specifically, when the
husband's resources are high, high male power is not met   by
violence on the part of the wife; whereas if the husband's
resources are low, male power tends to be met by female
violence. The other side of the coin is shown when the
wife's resources are controlled, but the correlations are
all very low. Nevertheless, we interpret the positive
correlation between male power and wife's violence as
reflecting resistance to male domination on the part of
working class wives with high resources, and the low
negative correlations as reflecting acceptance of male
dominance on the part of working class wives with low
resources.

SUMMARY AND CONCLUSIONS

The research presented in this paper was designed to
explore two closely related issues concerning physical
violence in marriage. The first of these issues is the
extent to which the use of physical force is associated with
the maintenance of male dominance in the family. The second
issue is a test of the idea that husbands who lack certain
valued personal traits and material possessions (called
"resources") tend to substitute physical violence to
maintain a position of superiority. Together these two
ideas form the core of what we call the "ultimate resource
theory" of intrafamily violence.

Since this is cross-sectional research, the causal
relationships inherent in the ultimate resource theory
cannot be tested in any definitive way. Rather, we computed
correlations between power and violence and simultaneously
held constant certain other variables as a means of
discovering if the resulting pattern of relationships
accords with the idea that violence is the ultimate resource
underlying male dominance in American families.

The resulting correlations were generally low.
Therefore, what confidence one can have in these results
derives from the consistency with which we found patterns of
positive and negative correlations concordant with the
theory, and also from the fact that the largest correlations
(0.49 and 0.31) were found for those relationships that
constituted the most crucial test of the theory. With these
qualifications in mind, the findings can be summarized as
follows:

1. Little or no relationship exists between the
conjugal balance of power and the use of violence by either
spouse. This finding is consistent with the ultimate
resource theory in that the theory specifies that male
dominance will lead to violence only if the husband cannot
legitimize his superior power position through the

possession of validating resources.

2. The greater the husband's resources, the less his use of physical violence. Similarly, the greater the wife's resources, the less her use of violence. These findings are consistent with the ultimate resource theory in that they suggest that those who can call on resources that do not have the costly side effects of violence will use less violence.

3. Superiority in resources relative to the spouse was also examined for possible association with violence. This analysis revealed that the extent to which a husband's resources exceed those of his wife has little or no relation to violence by either spouse. However, the more the wife's resources exceed those of her husband, the more likely the husband is to have used physical force during the referent year. These findings suggest that the wife's possession of superior resources can undermine the ability of the husband's resources to validate superior power, thus leading to the substitution of a resource in which wives can rarely be superior to their husbands: physical violence.

4. Finally, the specific hypotheses derived from the ultimate resource theory predicted a tendency for male power to be associated with violence only when the husband lacks validating resources. We found this hypothesis true, but only for working class husbands. For husbands high in resources, as predicted, there was no correlation between power and use of violence. But for those working class husbands low in resources, the greater the husband's power, the more often he used physical force on his spouse in situations of conflict.

5. In almost all the analyses reported in this paper, and especially in the most direct test of the ultimate resource theory summarized in the preceding paragraph, the correlations were stronger in working class families, or sometimes present only in working class families.

What could account for the fact that the ultimate resource theory seems to apply only within working class families? Two possibilities come to mind. The first is based on social class differences in male authority norms and can be called the "middle class equalitarian norms" explanation. The second is based on class differences in types of violence and can be called the "working class instrumental violence" explanation.

Middle Class Power Norms. This explanation assumes that within the middle class a significant degree of support no longer exists for norms that give superior authority to husbands. If this is correct, then few middle class husbands will attempt to claim the traditional male authority. Therefore, physical force is not needed to back up an ascribed position of authority if the husband lacks other resources to validate his ascribed authority. Unfortunately, we find this explanation difficult to accept, because our personal observation of families, together with much other evidence (Bahr, Bowerman, and Gecas, 1974; Blood and Wolfe, 1960; Kolb and Straus, 1974; Scanzoni, 1970; Skolnick and Skolnick, 1974: Chapter 6) suggests that despite considerable lip service to sexual equality, the actual structure of middle class families remains basically male-dominant.

Working Class Instrumental Violence. This explanation begins from the assumption that what we have called "instrumental violence" (see Chapter 1, footnote 2) is more acceptable within the working class, where there is a continuing traditional emphasis on the "macho" or "he-man." By contrast, the rejection or weakness of such norms and values in the middle class may lead middle class husbands to restrict the instrumental use of violence to a significant degree.

This does not mean that physical violence between husband and wife is absent in the middle class. There is, in fact, a growing body of evidence that conjugal violence is part of the reality of American middle class family structure, although less frequent than in the working class.*11 But the nature of this violence may be different. It may be largely what we have called "expressive violence." In fact, the current popularity of "creative aggression," "catharsis," and the idea that it is healthy for the individual and good for the marriage to "let it all hang out," tends to legitimize expressive violence as something that must be got out of one's system (Straus, 1974a). If the foregoing is correct, then marital violence in the middle class would be primarily expressive, whereas marital violence in the working class would be primarily instrumental. Therefore, since this explanation of instrumental violence is the focus of the ultimate resource theory, it follows that this theory should apply only within the working class, because that is the class in which instrumental violence is presumed to be the predominant type of violence.

Unfortunately, this second explanation for the finding that the ultimate resource theory applies only to the working class is also difficult to accept because our personal impression is that while there may be less instrumental violence in middle class families, it is far from completely absent. However, although neither middle class equalitarian norms nor working class instrumental violence by themselves seem sufficient to explain the support of the ultimate resource theory only for working class families, the combined effects of class difference in power norms and in norms concerning instrumental violence may be sufficient. Specifically, because of the weakening

of male-dominance norms in the middle class, a challenge to
a husband's superior authority may be less of a threat to
the identity and masculinity of middle class husbands than
of the working class husbands. Middle class husbands may be
able to adapt to what they formerly paid lip service, and
still retain their self-esteem. If this is the case,
husbands in the middle class have less need to defend an
ascribed position of authority. In addition, to the extent
that instrumental violence is subject to more severe
limitations in the middle class, it will be a higher "cost"
resource because of more negative side effects. Therefore,
the lesser need to use this ultimate resource combined with
the greater cost of using violence may account for the
finding that the ultimate resource theory applied only
within the working class sample.

NOTES

*We are indebted to John H. Scanzoni for comments and
criticism that aided in the revision of this paper.

1. "Resource theory" is a specific instance of
"exchange theory" (Bahr, 1974; Heer, 1963). In exchange
theory terms, the reasoning just presented is that an
individual will attempt to obtain a desired outcome or
reward at minimum cost. Thus, if one spouse desires
compliance from the other in a particular exchange sequence,
the less costly the use of the particular resource serving
as a basis for his power, the more likely it is to be
invoked, directly or indirectly. However, in the absence of
"minimum cost" resources, it is necessary to invoke more
costly resources to achieve a goal. The use of violence (an
illegitimate resource) forcing another to comply with one's
requests is probably much more costly to an individual than
the use of more legitimate resources such as occupational
status, prestige, educational attainments, personal
attributes, etc., which entice the other to comply more
voluntarily.

2. For ease of communication, from this point on, when
the term "resources" is used it should be taken as meaning
"valued material possessions and personal characteristics
other than physical strength," that is, resources other than
the actual or potential use of physical force.

3. Similar ideas have been expressed many times before
and keep reemerging. For example, in Parsons' 1947 essay on
"Certain Primary Sources and Patterns of Aggression in the
Social Structure of the Western World," in Rollo May's Power
and Innocence (1972), in research on "locus of control"
(Goodstadt and Hjelle, 1973), and in van den Berghe
(1974:778-787). Parsons' analysis not only asserts the

basic proposition that aggressive acts are carried out
"...more out of weakness and handicap than out
of...strength," but also mentions several of the factors
included in the measure of individual resources used for
this study. Specifically, he discusses the use of
aggression as a mode of response to anxiety, arguing that
the secure and nonanxious person is less likely to aggress.
He also asserts that in a society valuing individual
achievement, failure to achieve is a potent source of
frustration and hence aggression.

4. The items indexing violence in the version of the
CTS used with this sample are: .I. Threw something (but not
at the other) or smashed something, J. Threatened to hit or
throw something, K. Threw something at the other, L.
Pushed, grabbed, or shoved, M. Hit or tried to hit the
other person, but not with anything, N. Hit or tried to hit
the other with something hard. The following response
categories and score weights are used for all items:
Never = 0, Once that year = 1, Two or three times = 2,
Often, but less than once a month = 3, About once a month
= 4, More than once a month = 5. The Violence Index
consists of the sum of these response category weights.
This index has a range of 0 to 25. However, to avoid giving
excessive weight to a few outlying cases with extremely high
levels of violence, the raw scores were recoded into a
modification of the "sten" score normalizing technique with
a range of 0 to 8 (see Straus, 1974a:footnote 6).

5. Because of time limitations in the questionnaire,
only six items were used, rather than the eight used by
Blood and Wolfe: What car to get? How family income is
spent in general? Where to go on a vacation? Which house
or apartment to take? Whether mother should work or quit
working? Things concerning the children's activities? The
response categories used were: Mother always = 1, Mother
more than father = 2, Father and mother exactly the
same = 3, Father more than mother = 4, Father always = 5.

6. These four indexes (i.e., Absolute and Relative for
husbands and for wives) were arrived at on the basis of an
empirical searching procedure. Specifically, we first
searched the questionnaire to identify everything that
seemed as though it would fit the idea of an intrinsic or
extrinsic resource. Sixteen such items or scores were
identified. We then carried out an "external criterion item
analysis" (Straus, 1964:354) to find those items that were
in fact correlated with our power measure. Each of the
eight items making up these indexes was selected because it
was found to be correlated with power for the husband or the
wife, or both. The items were standardized to a range of 0
to 100. Each respondent's score on a given index then
consists of the mean of the eight standardized items and can
therefore range from 0 to 100.

Another way of thinking about these scores is that each
is expressed as percentage of the maximum possible score.
Thus, a respondent with an Absolute Resource index of 28 has
an average of 28 percent of the maximum possible points for
the eight resources. A respondent with a score of 28 on the
Relative Resources index has 28 percent of the raw score
obtained by the respondent whose resources exceeded that of
his or her spouse by the greatest amount.

Finally, it is important to note that because of the
way in which these indexes were arrived at, they are simply
a way of summarizing into one convenient measure what would
otherwise require eight correlations or eight table rows.
In particular, these indexes cannot be used to "test" the
resource theory because they include only items already
known to be associated with power.

7. For purposes of this study we divided the sample
into occupational class groups based on the husband's
occupation. If the husband was engaged in manual work, we
classified the family as working class. If the husband was
engaged in nonmanual work, the family was classified as
middle class.

Readers should be aware of the following two criticisms
of this procedure. (1) Some would find it preferable to use
the concepts of "blue collar" versus "white collar" because
of the controversy over what constitutes a social class and
the basis for assignment to classes. (2) Basing the
classification of the couple on a characteristic of the
husband has a built-in sexual bias (Steinmetz and Straus,
1973). Our use of this procedure reflects the low
percentage of wives who were employed outside the home. Had
we tried to use both occupations, the number of
unclassifiable cases would have resulted in an excessive
loss of cases from the analysis.

8. The product moment correlations given in Figure 2
understate the extent to which these data are consistent
with the resource theory. As a check to see if curvilinear
patterns were present (which of course would show up as
correlations near zero), we plotted the mean power score for
each decile of the resource scores. The resulting graphs,
with the exceptions to be noted later, did not indicate
curvilinear relationships. However, they did suggest a
closer association of resources with violence than is shown
by the correlation coefficients. We think that correlations
are low because of the large variance associated with the
means we plotted. In addition, occasional nonlinear
relations are seen. For example, the correlations of the
husband's power with the wife's relative resources is
only -0.09 for the middle class sample. While this is in
the direction the resource theory predicts, it is also not
statistically significant and very low coefficient.
However, the plot for this relationship shows a gradual

decrease in husband's power as the wife's resources increase
relative to his, until the ninth decile, at which point
there is a precipitous drop in husband's power. Thus, the
low correlation reported in Figure 2 is due to this
threshold effect, and also variance around the ten means.
The only other nonlinear relationship we were able to
discern is that between power and the husband's violence
within the middle class sample. Husband's violence was
found to be greatest in wife dominant families, but also
tends to be high in extremely husband dominant families.
So, it seems as though middle class husbands resort to
physical force both when their ascribed superior position
has been taken away, and also when they have a power
position that goes beyond mere superiority to one in which
their wives have almost no decision power. See Straus,
1973, Figure 2, for a plot of this relationship and further
discussion.

9. It is important to recognize that the superior
resources of husbands were not achieved in open competition,
because of the innumerable impediments to achievement for
women in most societies. Therefore, even if one accepts
superior resources as providing a moral justification for
superior power, the sexist structuring of opportunity in the
society renders such an ethical justification invalid.

10. Those below the median on each resource index were
classified as low and those above, as high in resources.
Working class and middle class families were classified
separately to reflect the large class difference in these
resources, and on the assumption that being "high" or "low"
in resources is relative to the average level of resources
in the sector of society in which one participates.

11. A graphic illustration was recently provided in the
Bergman film, Scenes From a Marriage. Numerous
illustrations, together with statistical data, are in Gelles
(1974). In the present sample, the mean violence score is
0.90 for working class and 0.33 for middle class husbands,
and 0.65 for working class and 0.39 for middle class wives.
Expressed as a percentage who used violence in the referent
year, the figures are 20.5 percent for working class and 9.6
percent for middle class couples.

Part V Summary and Policy Implications

The ideas, research methods, and research results in this book could be summarized in a number of ways. For example, we could point out and further illustrate certain themes which run through almost all the chapters, such as the cultural norms legitimizing violence, or the conflicts inherent in the organization of the family, or the role of physical violence in maintaining male dominance.

The method finally chosen to highlight and summarize some of the main themes is to ask what the practical implications are of the theories and facts contained in this book. Consequently, the final chapter identifies six characteristics of American social structure that, together, bring about the high level of husband-wife violence. For each of these factors there is a discussion of what can be done to change things to reduce the level of marital violence. In all, 21 different "policy implications" were deduced. Considerable evidence exists that some of these policies would reduce violence; the other policies are proposed on the strength of reasonable speculation. Fortunately for those seeking to reduce the level of marital violence, the question of whether proof can be given that the policies will actually achieve a reduction is almost beside the point; most of the 21 policy recommendations are steps that are socially desirable in their own right. For example, we do not know how much a lower level of economic insecurity and unemployment will reduce assaults by husbands on their wives. But since full employment and a basic minimum income is a social good, we will have gained even if movement toward that social good has no effect on the level of marital violence.

Chapter 13

A Sociological Perspective
on the Prevention of Wife-Beating

Murray A. Straus

Our ideas about the causes of wife-beating obviously influence the steps we take to prevent it. If wife-beaters are thought to be mentally ill, then psychotherapy is clearly needed. If husbands hit their wives because modern society puts excessive strains on the nuclear family, then some reorganization is needed of the roles in the family and the family's relation to the society. It is important to recognize that this chapter is concerned only with the social causes of husband-wife violence, and only with changes in society that might prevent marital violence.

With this in mind, the chapter will summarize some of the ways in which wife-beating is produced by the very nature of our society and its family system, and at the same time attempt to formulate policies aimed at reducing the level of husband-wife violence.

Some recommendations below advocate general social changes rather than the more specific aspects of "Family Policy Analysis," as defined by Wilson and McDonald (1977). In most cases, however, the suggestions listed below are clearly manipulable by law or practice in the public realm, or by the policies and decisions of business and other private organizations.

CULTURAL NORMS PERMITTING WIFE-BEATING

A fundamental aspect of American social structure that must be understood and confronted is the existence of the cultural norm that, as noted in Chapter 3 and elsewhere, makes the marriage license also a hitting license. But the concept of marriage license as hitting license is contained not only in the folk culture. More important, as noted in Chapter 3 and 6, it remains embedded in the legal system despite many reforms favoring women.

A great deal of other evidence supports the existence
of the "hitting license" norm. I will have to assume that
the information presented in Chapter 3 and 6 makes the case
plausible. What then are the implications for prevention?
There seem to be at least two parallel "policy implications"
(PIs).

> PI 1. Make the public aware of this largely
> unperceived norm.

This policy implication has a paradoxical quality, but
it is proposed on the assumption that awareness can
contribute to the demise of the "hitting license norm,"
because such a norm is contrary to other norms and values
about the family. It will pave the way toward a second
policy implication, of specific benefit to husbands and
wives, but especially to the latter.

> PI 2. Redefine the marital relationship as one
> in which any use of physical force is as
> unacceptable as it is between oneself and
> those with whom one works, bowls, or plays
> tennis.

The specific policy changes implied by PI 2 are
illustrated in the consent decree recently signed by the New
York City Police Department (New York Times, 27 June
1978:1). This decree obligates the Police Department to
arrest men who commit felonious assaults or other felonies
against their wives when there is reasonable cause to
believe the husband committed the crime. In addition, the
agreement provides that the police notify the wife of her
rights, including the right to make a citizen's arrest with
the aid of the police. The police also will be required to
remain at the scene of the crime temporarily to protect the
wife or to assist her in obtaining medical assistance if she
requests it. If the husband has left the scene, the police
must try to locate him as they would any other suspect.

A more detailed discussion of changes in the criminal
justice system will be found in the discussion of PI 19.
For the individual wife, this means making clear to her
husband that physical force simply will not be tolerated.
In an unknown, but perhaps not insignificant proportion of
cases, this alone could serve to alter the situation because
the "hitting license" aspect of marriage is so much an
unperceived "taken-for-granted" norm, and is so contrary to
other widely acknowledged and valued norms concerning the
marriage relationship.

By themselves, such individual attempts at redefining
the marital relationship to render violence illegitimate are
unlikely to be sufficient. In the first place, normative

rules are only one structural determinant of behavior, and
often a minor determinant. In the second place, such rules
do not arise from thin air. Rather, they reflect, and tend
to be integrated with, a network of other cultural elements.
Perhaps even more, they reflect the realities of daily
living. Consequently, a truly useful approach to the
problem of wife-beating must address these more fundamental
causes. These elements are so closely interwoven that it is
nearly as difficult to discuss them separately as it will be
to change them. However, they can at least be grouped into
somewhat meaningful patterns.

WIFE-BEATING AS A REFLECTION OF SOCIETAL VIOLENCE

Governmental Violence. Even if one assumes that
nation-states ultimately depend on at least the possibility
of using physical force to uphold the law, the present level
of physical force is neither desirable nor necessary (Goode,
1971). The necessity for and efficacy of much governmental
violence is highly questionable, as illustrated by the
controversy over the death penalty, police toughness (to say
nothing of police brutality), and the still widespread
practice of physical punishment in the schools (Maurer,
1974; Mercurio, 1972). It is sobering to remember that the
United States Supreme Court recently upheld both physical
punishment and the death penalty. Finally, we must remember
that our government maintains a world-wide military
establishment.

These examples of governmental violence provide
powerful models for the behavior of individual citizens.
They form an important part of a more general normative
system that holds that violence can and should be used to
attain socially desirable ends (Blumenthal et al., 1972,
1975). Of course, it is extremely difficult to prove that
governmental violence provides a role model for individual
violence, but one type of evidence supporting this
conclusion is exemplified in Chapter 4 and in Archer and
Gartner (1976).

Huggins and Straus' study (see Chapter 4) looked at a
sample of English language children's books covering the
period 1850 to 1970. The original purpose was to see if the
level of interpersonal violence depicted in these books
showed an upward or downward trend over this 120-year
period. The results showed no trend of this type. However,
even though there were no "war stories" in the sample of
books, during and immediately following each major war the
frequency of interpersonal violence rose dramatically.
Similarly, Archer and Gartner (1976) found a postwar
increase in homicide rates for a large sample of nations.
They concluded that the increase in murder rates was due to
a carry over of the war-time authorized or sanctioned

killing. Therefore:

>PI 3. Reduce to the maximum extent possible the
>use of physical force as an instrument of
>government.

Media Violence. Violence in the mass media both
reflects the existing high level of aggression and violence
in American society and helps perpetuate that pattern. The
typical citizen watches "prime time" TV in which more than
half of all characters are involved in some violence, and
one of ten in killing (Gerbner and Gross, 1976). The amount
of gratuitous violence in current motion pictures is also
extremely high. The significance of these facts has been
explored by intensive research, including a number of
excellent longitudinal and experimental studies, during the
past 10 years. These studies have led almost all scientific
reviewers of the accumulated evidence to conclude that
violence in the media is part of a societal pattern that
keeps America a high-violence society (Surgeon General,
1972).

The message of the mass media is clearly that physical
force can and should be used to secure socially desirable
ends, not just in the "wild west," but in almost all aspects
of contemporary life. Although it is rare for the media to
depict husbands using physical force on wives, the more
general message is easily transferred to the marital
relationship. At present, I know of no direct evidence that
the high value implicitly placed on both instrumental and
expressive violence in the mass media is transferred to the
marital relationship; however, this transferral seems so
likely in view of the extensive evidence of the phenomenon
that psychologists call "transfer of training" that the
following policy implication seems warranted:

>PI 4. Limit violence in the mass media as much
>as is consistent with preserving freedom of
>expression and artistic integrity.

Essentially, PI 4 calls for reducing the extent to
which television and fiction and nonfiction works "exploit"
violence, that is, use violence to capture as large an
audience as possible.

Domestic Disarmament. It is by now commonly accepted
that America is a violent society. But this acceptance does
not automatically extend to the realization that, for the
typical citizen, the problem is not violence in the streets,
but violence in the home. The largest single category of
murderer-victim relationship is that of members of the same
family. There are complex reasons for this fact (Gelles and
Straus, 1978); however, for the moment I would like to
focus on the "gun-toting" aspect of American violence. One
reason that domestic murders are so common is that more than

half of all American households contain a gun, most of which
are "hand guns" rather than "sporting guns." The following
proposal is addressed to this situation:

>PI 5. Enact stringent gun control legislation,
>particularly restricting hand guns, but also
>requiring that all guns be kept locked and
>unloaded.

PI 5 has been aptly termed "domestic disarmament" by
Amatai Etzioni. This policy could go a long way toward
reducing the most extreme aspect of domestic violence:
murder. Of course, domestic disarmament will not reduce
violence _per se_, since one can still punch, kick, choke, or
knife. But an attack with a gun is much more likely to be
fatal than are other modes of attack.

THE FAMILY AS TRAINING GROUND FOR VIOLENCE

What has been said so far emphasizes the extent to
which violence in the family reflects the level of violence
in the society. But the other side of the coin is at least
equally important; the level of violence in all aspects of
the society, including the family itself, reflects what is
learned and generalized from what happens in the family,
beginning with infancy.

Physical Punishment. The implicit models for behavior
provided by actions of the government and depicted in the
mass media form two legs of the stool supporting American
violence. The third leg is the family itself. In fact, the
family may play the most crucial role, because the family is
the setting in which most people first experience physical
violence, and because that violence is experienced in a
strong emotional context. Specifically, at least 90 percent
of parents use physical punishment in their children's early
years. Moreover, for about half of all children, this
continues through the end of high school--essentially until
the child leaves home (Bachman, 1967; Steinmetz, 1974;
Straus, 1971).

The importance of physical punishment in training the
next generation of violent citizens was described in
Chapter 2. In the forthcoming book giving the results of
our national survey of violence in families (Straus, Gelles,
and Steinmetz, 1979), one chapter gives detailed evidence
supporting this relationship. We found that the more
physical punishment a child experienced, the more violent
his/her marriage years later. This correlation is present
for "ordinary" physical punishment, but it is particularly
strong when physical punishment is used heavily. Physical
punishment, then, lays the groundwork for the normative
legitimacy of intrafamily violence and provides a

role-model--indeed a specific "script" (Gagnon and Simon, 1973; Huggins and Straus, Chapter 4)--for both the perpetrators _and the victims_ of such actions. Gelles (1976), for example, found that one of the three main factors linked to a wife's tolerating abuse from her husband is the extent to which her parents hit her as a child (see also Lefkowitz _et al._, 1976). An important policy implication of the facts just presented should be:

> PI 6. Gradually eliminate physical punishment as a mode of child rearing.

I have used the term "gradually" in formulating this policy implication even though my own values favor immediate cessation of physical punishment. Many practical difficulties stand in the way of immediate cessation, difficulties that, if disregarded, could have serious consequences. Specifically, we could not expect to eliminate physical punishment until parents can be provided alternative techniques for controlling the behavior of children, to protect them from danger and to teach the practical skills and ethical values for which society holds parents responsible. That a few parents manage to bring up children without physical punishment does not imply that most parents can do so. Such methods must be validated before we risk undermining the vital tasks of socialization carried out by parents. Fortunately, some effective techniques are beginning to emerge (see references following PI 8).

Sibling Violence. Almost as universal as physical punishment is physical fighting between children in the family. Perhaps such fighting is inevitable in early childhood. But it is not inevitable that attacks on each other by brothers and sisters be regarded as much less reprehensible than attacks on or by unrelated children. This difference in the way identical acts of violence are evaluated and handled symbolizes and reinforces the legitimacy of violence between family members. As a result, violence toward siblings continues long after violence toward peers has disappeared. For example, among the sample studied by Straus (1974a), almost two-thirds had hit or been hit by a brother or sister during the year they were _seniors_ in high school, compared with the one-third who reported hitting or being hit by someone outside the family. Thus, right through high school, many young people experience a second aspect of intrafamily violence that implies that nothing is terribly wrong about the use of physical force between family members. To the extent that this occurs, then:

> PI 7. Encourage parents to control acts of physical force between their children and to avoid explicitly or implicitly defining such acts as permissible.

As in the case of physical punishment, implementing PI 7 is not merely a matter of ceasing to do something. One of the circumstances highlighted by the sociological perspective is that elements of the social structure are interwoven, and therefore one of them cannot be treated in isolation. In this case, we must ask: "What is there about the situation of children in a family that generates such a high level of violence?" and "How can children resolve their disagreements without physical fights?" Until children are equipped with the skills to do that, it is as unrealistic for parents to implore "don't fight" as it is for family life educators to implore parents not to spank. Consequently:

> PI 8. Provide parents and children with techniques other than force and coercion for coping with and resolving the inevitable conflicts of family life.

Many obstacles bar the way for implementing PI 8, one of the most important of which is discussed in section E of this chapter--the failure to recognize the inevitability of intrafamily conflict, and hence to take steps for coping with conflict nonviolently. But even if that were not a factor, what techniques are available? Although still a matter of research and controversy, promising methods for resolving parent-child and sibling-sibling conflict have been developed over the last few years (Blechman et al., 1976a, b; O'Dell, 1974; Patterson et al., 1975).

"Somato-Sensory" Deprivation. Harry Harlow once epitomized the results of his classic experiments with monkeys reared in isolation by saying that monkeys deprived of warm social contact in infancy "...would rather fight than love." The same idea has surfaced in a number of different ways in the history of social science; for example, in the work on the authoritarian personality of Adorno et al. (1950). Part of what Adorno's "F scale" measures is the propensity to use physical violence for socially desirable ends. People who get high "F scale" scores, for example, tend to favor the death penalty and to feel that sex criminals should be both imprisoned and "...publicly whipped, or worse." Adorno et al. found that these same people also received relatively less love and affection from their parents than did those low on the "F scale."

Most recently, Prescott (1975) has pointed to neurophysiological and cross-cultural evidence showing that the more a person is deprived of "somatosensory gratification," such as intimate physical contact, love, and affection, the greater the level of aggression, including physical aggression. For example, a tabulation of data for 49 societies revealed that the societies that do not provide much physical affection to their children also tend to show a high level of violence between adults. Since a loving and affectionate childhood tends to inoculate persons and societies against violence, it seems likely that this background would be particularly efficacious against violence in the family.

The policy implication that follows from this finding is not that parents "should be" warm and affectionate because by now that has become part of the standard American child-rearing ideology (as compared with the "school of hard knocks" and the "don't spoil the child" conceptions). Rather, the policy implication recognizes that, despite the ideology of warmth and affection, millions of children are in fact deprived of just that (Adorno et al., 1950; Henry, 1963; Lewis, 1971). Consequently:

> PI 9. Sponsor research to determine the social and psychological conditions that cause some parents to be cold and distant rather than warm and loving, and translate the results into programs to assist such parents.

THE INEVITABILITY OF CONFLICT IN FAMILIES

Conflict, in the sense of differences in objectives or "interests" between persons and between groups, is an inevitable part of all human association (Coser, 1956; Dahrendorf, 1959; Simmel, 1908). Some groups tend to be characterized by more conflict than do others. Somewhat paradoxically, the more intimate the ties between members of a group, the higher the average level of conflict (Coser, 1956:67). Since the family is one of the most intimate groups, the level of conflict is particularly high. Chapter 1 describes some of the characteristics of the family that give rise to its typically high level of conflict.

These eleven characteristics of the family are by no means a complete list of factors that produce conflict. However, they should be sufficient to indicate that the family is typically the locus of a high level of conflict at the same time that it is the locus of a high level of interpersonal support and love. Modern society does not provide adequate mechanisms for nonviolent resolution of these conflicts. First, the family's privacy and separation from close ties with neighbors and relatives cuts it off from the assistance in resolving conflicts that such groups can provide. There is no one to turn to for help. Second, this same privacy and isolation from kin and neighbors means that few or no agents of social control exist to block the use of physical force. Consequently:

PI 10. Reduce the impact of government programs
and regulations that, directly or indirectly,
encourage geographic mobility or reduce ties
to the extended family.

This policy will be even more difficult to implement
than many of the others suggested in this chapter, for a
number of reasons. First, the art and science of "family
impact analysis" is only now beginning to be explored
(Minnesota Family Study Center, 1976). Aside from a few
obvious programs (such as those policies that give more
encouragement to building new neighborhoods than to
preserving the quality of existing neighborhoods), simply
identifying the relevant programs and government regulations
will be a slow, uncertain process. Second, those programs
that are identified will usually be serving some importan
purpose. Consequently, the policy would be not merely
matter of ending something, but even more a matter of
finding alternatives that do not encourage mobility and the
reduction of extended family ties. Finally, the aid and
support that intimate communities and kin provide are not an
unmixed blessing: they can be stifling at the same time
that they are helpful.

We have already suggested that our unwillingness to
recognize the high level of conflict in families is itself a
source of violence. As long as conflict within the family
is viewed as wrong, abnormal, or illegitimate, people will
be reluctant to learn techniques for engaging in conflict
nonviolently.

PI 11. Recognize the inevitability and
legitimacy of conflict within the family
rather than consider conflict an abnormal
deviation.

Once the inevitability and legitimacy of conflict
within families is recognized, the way is open for the
media, marriage counselors, churches, and human service
agencies to help families find constructive ways of
resolving conflicts. Many of the methods cited in the
references following PI 8, and those described in sections H
and I, are designed to do just that.

An important aspect of these methods is that they are
intended for normal families; they make no assumptions
about psychopathology. Instead, these methods assume that
the family members need to learn more efficient ways of
solving interpersonal problems and proceed to teach these
techniques by novel, nonmoralistic behavioral methods. They
focus on teaching people how to solve problems, not on what
the solution to the problem is.

Although the inevitability of marital conflict should be recognized, it is also important to avoid the trap represented by one wing of the "encounter group" movement, which has its parallel among a number of marriage counselors and writers of marital advice books, such as Bach and Wyden's The Intimate Enemy (1968). Bach and Wyden urge their readers to drop "outmoded notions of etiquette" and ventilate their anger. During one group session, one of the authors urged the women participants, "Don't be afraid to be a real shrew, a real bitch! Get rid of your pent up hostilities! Tell them where you're really at! Let it be total, vicious, exaggerated, hyperbole!" (Howard, 1970:54).

Although Bach and Wyden's book contains assertions to the contrary, the overall message of the book, as I read it, urges wives to do just what the quotation suggests. This advice is based on a "catharsis," or "ventilation" theory of aggression control. That theory begins with the assumption that all of us have in our nature a greater or lesser tendency toward aggression that somehow must find expression. If we attempt to repress this deep biologically based motivation, our innate aggression will only cause an explosion at some later time.

Unfortunately for those who have acted on such advice, almost no empirical research with any pretense of scientific rigor supports the theory, and much of it shows the reverse: that opportunities to observe aggression or to be aggressive tend to produce greater subsequent levels of aggression and violence (Berkowitz, 1973; Hokanson, 1970; Steinmetz and Straus, 1974; Straus, 1974). In general, aggression against another (either verbally or physically) tends to (a) produce counter aggression, (b) impedes getting to the real problem, and (c) if it does succeed in squelching the other person, reinforces the use of aggression as a mode of interaction.

There is, however, a kernel of truth underlying the "let it all hang out" and "ventilation" approaches to marriage. The difference must be perceived between assertion (standing up for one's interests) and aggression (acts carried out with the intention of hurting the other). Assertiveness is essential; but one can be assertive without being aggressive (although always with the risk of aggression being imputed). For example, the critical first steps of "getting help," "canceling the hitting license," and "making clear that one is prepared to leave," are all highly assertive, but nonaggressive acts. Second, assertiveness is necessary if there is to be any hope of resolving the conflict over which the violence occurs. If conflict arises over the children, sex, money, or running the household, then these issues must be faced.

Procedures for rational conflict resolution, often combined with systems for rewarding occurrences of desired behavior, are central concerns of the recent "marriage encounter" movement (Koch and Koch, 1976; Mace and Mace, 1974) and of "behavioral" therapists like Blechman et al., (1976a, b), Patterson (1975), and a number of others who are represented in the chapters of an important new book on Treating Relationships (Olson, 1976; see also Jacobson and Martin, 1976). One can say that a principal goal of these approaches to "treating relationships" is the improvement of interpersonal skills, including assertiveness, so that the legitimate interests of all parties can be furthered. This kind of therapy may also have the advantage of being less threatening and more attractive to husbands. If they accord with prevailing masculine role models, men are more reluctant than women to hash over their childhood or present emotions and their psychological status, as required in the traditional "insight" therapy. They prefer to examine actions and results more than history and personality, and these are precisely the foci of the new marriage encounter, marriage enrichment, and marriage counseling approaches.

SEX ROLE, SEXISM, AND WIFE-BEATING

Perhaps the most pervasive set of factors bringing about wife-beating are those connected with the sexist structure of the family and society. In fact, to a considerable extent, the cultural norms and values permitting and sometimes encouraging husband-to-wife violence reflect the hierarchical and male-dominant type of society that characterizes the Western world. The right to use force exists, as Goode (1971) concludes, to provide the ultimate support for the existing power structure of the family, in case those low in the hierarchy refuse to accept their place and roles. Nine of the specific ways in which the male-dominant structure of the society and of the family create and maintain a high level of marital violence were described in Chapter 6.

Defense of Male Authority

Since many men must fall back on the "ultimate resource" of physical force to maintain their authority (see Chapters 10 and 12 and Goode, 1971), it follows that a policy that reduced this need would be helpful:

>   PI 12. Eliminate the husband as "head of the family" from its continuing presence in the law, in religion, in administrative procedure, and as a taken-for-granted aspect of family life.

Although progress is being made in respect to the
achievement of husband-wife equality, the idea that the
husband is head of the family remains firmly rooted in
American culture (see the survey reported in Parade, 1971;
also Kolb and Straus, 1974 and the conclusion to Chapter 6).
In United Stated government statistics, the only time a
woman can be classified as the head of a household is when
no husband is physically present. No provision is made for
listing joint head of household. Only through the active
pursuit of the goals of the feminist movement is significant
change likely. Moreover, the importance of the feminist
movement goes well beyond husband-wife equality, and it will
be impossible to eliminate sexism in the family until it is
also eliminated in the society at large.

Although the elimination of sexism in the family is a
historical change of vast magnitude, aspects of sexism are
within the immediate control of individuals. For example,
both for her own protection and as a contribution to the
overall policy objective, no woman should enter marriage
without it being firmly and explicitly understood that the
husband is not the head of the family. Unless stated
otherwise, the implicit marriage contract includes the
"standard" clause about male leadership. Charging this
contract after marriage is not only difficult, but gives
rise to feelings of having been misled or cheated.

Although objections may be made to introducing these
ideas in junior and senior high school classes on the family
(as indicated by recent congressional pressure on the
National Science Foundation that resulted in ending support
for curriculum projects in Anthropology and Psychology),
many local school districts will find such content
appropriate. In addition, the feminist movement can
continue to challenge the implicit support of male dominant
family relations in magazines for young women such as
Seventeen, Bride, and Glamour.

Economic Constraints and Discrimination

Lack of economic alternatives to dependence on the
husband is another one of the three main factors that Gelles
(1976) found associated with beaten wives' remaining with
their husbands. Thus, for women to be in a position in
which they can refuse to tolerate physical coercion by their
husbands, occupational and economic equality are absolutely
essential. Consequently, one of the most fundamental policy
implications is:

> PI 13.   Eliminate the pervasive system of
> sex-typed occupations in which "women's
> occupations" tend to be poorly paid, and the
> equally pervasive difference between the pay
> of men and women in the same occupation.

Burdens of Child Care

Sexually based division of labor that assigns
child-rearing responsibilty to the wife, occupational
discrimination, lack of child-care facilities, inadequate
child support from either the government or the father--all
coerce women to remain married even when the victims of
violence.   A husband does not need to fear that if he beats
his wife and the wife leaves, he will be responsible for
both the care of the child and the need to earn sufficient
income.   So, a husband can hit (and otherwise oppress) his
wife with relative impunity. He can be reasonably confident
that if she does leave, he will not have the children unless
he insists on it; courts are reluctant to award children to
fathers in any circumstances. No shame is involved for a
father who claims that the child will be best off with the
mother, but for a mother to say the child is better off with
the father is not only shameful, but in many cases will
cause the child to be institutionalized or placed in a
foster home. Child care responsibility is only one of many
examples of sex-typed roles that bind women to violent
marriages. Therefore:

> PI 14. Reduce or eliminate the sex-typed
> pattern of family role responsibilities.

As in the case of sexual stereotyping in the paid labor
force, interest and ability rather than sex need to be the
primary criteria for who does what. Moreover, this is a
policy implication that, like that in respect to paid
employment, is desirable regardless of its effect on
wife-beating.   Just as many (but not all) women will find
greater fulfillment through equal participation in the paid
labor force, many (but again not all) men will find greater
fulfillment than they now experience in equal participation
in the household labor force.   That possibility is now
denied to men because of the shame attached to men's showing
major interest in household work and child care.

PI 14 is a long-range type of social change, and we
need not wait for it to come about. In the meantime, other
steps may be taken to aid women trapped in a violent
marriage by the necessity of assuming responsibility for
child care if the marriage breaks up:

> PI 15. Establish or subsidize a comprehensive
> and high quality system of day-care centers
> for preschool children.

Again, this policy is long overdue in its own right,
not just for its potential in preventing wife-beating. Such
facilities are needed by millions of women who enjoy fully
satisfactory marriages.

The three aspects of the sexist structure of the society are listed below; their implications for wife-beating were described in Chapter 6 and need not be repeated here.

Myth of the Single Parent Household

Preeminence of Wife Role for Women

Women as Children

These aspects and the many other ways in which women are disadvantaged (and therefore less able to end a violent marriage) suggest that fundamental changes should be made. PI 16, 17, and 18 are not policy analyses in the specific sense used by Wilson and McDonald (1972:1-2), but are guidelines for needed changes in public laws and private practices. The most important policy implication of all those put forth in this chapter is that:

> PI 16. Full sexual equality is essential for prevention of wife-beating.

At this point we must make clear an important limitation to much of what has been said. Sexual equality in itself is almost certainly not going to end conflict and violence between husbands and wives. Equality will reduce or eliminate certain kinds of conflict, but, at the same time, it will create new conflicts. Issues that are not now the subject of disagreement in millions of families--such as who will work for wages and who will work in the house, or more specific issues, such as who will do the laundry--can no longer be determined by referring to the traditional pattern of family roles. Rather, these issues become open questions, over which severe conflict can arise. It is by no means inconceivable that neither partner will want to be in the paid labor force, or that neither will want to do the laundry. Consequently, a reduction in the level of violence also requires that couples have interpersonal and conflict-management skills needed to cope with, and realize the benefits of, a less rigid family system. Millions of people lack these skills; almost all of us can improve them.

In addition, it would be shortsighted, even dangerous, to overlook the costs of freedom and flexibility. Freedom and flexibility in family patterns and sex roles remove some of the foundations of stability and security in life. Not everyone finds the benefits worth these costs. Erich Fromm's (1941) classic book Escape from Freedom was concerned with far more than the reasons that fascism had such wide support. At the other end of the continuum, the

millions of women opposed to the Equal Rights Amendment and
the feminist movement reflect the anxiety that many women
feel over the possible loss of familiar and stable guides to
life. Therefore:

> PI 17. As the society eliminates fixed sex
> roles, alternative sources of stability and
> security in self-definition will be needed.

Part of these needed social anchors will come from
occupational identification that, in the past, was difficult
or impossible for women. The difficulty was not only
because so few women were in socially valued occupational
roles, but also because for a woman to be highly identified
with an occupation raised doubts about her familial
commitment, her love for her husband and children, and her
femininity. However, occupation as a source of identity and
self-esteem has its limits. Vast numbers of occupations are
unlikely to be valued as a means of establishing a personal
identity--either by men or by women. Fortunately, other
roles and identities can give life needed structure and
social integration--particularly roles in relation to the
community, special purpose groups, and the larger kin group.
These will be discussed later. But before doing that, two
final aspects of sex roles need to be considered.

Compulsive Masculinity

"Compulsive masculinity" was described in Chapter 6. A
complementary "compulsive femininity" factor also exists, as
reflected in Marabel Morgan's Total Woman, the largest
selling work of non-fiction in 1973. Morgan lays great
stress on using femininity to control men. However, the
conception of women as subordinate and childlike that
underlies her view of femininity and her tactics for
manipulating men also teach (perhaps even more powerfully)
the natural inferiority of women. The book helps to
maintain the negative self-image that, despite the wiles
taught by Morgan, undercuts the ability of women to be truly
equal.

Negative Self-Image

Since compulsive masculinity and its associated
violence and compulsive femininity and its associated
negative self-image are patterns growing out of the
different experiences of men and women from early childhood
on, particularly in the way boys and girls are socialized
for their respective sex roles, it follows that:

PI 18. Parent-child interaction, parental
expectations, and all other aspects of
socialization should not be differentiated
according to the sex of the child.

Male Orientation of the Criminal Justice System

Not only is much male violence against wives
attributable to the sexist organization of society, but the
male-oriented organization of the criminal justice system
virtually guarantees that few women will be able to secure
legal relief (Fields, 1978).

But even if a woman goes to Family Court, unless she
has unusual understanding of and ability to manipulate the
system, there is often a three-week delay before her request
for a "peace bond" or an "order of protection" comes before
the judge. Such orders are therefore of no greater help in
securing immediate protection from another assault than the
police officers described in Chapter 3. Even without these
delays, many women cannot attend court because of the lack
of child-care arrangements during the long hours of waiting
for a case to come up, frequently repeated when the case is
rescheduled.

Chapters 3 and 6 detail many impediments to securing
legal protection against assault by a husband, including (a)
legal delays, especially in obtaining a "peace bond" or an
"order of protection"; (b) immunity from suit by one's
spouse; (c) the requirement that, despite abundant physical
evidence, the police officer must witness the attack before
an arrest can be made; (d) the frequent failure of police
to arrest even when they do witness an assault; (e) the
"cooling out" by police, prosecuting attorneys, and judges
of wives who attempt to bring complaints; and (f) the
refusal to make an award by public compensation review
boards (even in cases of permanent disability) if the injury
was inflicted by the husband. All of these factors indicate
the need for the following policy:

PI 19. Eliminate from the criminal justice
system the implicit toleration of
wife-beating shown in statutory and common
law; attitudes of the police, prosecutors,
and judges; and cumbersome and ineffective
procedures that make even the available legal
remedies and protection ineffective.

Some movement in the direction of PI 19 is now taking
place, but it is far from a general trend. A change in the
legal system requires a priority activity by well organized
feminist groups, as in the "NOW Wife Assault Program" in Ann
Arbor, Michigan (Fotjik, 1976; Resnik, 1976), or in the
occasional enlightened police department that recognizes the

need to reorient its mode of coping with "family disturbance" calls (Bard et al., 1975).

ECONOMIC FRUSTRATION AND VIOLENCE

American society, like most societies, is one in which,

from early childhood on, people learn to respond to frustration and stress by aggression. This response is not inevitable biologically

since in a few societies people learn to, and typically do, respond to frustration in other ways. Nevertheless,

aggressive response is typical of this society and is likely to remain so in the foreseeable future. For this reason, and because a policy directed to reducing frustration would be desirable in its own right, we should give high priority to enable as many persons as possible to avoid situations of extreme frustration of important life goals. This proposal is by no means the same as attempting to create a life without frustration. Such a life, even if it were possible, would be empty, and would probably be a source of violence in itself (see the discussion of the "Clockwork Orange" theory of violence in Gelles and Straus, 1978). However, a major blockage of a critical life goal is quite another thing.

Many critical life goals are (or perhaps should be) beyond the realm of social policy to facilitate. But a goal on which there is high consensus, as well as a high possibility of achieving change, is the provision of a meaningful occupational role and an adequate level of income for all families.

In industrial societies, the husband's position of leadership depends on the prestige and earning power of his occupation. Consequently, if the husband is unemployed or does not earn an amount consistent with other men in the family's network of associates, his leadership position is undermined. Data from a study by O'Brien (1971) show that, when this happens, husbands tend to try to maintain their superior position through the use of physical force. Data from my study of the parents of university students show that the percentage of husbands who struck their wives in the last year ranges from a low of 4 and 7 percent for those whose wives are almost completely or completely satisfied with their family income, up to 16 and 18 percent for those whose wives are slightly satisfied or not at all satisfied. There is also evidence that assaults on wives go up with unemployment (Parade, 1971:13; Straus, Gelles, and Steinmetz, 1979).

In discussing the sexist organization of the family as
a cause of wife-beating, we pointed out that if husbands no
longer had the burden of being the "head of the family" and
the main "breadwinner," they would not need to resort to
violence to maintain that position in situations where the
wife is more competent, earns more, or has a more
prestigious occupation. The same reasoning applies, perhaps
even more strongly, when the husband is unemployed.
Clearly, the most fundamental change needed is male
liberation from the bonds of traditional sex roles. At the
same time, we can pursue a policy that, aside from its
intrinsic worth, is likely to reduce wife-beating. It is
stark in its simplicity and powerful in its effect on human
welfare:

> PI 20. Full employment for all men and women in
>   the labor force at wage levels consistent
>   with the standards of the society, and a
>   guaranteed income for those unable to work.

Aside from its impact on wife-beating, in avoiding one
of the most severe frustrations that a person can experience
in an industrial society and in bypassing issues of power
within the family, full employment exerts a powerful effect
on self-esteem. Kaplan (1975) has shown that the lower an
adolescent's self-esteem, the greater the likelihood of his
being violent; Kaplan's data suggest that boys low in
self-esteem seek to achieve recognition from others through
violence. This behavior, of course, is tied to the equation
of masculinity with aggressiveness. Consequently, when
recognition through achievement in school, sports, or an
occupation is lacking, males can and do demonstrate their
"manhood" through violence. Again, the more fundamental
policy objective is to change the definition of masculinity.
But as long as that definition continues to be a part of our
culture, full employment can help avoid invoking this aspect
of "manhood" through providing meaningful employment as a
basis for self-esteem.

A more radical approach to this relationship between
economic frustration and wife-beating focuses on what
critics of American society see as the inhuman occupational
and economic system. Such critics are not opposed to full
employment, but they do oppose the economic and social
system that judges human worth by earnings and competitive
occupational achievement. As long as such a system
prevails, the bulk of the population is denied an adequate
level of self-esteem because only a minority, by definition,
can be at the top in occupational prestige and income. In
addition, the striving to get to the top pushes the more
human values to subordinate position. Ties of friendship,
kin, and community, for example, are regularly sacrificed in
moving to get a better job or accepting a promotion.
Consequently, the following policy is proposed:

PI 21. Reduce the extent to which society
evaluates people on the basis of their
economic achievements and reduce the
occupational and economic competition that
this entails.

The implication of PI 21 is not the end to all
competition. Competition can be pleasurable, if one can
choose the arena of competition and if there is a reasonable
chance of winning. Rather, the policy suggests the need to
end the forced and (for most of the population) no-win
competition that now characterizes our occupational-economic
system.

SUMMARY AND CONCLUSIONS

Physical violence between husband and wife is a common
but not an inevitable part of human nature. Only in rare
instances is it an outgrowth of pathological male
aggressiveness, or of female masochism. Rather, the typical
pattern of husband-wife violence, and its extreme in the
form of "wife-beating," is largely a reflection of the
nature of the society, its family system, and its typing of
sex roles and male/female personality traits. Consequently,
the focus of this chapter has been to deduce from these
social factors the policies that, if adopted, would reduce
the level of wife-beating. In all, 21 different policy
implications were outlined and are summarized in Table 1.

Table 1. Summary of Policy Implications for Prevention
Derived from Analysis of Six Social Structural Causal
Factors

Factor I. CULTURAL NORMS PERMIT AND LEGITIMIZE WIFE-BEATING

1. Make the public aware of this largely unperceived norm.
2. Redefine the marital relationship as one in which any
    use of physical force is as unacceptable as it is
    between oneself and those with whom one works, bowls,
    or plays tennis.

Factor II. WIFE-BEATING REFLECTS SOCIETAL VIOLENCE

3. Reduce to the maximum extent possible the use of
    physical force as an instrument of government.
4. Limit violence in the mass media to as much as is
    consistent with preserving freedom of expression and
    artistic integrity.
5. Enact stringent gun control legislation, particularly
    restricting hand guns, but also requiring that all guns
    be kept locked and unloaded.

Factor III. THE FAMILY IS THE PRIMARY SETTING IN WHICH VIOLENCE IS LEARNED

6. Gradually eliminate physical punishment as a mode of child rearing.
7. Encourage parents to control acts of physical force between their children and to avoid explicitly or implicitly defining such acts as permissible.
8. Provide parents and children with techniques other than force and coercion for coping with and resolving the inevitable conflicts of family life.
9. Sponsor research to determine the social and psychological conditions that cause some parents to be cold and distant rather than warm and loving, and translate the results into programs to assist such parents.

Factor IV. THE INEVITABILITY OF CONFLICT IN THE FAMILY

10. Reduce the impact of government programs and regulations that, directly or indirectly, encourage geographic mobility or reduce ties to the extended family.
11. Recognize the inevitability of conflict within the family rather than consider conflict an abnormal deviation.

Factor V. SEXUALLY STEREOTYPED ROLES AND SEXISM IN THE FAMILY AND THE SOCIETY.

12. Eliminate the husband as "head of the family" from its continuing presence in the law, in religion, in administrative procedure, and as a taken-for-granted aspect of family life.
13. Eliminate the pervasive system of sex-typed occupations in which "women's occupations" tend to be poorly paid, and the equally pervasive difference between the pay of men and women in the same occupation.
14. Reduce or eliminate the sex-typed pattern of family role responsibilities.
15. Establish or subsidize a comprehensive and high quality system of day-care centers for preschool children.
16. Full sexual equality is essential for prevention of wife-beating.
17. As the society eliminates fixed sex-roles, alternative sources of stability and security in self-definition will be needed.
18. Parent-child interaction, parental expectations, and all other aspects of socialization should not be differentiated according to the sex of the child.
19. Eliminate from the criminal justice system the implicit toleration of wife-beating shown in statutory and common law; the attitudes of the police, prosecutors, and judges; and cumbersome and ineffective procedures that make even the available legal remedies and

protection ineffective.

FACTOR VI.   FRUSTRATIONS BUILT INTO THE ECONOMIC SYSTEM

20. Full employment for all men and women in the labor
     force at wage levels consistent with the standards of
     the society, and a guaranteed income for those unable
     to work.
21. Reduce the extent to which society evaluates people on
     the basis of their economic achievements, and reduce
     the occupational and economic competition that this
     entails.

     Although the primary focus of the chapter was on
policies that will _prevent_ wife-beating, the desperate
immediate situation of millions of wives must also be
addressed. Consequently, the last third of the longer paper
from which this chapter was excerpted (Straus, 1977) is
devoted to steps that individual wives married to an
assaultive husband can take, and to actions feminist and
community groups, police, and human service agencies can
take, to cope with the immediate problem.

     Changing a phenomenon as deeply embedded in the social
system as wife-beating is a vast undertaking. So many
actions are needed that one almost does not know where to
start.   In fact, a realistic approach recognizes that there
is no one place to start. Rather, a broad public awareness
and commitment to change is necessary, so that individuals
and groups in all spheres of life can attend to changes in
each of these spheres. For example, change in the legal and
law enforcement system will not in itself end wife-beating.
But, the police, lawyers, judges, and legislators can act to
remove some of the many barriers that now prevent women from
receiving legal protection from beatings. Thus, in most
states, unless the assailant uses a weapon, the police
cannot make an arrest, even if the wife is obviously injured
and the husband makes no attempt to deny her charges.   (She
can, however, make a "citizen's arrest" and insist that the
police help her--provided she has sufficient presence of
mind, self-confidence, and determination, and some place to
hide when the husband is released from jail an hour or two
later!.)   The law regulating the evidence needed to make an
arrest for wife-beating can be changed, just as laws
regarding the evidence needed for a rape conviction have
recently changed. Similarly, putting a husband in jail
deprives the wife of her means of support; this fact is
often pointed out to women and is one reason so few severely
beaten wives press charges.   However, in some states, a
prisoner can be released for employment during working
hours, and such laws could be enacted in other states if the
society were truly determined to end wife-beating.

This final chapter has attempted to trace out the policy implications of our knowledge of one aspect of family violence: wife-beating. There is good reason for the emphasis on wife-beating. Women are under greater risk than men of serious injury from physical attack, and they have few alternatives for putting up with beatings by their husbands. In this and in previous chapters we pointed out a variety of social and economic constraints that lock women into marriage to a much greater extent than men. In short, as noted in Chapter 2, women are victimized by violence in the family to a much greater extent than are husbands, and should therefore be the focus of the most immediate remedial steps. However, a fundamental solution to the problem of wife-beating cannot be restricted to restraining assaults by husbands. Rather, the evidence indicates that violence is embedded in the very structure of society and the family system itself. The solution to wife-beating, like other forms of intrafamily violence, lies in the complex interplay of cultural and social organizational factors surrounding family life.

NOTES

*Revised version of part of "A Sociological Perspective and Treatment of Wife-Beating." Reprinted with permission from Maria Roy, (ed.) Battered Women. New York: Van Nostrand-Reinhold, 1977. This paper was first presented at the 1977 annual meeting of the American Psychiatric Association.

I am grateful to Maria Roy and to Professors Richard J. Gelles and Howard M. Shapiro, and Jean Giles-Sims for comments and criticisms of the first draft.

References

References

ABBOTT, SUSAN 1976 "Full-time farmers and week-end wives: An analysis of altering conjugal roles." Journal of Marriage and the Family 38 (February):165-174.

ADORNO, T. W., E. FRENKEL-BRUNSWIK, D. J. LEVINSON, and N. SANFORD 1950 The Authoritarian Personality. New York: Harper and Row.

ALDOUS, JOAN 1974 "The making of family roles and family change." The Family Coordinator 23 (July):231-235.

APPLEY, MORTIMER H. and RICHARD TRUMBULL (eds.) 1967 Psychological Stress: Issues in Research. New York: Appleton-Century-Crofts.

ARCHER, DANE and ROSEMARY GARTNER 1976 "Violent acts and violent times: A contemporative approach to postwar homicide rates." American Sociological Review 41 (December):937-963.

ARDREY, ROBERT 1966 The Territorial Imperative. New York: Atheneum Publishers.

BACH, GEORGE R. and PETER WYDEN 1968 The Intimate Enemy. New York: Morrow. Pp.17-33. Also reprinted in Steinmetz and Straus, 1974.

BACHMAN, JERALD G. 1967 Youth in Transition. Ann Arbor, Michigan: Institute for Social Research, University of Michigan.

BAHR, STEPHEN J. 1974 "Effects on power and division of labor in the family." Chap. 7 in Lois W. Hoffman and F. Ivan Nye (eds.), The Employed Mother in America (Second Edition). Chicago: Rand McNally.

BAHR, STEPHEN J., CHARLES E. BOWERMAN, and VIKTOR GECAS 1974 "Adolescent perceptions of conjugal power." Social Forces 52 (March):357-367.

BALSWICK, JACK O. and CHARLES W. PEEK 1971 "The inexpressive male: A tragedy of American society." The Family Coordinator (October):363-368. Also reprinted in Arlene and Jerome Skolnick (eds.), Intimacy, Family, and Society. Boston: Little, Brown and Co., 1974, PP. 237-244.

BANDURA, ALBERT 1973 Aggression: A Social Learning Analysis. New Jersey: Prentice-Hall

BANDURA A. and R. H. WALTERS 1959 Adolescent Aggression. New York: Ronald Press.

BANDURA, ALBERT and R. H. WALTERS 1963 Social Learning and Personality Development. New York: Holt, Rinehart and Winston.

BARD, MORTON 1969 "Family intervention police teams as a community mental health resource." The Journal of Criminal Law, Criminology and Police Science 60 (2):247-250.

235

BARD, MORTON 1971 "The study and modification of
    intra-familial violence." Pp.154-164 in Jerome L.
    Singer (ed.), The Control of Aggression and Violence.
    New York: Academic Press. Also reprinted in Steinmetz
    and Straus, 1974.
BARD, MORTON, et al. 1975 The Function of the Police in
    Crisis Intervention and Conflict Management: A
    Training Guide. Washington, D.C.: U.S. Department of
    Justice.
BART, PAULINE B. 1975 "Rape doesn't end with a kiss." VIVA
    (June):39-42 and 100-102.
BASOWITZ, HAROLD et. al. 1955 Anxiety and Stress: An
    Interdisciplinary Study of a Life Situation. New York:
    McGraw-Hill.
BELLAK, LEOPOLD and MAXINE ANTELL 1974 "An intercultural
    study of aggressive behavior on children's
    playgrounds." American Journal of Orthopsychiatry 44
    (4):503-511.
BEM, S. L. and D. J. BEM 1970 "Training the woman to know
    her place: The power of a non-conscious ideology." in
    D. J. Bem, Beliefs, Attitudes, and Human Affairs.
    Belmont, California: Brooks/Cole.
BENEDICT, RUTH 1938 "Continuities and discontinuities in
    cultural conditioning." Psychiatry I:161-167.
    Reprinted in Clyde Kluckhohn and Henry A. Murray
    (eds.), Personality in Nature, Society, and Culture.
    New York: Alfred A. Knopf.
BERGER, ARTHUR A. 1974 The Comic-Stripped American.
    Baltimore: Penguin Books.
BERGER, PETER and HANSFRIED KELLNER 1964 "Marriage and the
    construction of reality." Diogenes 46:1-25.
BERKOWITZ, LEONARD 1973 "The case for bottling up rage."
    Psychology Today 7 (July):24-31.
BERNSTEIN, PHILIP S. 1950 What the Jews Believe. New York:
    Farrar, Straus and Young.
BETTELHEIM, BRUNO 1967 "Children should learn about
    violence." Saturday Evening Post 240 (March):10-12.
    Also reprinted in Steinmetz and Straus, 1974.
BETTELHEIM, BRUNO 1973 "Bringing up children." Ladies Home
    Journal 10 (October):32 ff.
BICKMAN, LEONARD 1975 "Bystander intervention in a
    crime." Paper presented at International Advanced Study
    Institute on Victimology and the Needs of Contemporary
    Society, Bellagio, Italy, July 1-12, 1975.
BLAU, PETER M. 1964 Exchange and Power in Social Life.
    New York: John Wiley and Sons.
BLAU, PETER 1975 Approaches to the Study of Social
    Structure. New York: Free Press.
BLECHMAN, ELAINE A., DAVID H. L. OLSON, and I. D.
    HELLMAN 1976 "Stimulus control over family
    problem-solving behavior." Behavior Therapy.
BLECHMAN, ELAINE A., DAVID H. L. OLSON, C. Y.
    SCHORNAGEL, M. J. HALSDORD, and A. J. TURNER 1976
    "The family contract game: Technique and case study."
    Journal of Consulting and Clinical Psychology,
    44:449-455.

BLOOD, ROBERT O. 1963 "The husband-wife relationship." Pp.
282-308 in F.   Ivan Nye and Lois W. Hoffman (eds.),
The Employed Mother in America.   Chicago: Rand
McNally.
BLOOD, ROBERT O. 1965 "Long-range causes and consequences
of the employment of married women." Journal of
Marriage and the Family 27 (February):43-47.
BLOOD, ROBERT O. 1967 Love Match and Arranged Marriage.
New York: Free Press.
BLOOD, ROBERT O. and ROBERT L. HAMBLIN 1958 "The effects
of the wife's employment on the family power
structure." Social Forces 36 (May):347-352.
BLOOD, ROBERT O.   and DONALD M. WOLFE 1960 Husbands and
Wives: The Dynamics of Married Living. New York:
Free Press.
BLUMBERG, MYRNA 1964-65 "When parents hit out."   20th
Century (Winter):39-41.   Also reprinted in Steinmetz
and Straus, 1974.
BLUMENTHAL, MONICA. D., ROBERT L. KAHN, FRANK M. ANDREWS,
and KENDRA B.   HEAD 1972 Justifying Violence: The
Attitudes of American Men.   Ann Arbor, Michigan:
Institute for Social Research, University of Michigan.
BLUMENTHAL, MONICA D., LETHA B. CHADIHA, GERALD A.   COLE,
and TOBY EPSTEIN JAYARATNE 1975 More about Justifying
Violence: Methodological Studies of Attitudes and
Behavior.   Ann Arbor, Michigan: Institute for Social
Research, University of Michigan.
BOHANNAN, PAUL 1960 "Patterns of murder and suicide."
Chapter 9 in Paul Bohannan (ed.), African Homicide and
Suicide. New York: Atheneum.
BOTT, ELIZABETH 1957 Family and Social Network.   London:
Tavistock.
BRIM, ORVILLE G., JR., ROY FAIRCHILD, and EDGAR F. BORGOTTA
1961 "Relations between family problems." Marriage and
Family Living 23:219-226.
BROWN, BRUCE W. 1973 "The image of the contemporary male
as depicted in advertising during sports events."
Unpublished paper, Wilkes College, Wilkes-Barre,
Pennsylvania
BROWN, BRUCE W. 1977 "Education,   employment,   and
prescriptions for marital decision-making: 1900-1974."
Paper presented at the annual meeting of the American
Sociological Association, Chicago, September 1977.
BROWN, BRUCE W. 1978 "Wife-employment and the emergence of
equalitarian marital role prescriptions: 1900-1974."
Journal of Comparative Family Studies (in press).
BROWN, R. C. and J. T.   TEDESCHI 1974 "Determinants of
perceived aggression." Unpublished manuscript, Georgia
State University.
BROWNMILLER, SUSAN 1975 Against Our Will. New York: Simon
and Schuster.
BUCKLEY WALTER (ed.) 1968 Modern Systems Research for the
Behavioral Scientist. Chicago: Aldine.

BULCROFT, RICHARD and MURRAY A. STRAUS 1975 "Validity of
    husband, wife, and child reports of intrafamily
    violence and power." Mimeographed Paper.
BURGESS, ANN W. and LYNDA LYTLE HOLMSTROM 1974 Rape:
    Victims of Crisis. Bowie, Md.: Robert J. Brady Co.
BURIC, OLIVERA and ANDJELKA ZECEVIC 1967 "Family
    authority, marital satisfaction, and the social network
    in Yugoslavia." Journal of Marriage and the Family 29
    (May):325-336.
BURKE, RONALD J. and TAMARA WEIR 1976 "Relationship of
    wives' employment status to husband, wife, and pair
    satisfaction and performance." Journal of Marriage and
    the Family 38 (May):279-287.
BURR, WESLEY R. 1973 Theory Construction and the Sociology
    of the Family. New York: John Wiley and Sons.
BUSS, A. H. 1971 "Aggression pays." In J. L. Singer
    (eds.), The Control of Aggression and Violence. New
    York: Wiley and Sons.
CALONICO, JAMES M. and DARWIN L. THOMAS 1973 "Role-taking
    as a function of value similarity and affect in the
    nuclear family." Journal of Marriage and the Family 35
    (4):655-665.
CALVERT, ROBERT 1974 'Criminal and civil liability in
    husband-wife assaults." Also reprinted in Steinmetz and
    Straus, 1974.
CAMERON, P. and C. JANKY 1972 "The effects of viewing
    'violent' T.V. upon children's at-home and in-school
    behavior." Unpublished manuscript. University of
    Kentucky.
CAMPBELL, JAMES S. 1969 "The family and violence." Pp.
    251-261 in Steinmetz and Straus, 1974.
CARILLO-BERON, CARMEN 1974 A Comparison of Chicano and Anglo
    Women. San Francisco: R and E Research Associates.
CENTERS, RICHARD, BERTRAM H. Raven, and AROLDO RODRIGUES
    1971 "Conjugal power structure: A re-examination."
    American Sociological Review 36 (April):263-278.
COHEN, PERCY S. 1969 Modern Social Theory. London:
    Heinemann Educational Books Ltd.
COOPER, DAVID 1971 The Death of the Family. New York:
    Random House.
COOTE, ANNA 1974 "Police, the law, and battered wives."
    Manchester Guardian (May 23):11.
COSER, LEWIS A. 1956 The Functions of Social Conflict. New
    York: Free Press.
COSER, LEWIS A. 1967 Continuities in the Study of Social
    Conflict. New York: Free Press.
COSER, LEWIS A. 1969 "The functions of social conflict."
    Pp.218-219 in L. A. Coser and B. Rosenberg (eds.),
    Sociological Theory: A Book of Readings. New York:
    Macmillan.
COTTRELL, L. S. 1942 "The adjustment of the individual to
    his age and sex roles." American Sociological Review 7
    (October):617-620.
CROMWELL, RONALD E. and DAVID H. L. OLSON (eds.) 1975
    Power in Families. New York: Sage.

CROOG, SYDNEY H.   1970   "The family as a source of stress."
     Pp.   19-53 in Sol Levine and Norman A.   Scotch (eds.),
     Social Stress. Chicago: Aldine.
CUBER, JOHN F.   and   PEGGY HAROFF   1965   Sex   and   the
     Significant Americans. Baltimore: Penguin.
CURTIS, LYNN A.   1974   Criminal Violence: National Patterns
     and Behavior. Lexington, Mass.: Lexington Books.
DAHRENDORF, RALF 1959 Class and Class Conflict in Industrial
     Society. London: Routledge and Kegan Paul.
DAVIS, ALAN J.   1970   "Sexual assaults in   the   Philadelphia
     prison system." In John H. Gagnon and William Simon
     (eds.), The Sexual Scene. Chicago: Aldine.
DENZIN, NORMAN K.   1970   "Rules of conduct and the study of
     deviant   behavior: some   notes   on   the   social
     relationship." Pp.   120-159 in J.   Douglas (ed.),
     Deviance and Respectability. New York: Basic Books.
DIXON, W. J.   (ed.) 1965 BMD--Biomedical Computer Program.
     Pp.   459-481. Los Angeles: U.C.L.A.
DOHRENWEND, BRUCE P.   1961 "The social psychological nature
     of stress: A framework for causal inquiry." Journal of
     Abnormal and Social Psychology 62 (March):294-302.
DOLLARD, JOHN C. et. al. 1939 Frustration and Aggression.
     New Haven: Yale University Press.
DURKHEIM, EMILE   1950   Rules   of   Sociological   Method.
     Glencoe: Free Press.
EDELHERTZ, H.   and G. GEIS 1974 Public Compensation to
     Victims of Crime. New York: Praeger Publishers.
EMBREE, JOHN F.   1950   "Thailand   -   a   loosely   structured
     social system." American Anthropologist 52:181.
EPSTEIN, S.   and   S. P.   TAYLOR 1967 "Instigation   to
     aggression as a function of degree of defeat and
     perceived aggressive intent of the opponent." Journal
     of Personality 35:264-289.
ERIKSON, KAI 1966 Wayward Puritans. New York: Wiley.
ERLANGER, HOWARD S.   1974   "Social   class   differences   in
     parents' use of physical punishment." Pp.   150-158 in
     Steinmetz and Straus, 1974.
ETZIONI, AMITAI 1971 "Violence." Chapter 14 in Robert K.
     Merton and Robert A.   Nisbet (eds.), Contemporary
     Social Problems, Third Edition. New York: Harcourt
     Brace Jovanovich.
FARRINGTON, KEITH 1975 "Toward a general stress theory of
     intra-family violence." A paper presented at the 1975
     annual meeting of the National Council on Family
     Relations, Salt Lake City, Utah.
FARRINGTON, KEITH and JOYCE E. FOSS 1977 "In search of the
     'missing' conceptual framework in family sociology:
     the social conflict framework." Paper presented at the
     Theory Development and Methods Workshop, annual meeting
     of the National Council on Family Relations, October,
     1977, San Diego, California.
FENNELL, NUALA 1974 Irish Marriage. Dublin: The Mercier
     Press Ltd.

FERNANDEZ-MARINA, RAMON, EDUARDO P. MALDONADO, and RICHARD
    D.   TRENT 1958 "Three basic themes in Puerto Rican and
    Mexican-American family values." Journal of Social
    Psychology 48:167-181.
FERREIRA, ANTONIO J. 1963 "Family myth and homeostatis."
    Archives of General Psychiatry 9:457-463.
FESHBACH, SEYMOUR 1970 "Aggression." Chapter 22 in Paul H.
    Mussen (ed.), Carmichael's Manual of Child Psychology.
    Third Edition. New York: John Wiley and Sons.
FESHBACH, SEYMOUR and ROBERT D. SINGER 1971 Television and
    Aggression. San Francisco: Jossey-Bass.
FIELD, MARTHA H.   and   HENRY F.   FIELD 1973 "Marital
    violence and the criminal process: Neither justice or
    peace." The Social Service Review 47 (June):221-240.
FIELDS, MARJORY D.   1978   "Wife   beating   government
    intervention policies and practices." Testimony at
    hearings on "Research Into Domestic Violence,"
    Committee on Science and Technology, U.S. House of
    Representatives, February 14-16.
FOTJIK, KATHLEEN M. 1976 "Wife beating: How to develop a
    wife assault task force and project." Ann Arbor,
    Michigan: Ann Arbor-Washtenaw County NOW Wife Assault
    Task Force.
FOX, GREER LITTON 1973 "Another look at the comparative
    resources model: Assessing the balance of power in
    Turkish marriages." Journal of Marriage and the Family
    35 (4):718-729.
FRANCKE, LINDA BIRD 1977 "The body count in the battle of
    the sexes." New York Times (September 29):44.
FRENCH JOHN R. P. and BERTRAM H. RAVEN 1959 "The bases of
    social power." Pp. 150-167 in Dorwin Cartwright (ed.),
    Studies in Social Power. Ann Arbor: Research Center
    for Group Dynamics Institute for Social Research,
    University of Michigan.
FREUD, S. 1959 Why war? Letter to Professor Albert
    Einstein, 1932. In Collected Papers. Volume 5. New
    York: Basic Books.
FROMM, ERICH 1941 Escape from Freedom. New York: Holt,
    Rinehart and Winston.
FURSTENBERG, FRANK F., JR. 1966 "The American family: A
    look backward." American Sociological Review 31
    (June):326-337.
GAGNON, JOHN H. and WILLIAM SIMON 1973 Sexual Conduct:
    The Social Sources of Human Sexuality. Chicago:
    Aldine.
GECAS, VIKTOR 1972 "Motives and aggressive acts in popular
    fiction: Sex and class differences." American Journal
    of Sociology 77 (January):680-696.
GELLES, RICHARD J. 1973 "Child abuse as psychopathology:
    A sociological critique and reformulation." American
    Journal of Orthopsychiatry 43 (July):611-621. Also
    reprinted in Steinmetz and Straus, 1974.
GELLES, RICHARD J. 1974 The Violent Home: A Study of
    Physical Aggression Between Husbands and Wives.
    Beverly Hills, California: Sage Publications.

GELLES,RICHARD J.   1976 "Abused wives: Why do they stay?"
    Journal   of   Marriage   and   the   Family   38
    (November):659-668.
GELLES, RICHARD J.   1977 "Violence Towards Children in the
    United   States."   Paper presented at the American
    Association for the Advancement of Science, Denver.
GELLES, RICHARD J. and MURRAY A. STRAUS 1974 "Toward an
    integrated theory of intrafamily violence." Paper read
    at the 1974 Theory Construction Workshop at the Annual
    Meeting of the National Council on Family Relations,
    St. Louis, Missouri.
GELLES, RICHARD J.   and MURRAY A.   STRAUS 1975 "Family
    experience and public support of the death penalty."
    American Journal of Orthopsychiatry 45 (July):596-613.
GELLES, RICHARD J. and MURRAY A. STRAUS 1978 "Determinants
    of violence in the family: Toward a theoretical
    integration." Chapter in Wesley R. Burr, Rueben Hill,
    F. Ivan Nye, and Ira L. Reiss (eds.), Contemporary
    Theories About the Family. New York: Free Press.
GERBNER, GEORGE and LARRY GROSS 1976 "The scary world of
    TV's   heavy   viewer."   Psychology   Today   9
    (April):41-49,89.
GIANOPULOS, ARTIE and HOWARD E. MITCHELL 1957 "Marital
    disagreements in working wife marriages as a function
    of husband's attitudes toward wife's employment."
    Marriage and Family Living 17 (November):373-378.
GIL, DAVID G. 1971 "Violence against children." Journal of
    Marriage and the Family 33 (November):637-648.
GIL, DAVID G. 1975 "Unraveling child abuse." American
    Journal of Orthopsychiatry 45 (April):346-356.
GLAZER-MALBIN, NONA 1975 Old Family, New Family. Pp.
    27-66 "Man and woman: Interpersonal relationships in
    the marital pair." New York: D. Van Nostrand.
GOLDFARB 1970 "We're more violent than we think."
    MacLean's Magazine (August):25-28.
GOODE, WILLIAM J. 1962 "Marital satisfaction and
    instability: A cross-cultural analysis of divorce
    rates." International Social Science Journal 14
    (3):507-526.
GOODE, WILLIAM J. 1971 "Force and violence in the family."
    Journal of Marriage and the Family 33
    (November):624-636. Also reprinted in Steinmetz and
    Straus, 1974.
GOODSTADT, B. and L. HJELLE 1973 "Power to the powerless:
    Locus of control and the use of power." Journal of
    Personality and Social Psychology 27 (July):190-196.
GORDON, WHITNEY H. 1964 A Community in Stress. New York:
    Living Books.
GRAHAM, HUGH DAVIS and TED ROBERT GURR (eds.) 1969 Violence
    in America: Historical and Comparative Perspectives.
    National Commission on the Causes and Prevention of
    Violence: Reports. Vol. I and II. Washington, D.C.:
    U.S. Government Printing Office.
GREBLER, LEO, JOAN W. MOORE, and RALPH C. GUZMAN 1970 The
    Mexican-American People. New York: Free Press.

GREEN, ARNOLD W.   1941 "The cult of personality and   sexual
    relations." Psychiatry 4:343-348.
GRINKER, ROY R.   and JOHN P.   SPIEGEL 1945 Men   Under
    Stress. Philadelphia: The Blakiston Company.
GUTMACHER, MANFRED 1960 The Mind of the Murderer. New York:
    Farrar, Straus and Cudahy.
HAWKES, GLENN R. and MINNA TAYLOR 1975 "Power structure in
    Mexican and Mexican-American farm families." Journal of
    Marriage and the family 37:807-811.
HAWKINS, JAMES L.   1968 "Association between companionship,
    hostility,   and   marital   satisfaction." Journal of
    Marriage and the Family 30:647-650.
HEER, DAVID M. 1958 "Dominance and the working   wife."
    Social Forces 36 (May):341-347.
HEER, DAVID M. 1963 "The measurement and bases of family
    power:An   overview."   Marriage   and   Family Living
    25:133-139.
HEIDER, FRITZ   1958   The   Psychology of   Interpersonal
    Relations. New York: Wiley and Sons.
HENNON, CHARLES B. 1976 "Interpersonal violence and   its
    management by cohabiting couples." Paper presented at
    1976 Western Social Science Meetings, Tempe, Arizona.
HENRY, ANDREW and JAMES SHORT 1954 Suicide and Homicide.
    Glencoe, Ill.: Free Press.
HENRY, JULES 1963 Culture Against Man. New York: Random
    House.
HEPBURN, JOHN R. 1971 "The   subculture of   violence."
    Criminology 9 (May):87-98.
HEPBURN, JOHN R. 1973 "Violent behavior in interpersonal
    relationships."   The   Sociological   Quarterly   14
    (Summer):419-427.
HERON, WOODBURN 1957 "The   pathology of   boredom."
    Scientific American 196 (January):52-56.
HICKS, MARY W. and MARILYN PLATT 1970 "Marital happiness
    and stability: A review of the research in the
    sixties." In Carlfred B. Broderick (ed.), A Decade of
    Family Research and Action. Minneapolis, Minn:
    National Council on Family Relations.
HILL, REUBEN 1958 "Generic features of families   under
    stress." Social Casework 39 (February-March):139-150.
HOFFMAN, LOIS W. 1960 "Effects of employment of mothers on
    parental power relations and the division of household
    tasks." Marriage and Family Living 22 (February):27-35.
HOFFMAN, LOIS W. 1960 "Parental power relations and the
    division of household tasks." Pp.   215-230 in F. Ivan
    Nye and Lois W. Hoffman (eds.), The Employed Mother in
    America. Chicago: Rand McNally.
HOKANSON, J. E. 1970 "Psychophysiological evaluation of
    the catharsis hypothesis." In E. I. Megargee and J.
    E. Hokanson (eds.), The Dynamics of Aggression.   New
    York: Harper and Row.
HOLMES, THOMAS H.   and RICHARD H. RAHE 1967 "The social
    readjustment rating scale." Journal of Psychosomatic
    Research 11:312 ff..

HOMANS, GEORGE C. 1961 Social Behavior, Its Elementary Forms. New York: Harcourt, Brace and World.

HORNER, MATINA S. 1972 "Toward an understanding of achievement-related conflicts in women." Journal of Social Issues 28:157-175.

HOWARD, ALAN and ROBERT A. SCOTT 1965 "A proposed framework from the analysis of stress in the human organism." Behavioral Science 10:141-160.

HOWARD, JANE 1970 Please Touch: A Guided Tour of the Human Potential Movement. New York: Dell Publishing.

HOWELLS, WILLIAM DEAN 1964 The Rise of Silas Lapham. New York: Holt, Rinehart and Winston.

JACOBSON, NEIL S. and BARCLAY MARTIN 1976 "Behavioral marriage therapy: Current status." Psychological Bulletin 83 (July):540-556.

JANIS, IRVING L. 1958 Psychological Stress: Psychoanalytic and Behavioral Studies of Surgical Patients. New York: John Wiley and Sons.

JONES, E. E. and K. E. DAVIS 1965 "From acts to dispositions." In L. Berkowitz (ed.), Advances in Experimental Social Psychology. Vol. 2. New York: Academic Press.

KANDEL, DENISE B. and GERALD S. LESSER 1972 "Marital decision-making in American and Danish urban families: A research note." Journal of Marriage and the Family 34 (February):134-138.

KANOUSE, DAVID E. and L. REID HANSON 1971 "Negativity in evaluations." In E. E. Jones et al. (eds.), Attribution: Perceiving the Causes of Behavior. Morristown, N.J.: General Learning Press. University of Nebraska Press.

KAPLAN, HOWARD B. 1975 Self Attitudes and Deviant Behavior. Pacific Palisades, California: Goodyear.

KARDINER, ABRAM 1963 The Psychological Frontiers of Society. New York: Columbia University Press.

KELLEY, HAROLD H. 1967 "Attribution theory in social psychology." In D. Levine (ed.), Nebraska Symposium on Motivation, 15. Lincoln, Neb.: University of Nebraska Press.

KELLEY, HAROLD H. 1971 "Attribution in social interaction." In E. E. Jones et al. (eds.), Attribution: Perceiving the Causes of Behavior. Morristown, N.J.: General Learning Press.

KELLEY, HAROLD H. and JOHN W. THIBAUT 1969 "Group problem-solving." Chapter 29 in Gardner Lindzey and Eliot Aronson (eds.), The Handbook of Social Psychology, 2nd Edition, Volume 4. Reading, Mass.: Addison-Wesley.

KELLEY, HAROLD H., J. W. THIBAUT, R. RADLOFF, and D. MUNDY 1962 "The development of cooperation in the 'minimal' social situation." Psychological Monographs 76 (19) (Whole no. 538).

KEMPE, C. HENRY et. al. 1962 "The battered-child syndrome." Journal of the American Medical Association 181 (July 7):17-24.

KIRKPATRICK, CLIFFORD and EUGENE KANIN 1957 "Male sex
     aggression on a university campus." American
     Sociological Review 22:52-58.
KLAUSNER, SAMUEL Z. (ed.) 1968 Why Man Takes Chances:
     Studies in Stress-Seeking. Garden City, New York:
     Doubleday.
KOCH, JOANNE and LEW KOCH 1976 "The urgent drive to make
     good marriages better." Psychology Today 10
     (September):33-35 ff.
KOHN, MELVIN L. 1969 Class and Conformity: A Study in
     Values. Homewood, Illinois: Dorsey Press.
KOLB, TRUDY M. and MURRAY A. STRAUS 1974 "Marital power
     and marital happiness in relation to problem-solving
     ability." Journal of Marriage and the Family 36
     (November):756-766.
KOMAROVSKY, MIRRA 1962 Blue Collar Marriage. New York:
     Random House.
KOMAROVSKY, MIRRA 1973 "Cultural contradictions and sex
     roles: The masculine case." American Journal of
     Sociology (Jan.):873-884. Also reprinted in Arlene and
     Jerome Skolnick (eds.), Intimacy, Family, and Society.
     Boston: Little, Brown and Co., 1974, Pp. 245-257.
KUHN, DEANNA 1976 "Sex-role concepts of two- and three-year
     olds." Paper presented at the annual meeting of the
     Western Psychological Association, Los Angeles, April,
     1976.
LAING, R. D. 1972 The Politics of the Family. New York:
     Vantage.
LAROSSA, RALPH 1977 Conflict and Power in Marriage:
     Expecting the First Child. Beverly Hills: Sage.
LARSON, LYLE E. 1974 "System and subsystem perception of
     family roles." Journal of Marriage and the Family
     36(February):123-138.
LASLETT, BARBARA 1973 "The family as a public and private
     institution: A historical perspective." Journal of
     Marriage and the Family 35 (August):480-492.
LAZARUS, RICHARD S. 1966 Psychological Stress and the
     Coping Process. New York: McGraw-Hill.
LEFKOWITZ, MONROE M., LEOPOLD O. WALDER, L. ROWELL
     HOUSEMANN, and LEONARD D. ERON 1976 "Parental
     punishment: A longitudinal analysis of effects." Paper
     read at the International Society For Research on
     Aggression conference, Paris.
LEMASTERS, ERSEL E. 1957 "Parenthood as crisis." Marriage
     and Family Living 19 (November):352-355.
LEMASTERS, ERSEL E. 1971 "The passing of the dominant
     husband-father." Impact of Science on Society
     (January-March):21-30.
LEVINE, SOL and NORMAN A. SCOTCH 1967 "Toward the
     development of theoretical models: II." Milbank
     Memorial Fund Quarterly 45 (2):163-174.
LEVINGER, GEORGE 1966 "Sources of marital dissatisfaction
     among applicants for divorce." American Journal of
     Orthopsychiatry 26 (October):803-807.

LEWIS, OSCAR   1959   "Family dynamics in a Mexican   village."
    Marriage and Family Living 21:218-226.
LEWIS, OSCAR 1960 Tepoztlan: Village in Mexico.   New   York:
    Holt, Rinehart and Winston.
LEWIS, OSCAR   1963   The   Children   of   Sanchez.   New   York:
    Vintage Books.
LEWIS, OSCAR   1967   La Vida.   New York: Random House.
LEWIS,   ROBERT   A.   1971   "Socialization   into   national
    violence: Familial   correlates   of   hawkish attitudes
    toward war." Journal of Marriage and the Family 33
    (November):699-708.   Also   reprinted   in Steinmetz and
    Straus, 1974.
LOPATA, HELENA Z.   1971   Occupation: Housewife.   New York:
    Oxford University Press.
LORENZ, KONRAD   1966   On Aggression.   New   York: Harcourt
    Brace Jovanovich.
LUPRI, EUGENE   1969   "Contemporary authority patterns in the
    West   German   family: A   study   in   cross-national
    validation." Journal of Marriage and the Family 31
    (February):134-144.
LYNN, KENNETH   1969   "Violence in American literature and
    folklore."   Chapter 6   in   Hugh D.   Graham and Ted R.
    Gurr   (eds.),   Violence   in   America: Historical   and
    Comparative   Perspectives Vol.   I.   Washington D.C.:
    U.S.   Government Printing Office.
MACE,   DAVID   and   VERA   MACE   1974   We   Can   Have   Better
    Marriages--If   We   Really   Want   Them.   Nashville,
    Tennessee: Abingdon Press.
MADSEN, WILLIAM 1964 Mexican-Americans of South Texas.   New
    York: Holt, Rinehart and Winston.
MARTIN, DEL 1976   Battered   Wives.   San   Francisco: Glide
    Publications.
MARX, KARL   1964   The German   Ideology.   Moscow: Progress
    Publishers.
MASELLI, M. D.   and   J. ALTROCHI 1969 "Attribution   of
    intent." Psychological Bulletin 71:445-454.
MATZA, DAVID 1969 Becoming Deviant. Englewood Cliffs, N.J.:
    Prentice-Hall.
MAURER,   ADAH   1974   "Corporal   punishment."   American
    Psychologist 29 (August):614-626.
MAY, ROLLO   1972   Power and Innocence: A   Search   for   the
    Sources of Violence.   New York: Norton.
MCGRATH, JOSEPH E. (ed.)   1970   Social   and   Psychological
    Factors in Stress.   Pp.   10-21 "A conceptual formulation
    for research on stress." New York: Holt, Rinehart   and
    Winston.
MCKINLEY, DONALD GILBERT   1964   Social   Class   and   Family
    Life.   New York: Free Press.
MECHANIC, DAVID   1962   Students Under Stress: A   Study   in
    the   Social   Psychology of Adaptation.   New York: Free
    Press.
MECHANIC, DAVID   1968   Medical Sociology.   New   York: Free
    Press
MERCURIO, JOE 1972 Caning: Educational Rite and   Tradition.
    Syracuse: Syracuse University Press.

MERTON, ROBERT K. 1957 Social Theory and Social Structure.
    Glencoe, Ill.: Free Press.
MICHEL, ANDREE 1970 "Working wives and family interaction
    in French and American families." International Journal
    of Comparative Sociology 11 (June):157-165.
MIDDLETON, RUSSELL and SNELL W. PUTNEY 1960 "Dominance in
    decisions in the family: Race and class differences."
    American Journal of Sociology 65 (May):605-609
MINNESOTA FAMILY STUDY CENTER 1976 A Program For Training
    Family Impact Analysis. Minneapolis: University of
    Minnesota (mimeographed).
MIRANDE, ALFREDO 1977 "The Chicano family: A reanalysis of
    conflicting views." Journal of Marriage and the Family
    39:747-756.
MORGAN, MARABELL 1973 The Total Woman.   Old Tappan, New
    Jersey: Fleming H. Revell.
NIEBUHR, REINHOLD 1952 The Irony of American History.   New
    York: Charles Scribner's Sons.
NYE, F. IVAN 1958-59 "Employment status of mothers and
    marital conflict, permanence, and happiness." Social
    Problems VI (Winter):260-267.
NYE, F. IVAN 1963 "The adjustment of adolescent children."
    Pp. 133-141 in F. I. Nye and L. W. Hoffman (eds.),
    The Employed Mother in America.   Chicago: Rand
    McNally.
O'BRIEN, JOHN E. 1971 "Violence in divorce-prone families."
    Journal   of   Marriage   and   the   Family   33
    (November):692-698.   ·
O'DELL,   STAN 1974   "Training   parents   in   behavior
    modification: A review." Psychological Bulletin 81
    (July):418-433.
OLSON, DAVID H. L. 1969 "The measurement of family power by
    self-report   and   behavioral   methods."   Journal of
    Marriage and the Family 31(August):545-550.
OLSON, DAVID H. L. (ed.) 1976 Treating Relationships.
    Lake Mills, Iowa: Graphic Publications.
OLSON, DAVID H. L. and CAROLYN RABUNSKY 1972 "Validity of
    four measures of family power." Journal of Marriage and
    the Family 34 (May):224-234.
OPPONG, CHRISTINE 1970 "Conjugal power and resources: An
    urban African example." Journal of Marriage and the
    Family 32 (November):676-680.
OWENS, DAVID M. and MURRAY A. STRAUS 1975 "The social
    structure of violence in childhood and approval of
    violence as   an   adult." Aggressive Behavior   1
    (2):193-211.
PALMER, STUART 1970 Deviance and Conformity: Roles,
    Situations and Reciprocity. New Haven: College and
    University Press.
PALMER, STUART 1972 The Violent Society.   New   Haven,
    Conn.: College and University Press.
PARADE MAGAZINE 1971 "A special Roper Poll on women's
    rights." Boston Sunday Globe (September 26):4.
PARKIN, FRANK 1971 Class Inequality and Political Order.
    New York: Praeger Publishers.

PARNAS, RAYMOND I. 1967 "The police response to the domestic disturbance." Wisconsin Law Review 914 (Fall):914-960.

PARSONS, TALCOTT 1947 "Certain primary sources and patterns of aggression in the social structure of the Western world." Psychiatry 10 (May):167-181. Also Pp. 298-322 In T. Parsons (eds.), Essays in Sociological Theory, Revised Edition. New York: The Free Press, 1966.

PARSONS, TALCOTT and EDWARD A. SHILS 1953 Toward a General Theory of Action. Cambridge, Mass.: Harvard University Press.

PATTERSON, GERALD R. 1975 Families: Applications of Social Learning to Family Life. Revised Edition. Eugene, Oregon: Castalia.

PATTERSON, GERALD R., J. B. REID, R. R. JONES, and R. E. CONGER 1975 A Social Learning Approach to Family Intervention. Volume I: Families with Aggressive Children. Eugene, Oregon: Castalia.

PENALOSA, FERNANDO 1968 "Mexican family roles." Journal of Marriage and the Family 30:680-689.

PINEO, A. C. 1961 "Disenchantment in the later years of marriage." Marriage and Family Living 23:3-11.

POGREBIN, LETTY COTTIN 1974 "Do women make men violent?" Ms 3 (November):49-55, 80.

PRESCOTT, JAMES W. 1975 "Body pleasure and the origins of violence." The Futurist (April):64-74.

RAMIREZ, MANUEL 1967 "Identification with Mexican family values and authoritarianism in Mexican-Americans." The Journal of Social Psychology 73:3-11.

RAUSCH, HAROLD L., WILLIAM A. BERRY, RICHARD K. HERTEL, and MARY ANN SWAIN 1974 Communication, Conflict, and Marriage. San Francisco: Jossey-Bass.

REINHOLD, ROBERT 1977 "The trend toward sexual equality: depth of transformation uncertain." New York Times (November 30):1.

REISS, ALBERT J., JR. 1968 "Police brutality--answers to key questions." Transaction 5 (July-August):10-19.

RESNIK, MINDY 1976 "Wife beating: Counselor training manual No.1." Ann Arbor: AA NOW/Wife Assault.

RICHMOND, MARIE L. 1976 "Beyond resources theory: Another look at factors enabling women to affect family interaction." Journal of Marriage and the Family 38 (May):257-266.

ROBERTS, STEVEN V. 1971 "Crime rates of women up sharply over men's." New York Times (June 13):1, 72.

RODMAN, HYMAN 1967 "Marital power in France, Greece, Yugoslavia and the United States: A cross-national discussion." Journal of Marriage and the Family 39 (May):320-324.

RODMAN, HYMAN 1972 "Marital power and the theory of resources in cultural context." Journal of Comparative Family Studies III (Spring):50-69.

ROGERS, MARY F. 1974 "Instrumental and infra-resources: The bases of power." American Journal of Sociology 79 (May):1418-1433.

ROSENTHAL, A. M. 1964 Thirty-Eight Witnesses. New York: McGraw-Hill.

ROSS, DOROTHEA and SHEILA ROSS 1972 "Resistance by pre-school boys to sex-inappropriate behavior." Journal of Educational Psychology 63 (August):342-346.

RUEGER, ROSS 1973 "Seeking freedom from the male myth." Human Behavior 2 (April):75-77.

RYAN, BRYCE F. and MURRAY A. STRAUS 1954 "The integration of Sinhalese society." Research Studies of the State College of Washington 22 (December):179-227.

RYDER, R. G. 1968 "Husband-wife dyads versus married strangers." Family Process 7:233-237.

SAFILIOS-ROTHSCHILD, CONSTANTINA 1967 "A comparison of power structure and marital satisfaction in urban Greek and French families." Journal of Marriage and the Family 29 (May):345-352.

SAFILIOS-ROTHSCHILD, CONSTANTINA 1970 "The study of family power structure: a review 1960-1969." Journal of Marriage and the Family 32 (November):539-552.

SAFILIOS-ROTHSCHILD, CONSTANTINA (ed.) 1972 Toward a Sociology of Women. Pp. 63-70 "Instead of a discussion: companionate marriages and sexual equality: are they compatible?" Lexington, Mass.: Xerox Corporation.

SAFILIOS-ROTHSCHILD, CONSTANTINA 1976 "A macro- and micro-examination of family power and love: an exchange model." Journal of Marriage and the Family 38 (May):355-362.

SCANZONI, JOHN H. 1968 "A social system analysis of dissolved and existing families." Journal of Marriage and the Family 30 (August):452-461.

SCANZONI, JOHN H. 1970 Opportunity and the Family. New York: Free Press.

SCANZONI, JOHN H. 1972 Sexual Bargaining. Englewood Cliffs, N.J.: Prentice-Hall.

SCANZONI, JOHN H. 1975 "Sex roles, economic factors and marital solidarity in black and white marriages." Journal of Marriage and the Family 37 (February):130-144.

SCHULZ, DAVID 1969 Coming up Black: Patterns of Ghetto Socialization. Englewood Cliffs, N.J.: Prentice-Hall.

SCOTT, MARVIN B. and STANFORD LYMAN 1970 "Accounts, deviance and social order." Pp. 89-119 in J. Douglas (ed.), Deviance and Respectability. New York: Basic Books.

SCOTT, ROBERT A. and ALAN HOWARD 1970 "Models of stress." Pp. 259-278 in Sol Levine and Norman A. Scotch (eds.), Social Stress. Chicago: Aldine.

SEIDENBERG, ROBERT 1972 "The trauma of eventlessness." Psychoanalytic Review 59 (Spring):95-109.

SELYE, HANS 1956 The Stress of Life. New York: McGraw-Hill.

SHAPIRO, HOWARD and ARNOLD DASHEFSKY 1974 Ethnic
    Identification Among American Jews. Lexington, Mass.:
    Lexington Books.
SHAVER, KELLEY G. 1975 An Introduction to Attribution
    Processes. Cambridge, Mass.: Winthrop.
SHEARER, LLOYD 1975 "Ingeborg Dedichen: She was the great
    love of Aristotle Onassis." Parade (July):4-5.
SHOSTROM, EVERETT L. and JAMES KAVANAUGH 1971 Between Man
    and Woman. Los Angeles: Nash Publishing.
SIMMEL, GEORG 1950 The Sociology of Georg Simmel (ed. Kurt
    H. Wolff). New York: Free Press.
SIMMEL, GEORG (1908) 1955 Conflict and the Web of Group
    Affiliations. Glenco, Ill.: Free Press.
SIPES, RICHARD G. 1973 "War, sports and aggression: An
    empirical test of two rival theories." American
    Anthropologist 75 (February):64-68.
SKINNER, B. F. 1953 Science and Human Behavior. New York:
    Free Press.
SKOLNICK, ARLENE 1973 The Intimate Environment: Exploring
    Marriage and The Family. Boston: Little, Brown and
    Co.
SKOLNICK, ARLENE and JEROME H. SKOLNICK (eds.) 1974
    Intimacy, Family, and Society. Boston: Little, Brown
    and Com.
SPREY, JETSE 1969 "The family as a system in conflict."
    Journal of Marriage and the Family 31
    (November):699-706.
SPREY, JETSE 1971 "On the management of conflict in
    families." Journal of Marriage and the Family 33
    (November):722-731. Also reprinted in Steinmetz and
    Straus, 1974, Pp. 110-119.
SPREY, JETSE 1972 "Family power structure: A critical
    comment." Journal of Marriage and the Family 34
    (May):235-238.
STAPP, JOY and AYALA PINES 1976 "Career or family? The
    influence of goals on liking for a competent woman."
    Paper presented at the annual meeting of the Western
    Psychological Association, Los Angeles, April 1976.
STARK, RODNEY and JAMES MCEVOY III 1970 "Middle class
    violence." Psychology Today 4 (November):52-65.
STEELE, BRANDT F. and CARL B. POLLOCK 1968 "A psychiatric
    study of parents who abuse infants and small children."
    Pp.103-147 in Ray E. Helfer and C. Henry Kempe
    (eds.), The Battered Child. Chicago: University of
    Chicago Press.
STEINMETZ, SUZANNE K. 1974 "Occupational environment in
    relation to physical punishment and dogmatism." Pp.
    166-172 in Steinmetz and Straus, 1974.
STEINMETZ, SUZANNE K. 1977 The Cycle of Violence:
    Assertive, Aggressive and Abusive Family Interaction.
    New York: Praeger.
STEINMETZ, SUZANNE K. and MURRAY K. STRAUS 1973 "Changing
    sex roles and their implications for measurement of
    family socioeconomic status." Paper presented at the
    1972 meeting of the American Sociological Association.

STEINMETZ, SUZANNE K.   and   MURRAY A. STRAUS 1973 "The
    family   as   cradle   of   violence." Society (formerly
    Transaction)   10   (September-October):50-56.   (A
    pre-publication adaptation of part of the introduction
    to Violence in the Family.)
STEINMETZ, SUZANNE K.   and MURRAY A. STRAUS (eds.)   1974
    Violence   in   the   Family. New York: Harper and Row
    (originally published by Dodd, Mead and Co.).
STRAUS, MURRAY A.   1964 "Measuring families." Chap. 10 in
    Harold   T.   Christensen (ed.), Handbook of Marriage and
    the Family. Chicago: Rand McNally.
STRAUS, MURRAY A.   1971 "Some   social   antecedents   of
    physical punishment: A linkage theory interpretation."
    Journal   of   Marriage   and   the   Family   33
    (November):658-663.   Also   reprinted in Steinmetz and
    Straus, 1974.
STRAUS, MURRAY A.   1973 "A general systems theory approach
    to a theory of violence between family members." Social
    Science Information 12 (June):105-125.
STRAUS, MURRAY A.   1974a "Leveling, civility, and violence
    in   the   family." Journal of Marriage and the Family 36
    (February):13-29, plus addendum in August 1974 issue.
    Also reprinted in Nursing Education, 1974; and in
    Richard W. Cantrell and David F.   Schrader (eds.),
    Dynamics of Marital Interaction, Kendall/Hunt, 1974,
    and in Kenneth C. W. Kammeyer, (ed.), Confronting the
    Issues: Sex Roles, Marriage and the Family. Boston:
    Allyn and Bacon, 1976.
STRAUS, MURRAY A.   1974b "Cultural and social organizational
    influences on violence between family members." In
    Raymond   Prince   and   Dorothy   Barrier   (eds.),
    Configurations: Biological and Cultural Factors in
    Sexuality and Family. New York: D.C. Heath.
STRAUS, MURRAY A.   1975 "Husband-wife interaction in nuclear
    and joint households." Pp.   134-135 in D. Narain
    (ed.), Explorations in the Family and Other Essays:
    Professor K. M. Kapadia Memorial Volume. Bombay:
    Thacker.
STRAUS, MURRAY A.   1976 "Sexual inequality, cultural norms,
    and wife-beating." Victimology 1 (Spring):54-76. Also
    reprinted in Emilio C. Viano (ed.), Victims and
    Society, Washington, D.C.: Visage Press, 1976, and in
    Jane Roberts Chapman and Margaret Gates (eds.), Women
    Into Wives: The Legal and Economic Impact on Marriage.
    Sage Yearbooks in Women Policy Studies, Volume 2.
    Beverly Hills: Sage, 1977.
STRAUS, MURRAY A.   1977a "A sociological perspective on the
    prevention and treatment of wife-beating." In Maria Roy
    (ed.),   Battered Women.   New   York: Van
    Nostrand-Reinhold.

STRAUS, MURRAY A. 1977b "Societal morphogenesis and intrafamily violence in cross-cultural perspective." In Leonore Loeb Adler (ed.), Issues in Cross-Cultural Research. New York: Annals of the New York Academy of Sciences 285:717-730. Also reprinted in Karen Kowalski, (ed.), Women's Health Care. Wakefield, Mass.: Nursing Dimension, Vol. 7, 1969, Pp. 45-63.

STRAUS, MURRAY A. 1977c "Normative and behavioral aspects of violence between spouses: Preliminary data on a nationally representative USA sample." Paper read at the Symposium on Violence in Canadian Society, March 12.

STRAUS, MURRAY A. 1977d "Exchange and power in marriage in cultural context: A multimethod and multivariate analysis of Bombay and Minneapolis families." Paper read at the 1977 meeting of the Association for Asian Studies, New York.

STRAUS, MURRAY A. 1979 "Measuring intrafamily conflict and violence: the Conflict Tactics (CT) scales." Journal of Marriage and the Family, 41:75-88.

STRAUS, MURRAY A., RICHARD J. GELLES, and SUZANNE K. STEINMETZ 1980 Behind Closed Doors: Violence in the American Family. New York: Anchor/Doubleday. In press.

STRAUS, MURRAY A. and LAWRENCE J. HOUGHTON 1960 "Achievement, affiliation, and co-operation values as clues to trends in American rural society, 1924-1958." Rural Sociology 25 (December):394-403.

STRAUS, MURRAY A. and IRVING TALLMAN 1971 "SIMFAM: A technique for observational measurement and experimental study of families." In Joan Aldous et al. (eds.), Family Problem Solving. Hinsdale, Illinois: Dryden.

STRODTBECK, FRED L. 1958 "Family interaction, values and achievement." Pp. 135-194 in David C. McClelland, Alfred L. Baldwin, Urie Bronfenbrenner and Fred L. Strodtbeck (eds.), Talent and Society. New Jersey: D. Van Nostrand.

SURGEON GENERAL'S SCIENTIFIC ADVISORY COMMITTEE ON TELEVISION AND SOCIAL BEHAVIOR 1972 Report of the Surgeon General's Scientific Advisory Committee on Television and Social Behavior. Washington, D.C.: U.S. Government Printing Office.

TANAY, C. 1969 "A psychiatric study of homicide." American Journal of Psychiatry 125 (9):1252-1258.

TEDESCHI, J. T., R. SMITH and R. BROWN 1974 "A reinterpretation of research on aggression." Psychological Bulletin 81:540-562.

THIBAUT, JOHN W. and HAROLD H. KELLEY 1959 The Social Psychology of Groups. New York: John Wiley and Sons.

TRUNINGER, ELIZABETH 1971 "Marital violence: The legal solution." The Hastings Law Journal 23 (November):259-276.

TURK, J. L.   and   N. W. BELL   1972 "Measuring   power   in
    families." Journal of Marriage and the Family 34
    (May):215-222.
TURNER, RALPH 1968 "The   self-conception   in   social
    interaction." Pp. 92-106 in Gordon and Gergen (eds.),
    The Self in Social Interaction. New York: Wiley and
    Sons.
UNDERWOOD, B. J. 1957 Psychological Research.   New York:
    Appleton-Century-Crofts.
VAN DEN BERGHE, PIERRE L. 1974 "Bringing beasts back in:
    Toward a biosocial theory of aggression." American
    Sociological Review 39 (December):777-788.
WALSTER, ELAINE 1966 "Assignment of responsibility for an
    accident." Journal of Personality and Social Psychology
    3:73-79.
WEBER, MAX 1964 The Theory of Social and Economic
    Organization. New York: Free Press.
WEITZMAN, LENORE J.   1975 "To love, honor, and obey?
    Traditional legal marriage and alternative family
    forms." Family Coordinator 24 (November):531-548.
WELLER, ROBERT H. 1968 "The   employment   of   wives,
    dominance, and fertility." Journal of Marriage and the
    Family 31 (August):437-442.
WELSH, RALPH S.   1976 "Severe parental punishment and
    delinquency: a developmental theory." Journal   of
    Clinical Child Psychology 5 (Spring):17-21.
WESTLEY, WILLIAM A. 1953 "Violence and the   police."
    American Journal of Sociology 59 (July):34-41.
WHITE, LESLIE A. 1975 The Concept of Cultural Systems. New
    York: Columbia University Press.
WHITEHURST, ROBERT N. 1974 "Violence   in   husband-wife
    interaction." Pp. 75-82 in Steinmetz and Straus, 1974.
WHITEHURST, ROBERT N. 1974 "Alternative family structures
    and violence-reduction." Pp. 315-320 in Steinmetz and
    Straus, 1974.
WHITING, BEATRICE B.   1965 "Sex identity conflict and
    physical violence: A comparative study." American
    Anthroplogist 67 (December):123-140.
WILLIAMS, DONALD B. 1974 "Compensating victims of crimes
    of violence: Another look at the scheme." Pp. 147-153
    in I. Drapkin and E. Viano (eds.), Victimology: A
    New Focus. Volume II.   Society's Reaction to
    Victimization. Lexington, Mass.: Lexington Books.
WILLIAMS, ROBIN M. 1970 American Society: A Sociological
    Interpretation. New York: Alfred A. Knopf.
WILSON, LANCE R. and GERALD W. McDONALD 1977 Family Impact
    Analysis and Family Policy Advocate: The Process of
    Analysis. Family Impact Series. Minnesota Family
    Study Center, Report No. 4.
WINTER, W. D., FERREIRA, A. J., and N. BOWERS 1973
    "Decision-making in married and unrelated couples."
    Family Process 12:83-94.

WOLFE, DONALD M.   1959   "Power and authority in the family."
    Pp.   99-117 in D.   Cartwright (ed.), Studies in Social
    Power.   Ann Arbor, Michigan: University of Michigan
    Institute for Social Research.
WOLFF, HAROLD G.   1968   Stress and Disease.   Second Edition.
    Edited by Stewart Wolf and Helen Goodell.   Springfield,
    Ill.:   Charles C.   Thomas.
WOLFGANG, MARVIN E.   1956   "Husband-wife   homicides."
    Corrective Psychiatry and Journal of Social Therapy
    2:263-271.
WOLFGANG, MARVIN E.   1957 "Victim-precipitated   criminal
    homicide." Journal of Criminal Law, Criminology and
    Police Science 48 (June):1-11.   Also Pp.   72-87 in
    Marvin   E.   Wolfgang (ed.), Studies in Homicide.   New
    York: Harper and Row.
WOLFGANG, MARVIN E.   1969 "Violence and human behavior."
    Paper presented at the annual meeting of the American
    Psychological Association, Washington, D.C., August 30.
WOLFGANG, MARVIN and FRANCO FERRACUTI 1967 The Subculture of
    Violence.   New York: Barnes and Noble.
YAFFE, JAMES 1968 The American Jew.   New York: Paperback
    Library.
YARROW, MARIAN RADKE, CHARLOTTE GREEN SCHWARTZ,   HARRIET S.
    MURPHY, and LEILA CALHOUN DEASY 1955 "The psychological
    meaning of mental illness in the   family." Journal of
    Social Issues 11 (4):12-24.
YINGER, JOHN M.   1965 Toward a Field Theory of Behavior:
    Personality   and   Social   Structure.   New   York:
    McGraw-Hill.
YLLO, KERSTI A.   and MURRAY A. STRAUS 1980 "Interpersonal
    violence among married and cohabiting couples." Family
    Coordinator, April, in press.
YOUNG, MICHAEL   and   PETER WILLMOTT 1973 The   Symmetrical
    Family: A Study of Work and Leisure in the London
    Region.   London: Routledge and Kegan Paul.
ZUK, GERALD H.   1978 "A therapist's perspective on Jewish
    family values."   Journal   of Marriage and Family
    Counseling 4 (January):103-110.

Indexes

Author Index

257

Subject Index

About the Authors

CRAIG M. ALLEN is an Instructor in Sociology at Iowa State University. He has done research on family intervention techniques, parental discipline and locus of control in children, and children's modeling of cartoon characters. Currently, he is studying relationships among measures of conjugal power to determine if indexes based on contested power are more sensitive indicators of the marital power balance than indexes based on uncontested power. He is the author of "Role Specialization and Locus of Control," presented at the Third Annual Family Research Conference, Brigham Young University, 1974.

BRUCE W. BROWN is Assistant Professor of Sociology at Wilkes College in Wilkes-Barre, Pennsylvania. He has done research on historical analysis of the family, family measurement techniques, and discipline of children. He is now doing a study of how family life has been depicted in magazine advertising since 1920, which emphasizes both historical and life cycle changes in family companionship and intimacy. He is the author of "The Changing Role of the Male Marriage Partner as Depicted in the 20th Century Marriage Manual" (New York State Sociological Association, 1973); "Education, Employment, and Prescriptions for Marital Decision-Making: 1900-1974" (American Sociological Association, 1977); "Magazine Advertising: Its Use in the Historical Study of the Family" (Pennsylvania Sociological Society, 1979); "Wife-Employment and the Emergence of Equalitarian Marital Role Prescriptions: 1900-1974" (Journal of Comparative Family Studies, Spring 1978); and "Parent's Discipline of Children in Public Places" (Family Coordinator, July 1979). He is co-author, with Murray A. Straus, of Family Measurement Techniques (University of Minnesota Press, 1978); and with Joseph A. Panzanaro, of "Compulsory Pre-Marital Education?" (Wilkes College Quarterly, Summer 1979).

JOSEPH CARROLL is an Assistant Professor in Sociology at Colby-Sawyer College in New London, New Hampshire. He has done research on the intergenerational transmission of family violence, and climatological factors associated with aggression. He is now doing a study of causes of psychological distress and family problems that emphasizes the effect of varying degrees of integration into one's community. He is the author of "The Intergenerational Transmission of Family Violence: The Long-term Effects of Aggressive Behavior," 1977), and the "Effect of Climate on Homicide and Suicide: Humidity, Heat, and Cold" (Annual meeting of the Society for the Study of Social Problems, 1977).

KEITH FARRINGTON is a member of the Department of Sociology and Anthropology at Whitman College. His research interests include the causes and consequences of social stress, labeling and deviance, and violent behavior. He is the author or co-author of "The Scheduling of Personal Crises: Seasonal Changes in the Pace of Social Activities and Help-seeking at Mental Health Clinics" (presented at the annual meeting of the Society for the Study of Social Problems, New York City, August 1976), "Family Violence and Household Density: Does the Crowded Home Breed Aggression?" (presented at the annual meeting of the Society for the Study of Social Problems, Chicago, September 1977), and "In Search of the Missing Conceptual Framework in Family Sociology: The Social Conflict Framework" (presented at the annual meeting of the National Council on Family Relations, San Diego, October 1977). He is currently doing a macroscopic analysis of variations in the pace of social life and their effects.

JOYCE E. FOSS is an Assistant Professor in Sociology at Sangamon State State University in Springfield, Illinois. She has done research on sex roles and mental health, the impact of Women's Studies courses on attitudes toward women's roles, and community perceptions of hospital services. Currently she is doing a study of the types of power assertions used by husbands and wives, which emphasizes relationships between structural and processual aspects of power. She is the author of "Sex Differences in the Use of Mental Health Clinics: Real Illness or Patient Behavior?" (Society for the Study of Social Problems Annual Meeting, 1974); and co-author of "Review Essay: Theory Construction and the Sociology of the Family, by Wesley R. Burr" (Journal of Marriage and the Family, 1976), "In Search of the 'Missing' Conceptual Framework in Family Sociology: The Social Conflict Framework" Annual Meeting of the

National Council on Family Relations, 1977), and "Sex
Differences in Help-Seeking Behavior: A Test of Three
Competing Theories" (Society for the Study of Social
Problems Annual Meeting, 1978).

GERALD T. HOTALING is an Instructor in Sociology at the
University of Vermont. His research interests include
Family Violence, Mental Health and the Family, and Sex Roles
and Health Behavior. He is a member of the editorial board
of the journal Alternative Lifestyles: Changing Patterns in
Marriage, Family and Intimacy.

He is the author of "Family Vulnerability to Stigma as
a Factor in Help-Seeking Behavior" (Society for the Study of
Social Problems meetings 1975), "Facilitating Violence: Why
Intimates Attribute Aggression" (presented at the National
Council on Family Relations meetings 1975), "Social Class
and Value Orientation in the Phase Movement of Families
Through the Mental Health System" (Society for the Study of
Social Problems meeting 1976), "Sex Differences in
Help-Seeking Behavior" (Society for the Study of Social
Problems meeting 1978, with Saundra Atwell and Joyce E.
Foss), and "Adolescent Life Changes and Illness: A
Comparison of Three Models" (Eastern Sociological Society
meetings 1978, to be published by the Journal of Youth
Adolescence, 1978).

MARTHA D. HUGGINS is an Instructor at Union College in
the Department of Sociology. She recently spent two years
as a Visiting Professor in the Department of Sociology at
the Universidade Federal de Pernambuco, Brazil. The
Visiting Professorship was funded by the Fletcher School of
Law and Diplomacy, Tufts University, and the Ford
Foundation. The title of her dissertation is "Punishment
without Crime: Deviance, Social Change and Social Control
in Pernambuco, Brazil, 1860-1922." She is the co-author
(with Scott G. McNall) of "Guerilla Warfare: A Preliminary
Study of Predisposing and Precipitating Factors," and of a
paper presented at the 1977 Eastern Sociological Society
meeting on "The Relationship between Social and Political
Conditions and Historical Trends in Deviant Behavior in
Recife, Brazil."

RALPH LaROSSA is an Assistant Professor of Sociology at
Georgia State University in Atlanta. He has done research
on the psycho-social aspects of marriage and first pregnancy

and is currently involved in two projects: a participant observation study of the aging process and an in-depth interview study of the transition to parenthood. He is the author of Conflict and Power in Marriage: Expecting the First Child (Sage, 1977).

MURRAY A. STRAUS has been Professor of Sociology at the University of New Hampshire since 1968. He is the author of about 80 articles in the sociology of the family, violence, South Asia, rural sociology, and research methods; and the following books: Sociological Analysis: An Empirical Approach Through Replication (1968); Family Measurement Techniques (1969, revised edition, 1977); Family Analysis: Readings and Replications of Selected Studies (1969); Family Problem Solving (1971); and Violence in the Family (1974). He was Assistant Editor of Sociological Abstracts and founding editor of the journal Teaching Sociology. Straus was president of the National Council on Family Relations, vice-president of the Eastern Sociological Society, and member of the Council of the American Association for the Advancement of Science. He was recently given the E. W. Burgess award for outstanding contributions to research on the family. Together with Richard Gelles and Suzanne Steinmetz, he is the author of a book on Violence In the American Family based on data from the nationally representative sample of 2,143 families described in the article in this issue.